TOP TEN GOOD THINGS ABOUT LISTS

(Created by David Letterman's writers at Late Show*)*

10. Only possible way to keep track of the Baldwin brothers.

9. Odds are very small that you'll be killed while making or reading a list.

8. Thanks to the brave Americans who fought in the Revolutionary War, we live in a country free from the oppression of a list tax.

7. Without lists, Santa Claus wo̶u̶l̶d̶ ̶b̶e̶ ̶s̶crewed.

6. Occasiona̶l̶l̶y̶ ̶c̶o̶m̶e̶ ̶w̶i̶t̶h̶ ̶d̶e̶licious g̶o̶o̶e̶y̶ ̶c̶e̶n̶t̶e̶r̶s̶!̶ fles!

5. FBI's mo̶s̶t̶ ̶u̶s̶e̶d̶ ̶i̶n̶d̶i̶c̶ator for crimi̶n̶a̶l̶s̶

4. Fun rainy-̶d̶a̶y̶ ̶a̶c̶t̶i̶v̶i̶t̶y̶:̶ ̶make list of Larry King's ex-wives!

3. Lists provide easy way for *TV Guide* books to separate suckers like you from $6.99.

2. Reading lists keeps you busy during whatever crap NBC shows between *Friends* and *Seinfeld*.

1. Lame jokes seem funnier when grouped into lists of ten.

THE

TV GUIDE

BOOK
OF
LISTS

Edited by
Amy Paulsen and
Annabel Vered

HarperPaperbacks
A Division of HarperCollins*Publishers*

HarperPaperbacks
A Division of HarperCollinsPublishers
10 East 53rd Street, New York, N.Y. 10022-5299

ISBN 0-06-101091-X

HarperCollins®, 🔥®, and HarperPaperbacks™
are trademarks of HarperCollinsPublishers, Inc.

First printing: April 1998

Printed in the United States of America

Visit HarperPaperbacks on the World Wide Web at
http://www.harpercollins.com

❖ 10 9 8 7 6 5 4 3 2 1

Table of Contents

Introduction

The editors of *TV Guide* are serious journalists *and* serious couch potatoes. (Turns out you *can* be both, despite what they tell you at college.) More than anyone, we appreciate television's rich history of entertainment and information. At the same time, we revel in TV trivia and pride ourselves in our prolific knowledge of outrageous facts and obscure phenomena.

The TV Guide Book of Lists indulges our dual nature and serves two purposes: to document the incredible impact that TV has made over the past 50 years (see "The 100 Greatest Episodes of All Time," or "TV's 20 Most Romantic Moments"), and to disseminate all manner of curious and colorful TV information (see "13 Stars Who Appeared on *The Dating Game*," or "12 Actors Who Have Been Arrested").

Finally, this book comes to you at an important time. In this age of information, lists play a more and more critical role in our lives. Rather than try to explain it ourselves, we asked the king of lists, David Letterman, and his *Late Show* writers to count the ways that lists make the world a better place.

Top Ten Good Things About Lists

10. Only possible way to keep track of the Baldwin brothers.

9. Odds are very small that you'll be killed while making or reading a list.

8. Thanks to the brave Americans who fought in the Revolutionary War, we live in a country free from the oppression of a list tax.

7. Without lists, Santa Claus would be screwed.

6. Occasionally, lists make mention of a delicious golden brown breakfast food: waffles!

5. FBI's most wanted list is excellent motivator for criminals who lack drive.

4. Fun rainy-day activity: Make list of Larry King's ex-wives!

3. Lists provide easy way for TV Guide books to separate suckers like you from $6.99.

2. Reading lists keeps you busy during whatever crap NBC shows between Friends and Seinfeld.

1. Lame jokes seem funnier when grouped into lists of ten.

TV Trends and Star Style

21 Kinds of Clothes That Made the Man or Woman

Looks aren't everything, but in these cases, *having* a look made all the difference in the world.

1. Amanda's micro-mini power suits on *Melrose Place*

2. Cher's Bob Mackie gowns on *The Sonny and Cher Comedy Hour*

3. Columbo's rumpled raincoat on *Columbo*

4. Corporal Klinger's dresses on *M*A*S*H*

5. Daisy Duke's shorts on *The Dukes of Hazzard*

6. Ed Norton's white undershirt and porkpie hat on *The Honeymooners*

7. Emma Peel's shiny leather catsuit on *The Avengers*

8. Fonzie's leather jacket on *Happy Days*

9. Gilligan's sailor hat on *Gilligan's Island*

10. Goldie Hawn's bikini on *Laugh-In*

11. Granny's boots on *The Beverly Hillbillies*

12. Huggy Bear's pimp threads on *Starsky and Hutch*

13. Illya Kuryakin's black turtlenecks on *The Man from U.N.C.L.E.*

14. Jeannie's harem pants on *I Dream of Jeannie*

15. Minnie Pearl's country bonnet with price tag on *Hee Haw*

16. Pat Boone's white bucks on *The Pat Boone Show*

17. Sheena's leopard tunic on *Sheena, Queen of the Jungle*

18. Sister Bertrille's habit on *The Flying Nun*

19. Sonny Crockett's Versace suits with pastel T-shirts on *Miami Vice*

20. Tom Magnum's Hawaiian shirts on *Magnum, P.I.*

21. Xena's heavy metal breastplate on *Xena: Warrior Princess*

10 Most Outrageous Fashion Statements at the Academy Awards

A Calvin Klein sheath? Ho hum. A rented tux? Tsk-tsk. To make your mark at the Oscars, you have to dress to excess. Here are the ten who did it best.

1. 1969: Barbra Streisand's see-through Scaasi bell-bottomed pantsuit

2. 1974: Robert Opal's birthday suit (he was the streaker who interrupted host David Niven as he was introducing presenter Elizabeth Taylor)

3. 1988: Cher's Bob Mackie black-sequined gown with see-through netting around torso

4. 1989: Demi Moore's self-designed black spandex biker shorts leotard with a bustle in the back.

5. 1990: Kim Basinger's self-designed, single-sleeved white dress with a high-collared side.

6. 1992: Geena Davis's white satin assymetrical-hem gown with skirt and fluff balls by Bill Hargate

7. 1992: Juliette Lewis's cornrowed hair

8. 1995: Lizzy Gardiner's American Express card dress

9. 1996: Mel Gibson's tuxedo with tartan vest

10. 1997: Woody Harrelson's black Giorgio Armani hemp tuxedo

26 Cigar Smokin' Stars

Old fogies aren't the only ones who like to light up stogies. These days, cigars are the hottest accessory in Hollywood—for men *and* women.

1. James Belushi
2. Milton Berle
3. George Burns
4. Sid Caesar
5. David Caruso
6. Bill Cosby
7. Ted Danson
8. Robert Davi
9. Danny DeVito
10. Johnny Depp
11. Whoopi Goldberg
12. Lauren Hutton
13. Alan King
14. Ernie Kovacs
15. David Letterman
16. Lee Majors
17. Groucho Marx
18. Gerald McRaney

19. Chuck Norris

20. George Peppard

21. Luke Perry

22. Jason Priestley

23. Red Skelton

24. Dennis Rodman

25. Dan Rather

26. Tom Selleck

(Courtesy of Cigar Aficionado*)*

16 Who Admit They Had Plastic Surgery

Here's to the noble few who are real enough to admit that they're plastic.

1. Loni Anderson: eyes, breast reduction
2. Pamela Anderson Lee: breast implants
3. Bea Arthur: face-lift
4. Milton Berle: nose job
5. Robert Blake: face-lift
6. Carol Burnett: chin implant
7. Cher: nose job, breast enlargement, teeth
8. Phyllis Diller: brow lift, two nose jobs, under-eye lift, cheek implants, eye liner tattoo

9. Nicole Eggert: breast implants (later removed)

10. Mariel Hemingway: breast implants (later removed)

11. Jenny Jones: breast implants (later removed)

12. Angela Lansbury: face-lift and neck tightening

13. Melanie Mayron: nose job

14. Geraldo Rivera: had fat cells from butt injected around eyes and forehead to get rid of wrinkles—in front of a studio audience

15. Joan Rivers: face-lift, eyes done, liposuction on thighs, nose job, tummy tuck

16. Roseanne: breast reduction, nose job, face-lift, tummy tuck

20 Great Baldies

They bared their pates proudly, these fearless, peerless, hairless wonders.

1. Jason Alexander, *Seinfeld*

2. Ed Asner, *The Mary Tyler Moore Show*

3. Beldar the Conehead, *Saturday Night Live*

4. Daniel Benzali, *Murder One*

5. William Conrad, *Cannon*

6. Jackie Coogan, *The Addams Family*

7. Richard Deacon, *The Dick Van Dyke Show*

8. Danny DeVito, *Taxi*

9. Hector Elizondo, *Chicago Hope*

10. Dennis Franz, *NYPD Blue*

11. William Frawley, *I Love Lucy*

12. Alan Funt, *Candid Camera*

13. Werner Klemperer, *Hogan's Heroes*

14. Gavin MacLeod, *The Mary Tyler Moore Show*

15. Richard Moll, *Night Court*

16. Alan Rachins, *L.A. Law*

17. Telly Savalas, *Kojak*

18. Homer Simpson, *The Simpsons*

19. Patrick Stewart, *Star Trek: The Next Generation*

20. Jeffrey Tambor, *The Larry Sanders Show*

Six Bald or Balding Stars Who Have Worn Toupees on TV

Some still cover up; others have pulled the rugs out from over their heads.

1. Ted Danson, *Cheers*

2. Charles Grodin, *Charles Grodin*

3. Fred MacMurray, *My Three Sons*

4. Carl Reiner, *The Dick Van Dyke Show*

5. Burt Reynolds, *Evening Shade*

6. Willard Scott, *Today*

14 Former Models Who Made It Big on TV

If you don't hate them because they're beautiful, you probably find them mildly annoying for being so successful.

1. Josie Bissett: *Melrose Place*
2. Courteney Cox: *Friends*
3. Cindy Crawford: *House of Style*
4. Ted Danson: *Cheers*
5. Pam Dawber: *Mork & Mindy*
6. Susan Dey: *The Partridge Family, L.A. Law*
7. Farrah Fawcett: *Charlie's Angels*
8. Ali MacGraw: *Dynasty*
9. Tom Selleck: *Magnum, P.I.*
10. Cybill Shepherd: *Cybill, Moonlighting*
11. Brooke Shields: *Suddenly Susan*
12. Jaclyn Smith: *Charlie's Angels*
13. Sela Ward: *Sisters*
14. Vanna White: *Wheel of Fortune*

Nine Stars with Multiple Tattoos

Marking one's body with permanent ink is an act of absolute commitment: commitment to a mate, a motto, a butterfly, or a rose . . .

1. Pamela Anderson Lee: a "barbed wire" bracelet around her arm (for her movie *Barb Wire*) and a tattooed wedding band that spells "Tommy" on her ring finger, celebrating her marriage to rocker Tommy Lee

2. Tom Arnold: two "Roseanne" tattoos, one portrait of Roseanne over his heart, Grateful Dead on arm, Star of David on his chest

3. Cher: one necklace and three flowers, on arms, back, and bottom.

4. Johnny Depp: an Indian chief, "Betty Sue," and "Winona Forever"

5. Janeane Garofalo: "Think," curlicue tattoos, and bracelet tattoo on right arm

6. Lorenzo Lamas: the Harley logo, matching toe tattooes with wife Shauna Sand, shaped like two halves of a wedding ring to symbolize their love

7. Alyssa Milano: rosary beads on back, tattoos on each ankle

8. Roseanne: a garter and stockings, three "Tom" tattoos, and one "Property of Tom Arnold"

9. Antonio Sabato: A Japanese symbol that means "To live for today" and the Big Dipper

Five Stars Who Had Tattoos Removed or Altered

Oops.

1. Tom Arnold: removed the portrait of Roseanne and the Grateful Dead tattoo

2. Tony Danza: removed a tattoo of R. Crumb's Keep on Truckin' cartoon

3. Johnny Depp: Changed "Winona Forever" (for ex-flame Winona Ryder) to "Wino Forever"

4. Shannen Doherty: removed a tattoo that read ASH, which represented her ex-hubby, Ashley Hamilton

5. Roseanne: "Property of Tom Arnold" is now covered with a fairy garden motif

Two TV Characters Who Have Been Tattooed

1. Special Agent Dana Scully, *The X-Files:* a snake biting its tail

2. Rachel Green, *Friends:* a heart

One TV Star with Pierced Nipples

At least he claims he has them. We haven't actually checked.

1. Drew Carey

12 Men Who Have Worn Dresses—More Than Once!—on TV

Don't ask why, but a man in drag is a guaranteed crowd-pleaser.

1. Milton Berle: *The Milton Berle Show*
2. Dana Carvey: *Saturday Night Live*
3. David Duchovny: *Twin Peaks*
4. Dame Edna: *The Dame Edna Experience*
5. Jamie Farr: *M*A*S*H*
6. Tom Hanks: *Bosom Buddies*
7. Benny Hill: *The Benny Hill Show*
8. Martin Lawrence: *Martin*
9. Dennis Rodman: various TV appearances
10. Peter Scolari: *Bosom Buddies*
11. Jaleel White: *Family Matters*
12. Flip Wilson: *The Flip Wilson Show*

22 Famous TV Catchphrases

TV characters come and go, but their trademark lines live on forever.

1. "What, me worry?" Maynard G. Krebs, *Dobie Gillis*

2. "Book him, Dan-o." Steve McGarrett, *Hawaii Five-O*

3. "Beam me up, Scotty." Captain Kirk, *Star Trek*

4. "What a revoltin' development this is!" Chester Riley, *The Life of Riley*

5. "Sorry about that, Chief." Maxwell Smart, *Get Smart*

6. "Lucy, I'm home from the club!" Ricky Ricardo, *I Love Lucy*

7. "Dy-no-mite!" J.J. Evans, *Good Times*

8. "Aaaaay!" Fonzie, *Happy Days*

9. "Up your nose with a rubber hose." The Sweathogs, *Welcome Back, Kotter*

10. "Stifle yourself." Archie Bunker, *All in the Family*

11. "Boss, the plane, the plane!" Tattoo, *Fantasy Island*

12. "Danger, Will Robinson." Robot, *Lost in Space*

13. "That does not compute." Robot, *Lost in Space*

14. "Sock it to me!" the entire cast, *Laugh-In*

15. "Bang, zoom, to the moon!" Ralph Kramden, *The Honeymooners*

16. "Baby, you're the greatest!" Ralph Kramden, *The Honeymooners*

17. "How sweet it is!" Jackie Gleason, *The Jackie Gleason Show*

18. "Say goodnight, Gracie." George Burns, *The Burns and Allen Show*

19. "The devil made me do it!" Geraldine, *The Flip Wilson Show*

20. "Marcia, Marcia, Marcia!" Jan Brady, *The Brady Bunch*

21. "Nanu, nanu." Mork, *Mork & Mindy*

22. "Shazbat!" Mork, *Mork & Mindy*

THAT WAS THEN, THIS IS NOW

What a difference a couple of decades makes. Compare these '70s situations to those TV characters find themselves in today:

On *The Brady Bunch*, Greg feared telling the folks he wrecked the car.

On *Mad About You*, Paul's sister fears telling the folks she's a lesbian.

On *Happy Days*, sharing some Cokes meant sipping cola through straws from the same glass.

On *Beverly Hills, 90210*, sharing some coke means snorting an illegal substance through straws from the same mirror.

On *The Waltons*, Grandpa Walton was master of his domain because he had the payments on Walton's Mountain covered.

On *Seinfeld*, Jerry was master of his domain because he kept his hand outside the covers.

On *Little House on the Prairie*, Laura and Nellie, both eager to satisfy their hunger for sweets, fought over the last cookie.

On *Friends*, Monica and Rachel, both eager to satisfy their hunger for sex with their boyfriends, fight over the last condom.

On *The Bob Newhart Show*, "Hi, Bob!" meant another shot of Dr. Hartley arriving home in time for dinner.

On *Married . . . with Children*, "Hi, Bob!" means it's time for Bud to down another shot of tequila.

On *Sanford and Son*, when Fred dealt in junk, he bought and sold old furniture.

On *Law & Order*, when the perps deal in junk, they buy and sell illegal drugs.

On *Welcome Back, Kotter*, dressing down meant Horshack was in trouble again.

On *The Nanny*, dressing down means Fran isn't wearing a leopard print.

On *The Beverly Hillbillies*, the pill was Mr. Drysdale's leave-nothing-to-chance secretary, Miss Hathaway.

On *Roseanne*, the pill is older daughter Becky's leave-nothing-to-chance method of birth control.

(Vicki Jo Radovsky)

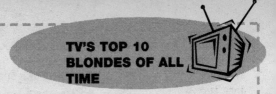
1. Elizabeth Montgomery (*Bewitched*): That flip was as sassy as her ever-twitching nose.

2. Farrah Fawcett (*Charlie's Angels*): On the strength of her "feathers" (and a toothy pinup), she flew straight into the stratosphere.

3. Candice Bergen (*Murphy Brown*): The poster child for blond ambition, Murphy plays it straight and sensible.

4. Barbara Eden (*I Dream of Jeannie*): The ultimate bottle blonde.

5. Heather Locklear (*Dynasty, T.J. Hooker, Melrose Place*): With that name, she was destined to be a golden-haired vixen.

6. Linda Evans (*The Big Valley, Dynasty*): She put the glamour back in stoicism—despite her helmet hair.

7. Goldie Hawn (*Laugh-In*): Goldie's locks topped a petite package of giggles and glitz. She *did* have more fun; so did we.

8. Ann Sothern (*Private Secretary*): Like her coif, unflappable Susie never wilted.

9. Suzanne Somers (*Three's Company*): Chrissy Snow's kooky topknot symbolized how bouncy a ditzy blonde could be.

10. Vivian Vance (*I Love Lucy*): Ethel, with her cool, calm 'do, was a perfect match for Lucy's headstrong red.

1. Tickle Me Elmo: Sales jumped 10% in October, 1996. More than a million dolls were sold by Christmas.

2. Listerine: The mouthwash maker has been deluged with hundreds of responses from consumers who are switching from Scope—which rated Rosie as one of America's least kissable celebrities—to their brand.

3. Drake's Cakes: Rosie calls them "heaven in a foil wrapper," and gives one to every audience member. Sales in 1997 have increased by as much as 11% over 1996.

4. Koosh Balls: Rosie flings them at audience members during the show. According to the makers of Koosh Balls, sales of Flingshots have doubled.

2

Career Moves

15 Former Professions That Turned Out to Be Dead Ends

Luckily, they decided to quit their day jobs and give acting a chance.

1. Bartender: Bruce Willis

2. Bellboy: Tom Hanks

3. Bouncer: John Goodman

4. Chef: Joe Lando

5. Coffin polisher: Denzel Washington

6. Fry cook: Lorenzo Lamas

7. Garbage collector: Norm Macdonald

8. Hairdresser: Danny DeVito

9. Hatcheck girl: Carol Burnett

10. Mechanic: Jay Leno

11. Oyster shucker: Ellen DeGeneres

12. Postman: Dennis Franz

13. Weatherman: David Letterman

14. Wig cleaner: Groucho Marx

15. Wig company receptionist: Kathy Kinney

15 Stars Who Have Dabbled as Singers

Luckily, they *didn't* quit their day jobs to give singing a chance.

1. Crystal Bernard: *The Girl Next Door*

2. Phyllis Diller: *Born to Sing*

3. Patty Duke: *Just Patty: The Best of Patty Duke*

4. Shelley Fabares: *The Best of Shelley Fabares*

5. Michael J. Fox: *Light of Day* soundtrack

6. Andy Griffith: *American Originals; I Love to Tell the Story: 25 Timeless Hymns*

7. David Hasselhoff: *Night Rock; David Hasselhoff*

8. Don Johnson: *Heartbeat; Let it Roll*

9. Leonard Nimoy: *Mr. Spock's Music From Outer Space; You Are Not Alone*

10. Telly Savalas: *Feelings*

11. William Shatner: *The Transformed Man*

12. David Soul: *Don't Give Up on Us*

13. Mr. T: *Be Somebody or Be Somebody's Fool*

14. Philip Michael Thomas: *Somebody*

15. Bruce Willis: *If It Don't Kill You, It Just . . .*

Nine TV Stars Who Had Success as Recording Artists

1. The Blues Brothers (Dan Aykroyd, John Belushi): *Best of the Blues Brothers; Briefcase Full of Blues; Highlights; Made in America; Red, White & Blues; The Definitive Collection*

2. David Cassidy: *Best of David Cassidy; Didn't You Used to Be . . . ; When I'm a Rock 'n' Roll Star*

3. Shaun Cassidy: *Greatest Hits*

4. Lisa Hartman: *Till My Heart Stops; Letterock; Hold On; Lisa Hartman*

5. Eddie Murphy: *Eddie Murphy; How Could It Be; Love's Alright; So Happy*

6. Rick Nelson: *All My Best; All Time Greatest Hits; Best of Rick Nelson; Garden Party; Greatest Hits; In Concert: Troubadour 1969*

7. John Schneider: *A Memory Like You; Greatest Hits; Take the Long Way Home; Too Good to Stop Now; Tryin' to Outrun the Wind; White Christmas; You Ain't Seen the Last of Me*

8. Cybill Shepherd: *Somewhere Down the Road;
   Vanilla; Cybill Does It . . . to Cole Porter*

9. Rick Springfield: *Beautiful Feelings; Comic
   Book Heroes; Greatest Hits; Living in Oz; Rock
   of Life; Success Hasn't Spoiled Me Yet; Tao;
   Working Class Dog*

Three Who Teamed with a Real Singer for a Song

1. Don Johnson (with Barbra Streisand): "Heartbeat"

2. Victoria Principal (with Andy Gibb): "All I
   Have to Do Is Dream"

3. Bruce Willis (with the Pointer Sisters):
   "Respect Yourself"

30 Books Written by TV Stars

Sooner or later, every celebrity (with or without a
ghostwriter) pens a book. It must be some kind of
union rule. . . .

1. *After All*, by Mary Tyler Moore
2. *The Autobiography of Larry Sanders*, by Garry
   Shandling
3. *Bob Hope's Dear Prez, I Wanna Tell You!*, by
   Bob Hope

4. *Couplehood*, by Paul Reiser

5. *Dirty Jokes and Beer*, by Drew Carey

6. *Don't Stand Too Close to a Naked Man*, by Tim Allen

7. *Enter Talking*, by Joan Rivers

8. *Enter Whining*, by Fran Drescher

9. *Fatherhood*, by Bill Cosby

10. *I'm Not Really Here*, by Tim Allen

11. *Knee Deep in Paradise*, by Brett Butler

12. *Leading with My Chin*, by Jay Leno

13. *Man of War* series, by William Shatner

14. *Miss America*, by Howard Stern

15. *Mountain, Get Out of My Way*, by Montel Williams

16. *My Point (and I Do Have One)*, by Ellen DeGeneres

17. *No Shirt, No Shoes, No Problem!*, by Jeff Foxworthy

18. *Parenthood*, by Paul Reiser

19. *Private Parts*, by Howard Stern

20. *The Rants*, by Dennis Miller

21. *SCTV: Behind the Scenes*, by Dave Thomas

22. *SeinLanguage*, by Jerry Seinfeld

23. *Sinbad's Guide to Life (Because I Know Everything)*, by Sinbad

24. *So Far . . .*, by Kelsey Grammer

25. *Still Talking*, by Joan Rivers

26. *Tek* series, by William Shatner

27. *True Story: A Comedy Novel*, by Bill Maher

28. *Vanna Speaks*, by Vanna White

29. *Wake Me When It's Funny*, by Garry Marshall

30. *You So Crazy*, by Martin Lawrence

10 Poets

Don't laugh. Inside that seemingly superficial TV star there may beat the heart of a poet. In fact, celebrity poetry readings at Hollywood coffee houses have proliferated in recent years, for better or verse.

1. Justine Bateman

2. David Carradine

3. Patti D'Arbanville

4. Robert Downey, Jr.

5. Woody Harrelson

6. Traci Lords

7. Judd Nelson

8. Michael J. Pollard

9. Carl Reiner

10. Katey Sagal

20 Infomercial Products Hawked by Television Personalities

Why do big-name stars like Cher, Faye Dunaway, and Farrah Fawcett make these cheesy infomercials? Well, either they really believe in the products they're promoting—or else they just want to make a quick buck.

1. "Avon's Anew," with Linda Gray

2. "Beautiful Skin," with Raquel Welch

3. "Beauty Breakthroughs II: For the '90s," with Meredith Baxter Birney, Lisa Hartman, and Ali MacGraw selling Victoria Jackson makeup products

4. "Bioflora" skin care products, with Joan Collins

5. "California Contour Systems," with Farrah Fawcett and Joan Rivers selling a cellulite product

6. "Danielo" cosmetics, with Jennifer O'Neill

7. "Jose Eber's Secret Color," with Faye Dunaway selling a mascaralike product applied to one's hair roots

8. "Focus on Beauty," with Cher, Larry Hagman, and Ted Danson selling Lori Davis hair products

9. "Growing in Love and Hidden Keys," with Connie Sellecca and John Tesh promoting a relationship improvement seminar

10. "Incredible Cover Kit," with Morgan Brittany selling makeup

11. "Lasting Kiss," with Loretta "Hot Lips" Swit selling specialty lipstick

12. "Loni Facial Systems," with Loni Anderson

13. "Micro-Diet," with Robin Leach and Dr. Joyce Brothers

14. "Murad," with Sarah Purcell selling skin care products

15. "Primage by Sevinor," with Linda Evans selling a treatment line developed by a plastic surgeon

16. "Principal Secret," with Victoria Principal selling her own line of skin-care products

17. "The Psychic Friends Network," with Dionne Warwick, Gary Coleman, and Yasmine Bleeth

18. "Total Gym," with Chuck Norris and Christie Brinkley

19. "Tyra" skin care system, with Jane Seymour

20. "Where There's a Will There's an A," with John Ritter, Michael Landon, and Burt Reynolds showing you how your kids can get better grades

17 Sirens Who Stripped for Playboy

Some women bare their assets to jump-start a stalled-out career, others to launch a new one. Still others figure that while they got it, they might as well flaunt it.

1. Pamela Anderson Lee
2. Joan Collins
3. Shannen Doherty
4. Erika Eleniak
5. Linda Evans
6. Farrah Fawcett
7. Sherilyn Fenn
8. Robin Givens
9. Mariel Hemingway
10. Pamela Sue Martin
11. Jenny McCarthy
12. Donna Mills
13. Dana Plato
14. Victoria Principal
15. Suzanne Somers
16. Shannon Tweed
17. Vanna White

34 TV Personalities Who Made Exercise Videos

Blame it on Jane Fonda: after her first exercise video, *Jane Fonda's Workout*, became a bestseller in 1982, countless celebrities invested in leotards and leg warmers and jumped on the video fitness bandwagon.

1. David Carradine: *David Carradine's Kung Fu and Tai Chi Workout*

2. Dixie Carter: *Dixie Carter's Yoga For Your Unworkout* and *Unworkout II*

3. Cher: *Cher Fitness: Body Confidence* and *Cher Fitness: A New Attitude*

4. Joan Collins: *Personal Workout* and *Secrets of Fitness and Beauty*

5. Cindy Crawford: *Shape Your Body Workout* and *The Next Challenge Workout*

6. Sandy Duncan: *5 Minute Workout*

7. Linda Evans: *The New You*

8. Fabio: *Fabio Fitness*

9. Lou Ferrigno: *Lou Ferrigno's Body Perfection*

10. Daisy Fuentes: *Totally Fit Workout*

11. Zsa Zsa Gabor: *It's Simple, Darling*

12. Jennie Garth: *Jennie Garth's Body in Progress*

13. Florence Henderson: *Florence Henderson's Looking Great/Feeling Great*

14. Marilu Henner: *Marilu Henner's Dancerobics*

15. Kathy Ireland: *Total Fitness Workout, Body Specifics, Reach, Absolutely Fit,* and *Advanced Sports Fitness*

16. Shirley Jones: *Lo-Cal Diet, Exercise and Beauty,* and *Lite Aerobic Workout*

17. Angela Lansbury: *Angela Lansbury's Positive Moves*

18. Heather Locklear: *Heather Locklear Presents Your Personal Workout*

19. Traci Lords: *Advanced Jazzthetics* and *Warm Up*

20. Joan Lunden: *Workout America*

21. Ali MacGraw: *Yoga, Mind and Body*

22. Shirley MacLaine: *Shirley MacLaine's Inner Workout*

23. Marla Maples: *Journey to Fitness*

24. Mary Tyler Moore: *Every Woman's Workout*

25. Eric Nies: *The Grind Workout: Fitness with Flava*

26. Regis Philbin: *My Personal Workout*

27. Stefanie Powers: *Stefanie Powers' Broadway Workout*

28. Joan Rivers: *Shopping for Fitness*

29. O.J. Simpson: *Minimum Maintenance Fitness for Men*

30. Jaclyn Smith: *Jaclyn Smith's Workout For Beauty and Balance*

31. Suzanne Somers: *Somersize*

32. Lucky Vanous: *The Ultimate Fat-Burning System*

33. Vanna White: *Get Slim . . .*

34. Carney Wilson: *Great Changes: Low-Impact Workout with Carnie Wilson and Idrea*

18 Who Tried Their Luck as Game Show Hosts

1. Don Ameche: *Take a Chance* (1950)

2. Milton Berle: *Jackpot Bowling* (1960–61)

3. Johnny Carson: *Your Vacation* (1954); *Who Do You Trust?* (1957–62)

4. Bill Cosby: *You Bet Your Life* (1992)

5. Walter Cronkite: *It's News to Me* (1954)

6. Jackie Gleason: *You're in the Picture* (1961, canceled after one episode)

7. Greg Kinnear: *College Mad House* (1989)

8. Ernie Kovacs: *Time Will Tell* (1954); *Take a Good Look* (1959–61)

9. Gypsy Rose Lee: *Think Fast* (1950)

10. Jack Paar: *Bank on the Stars* (1953)

11. Vincent Price: *E.S.P.* (1958); *Keep Talking* (1959)

12. Ahmad Rashad: *Caesar's Challenge* (1993–94)

13. Carl Reiner: *The Celebrity Game* (1964–65)

14. Rod Serling: *Liar's Club* (1969)

15. Dick Van Dyke: *Mother's Day* (1958–59); *Laugh Line* (1959)

16. Jerry Van Dyke: *Picture This* (1963)

17. Mike Wallace: *Majority Rules* (1949); *Guess Again* (1951); *There's One In Every Family* (1952–53); *I'll Buy That* (1953–54); *Who's the Boss?* (1954); *The Big Surprise* (1956–57); *Who Pays?* (1959)

18. Flip Wilson: *People Are Funny* (1984)

15 Stars Who Shouldn't Have Quit Their Series

1. Barbara Anderson, *Ironside*

2. David Caruso, *NYPD Blue*

3. Mike Evans, *The Jeffersons*

4. Farrah Fawcett, *Charlie's Angels*

5. David Hartman, *Good Morning America*

6. Steven Hill, *Mission Impossible*

7. Don Knotts, *The Andy Griffith Show*

8. Shelley Long, *Cheers*

9. Rob Morrow, *Northern Exposure*

10. Pernell Roberts, *Bonanza*

11. Suzanne Somers, *Three's Company*

12. McLean Stevenson, *M*A*S*H*

13. Sally Struthers, *All in the Family*

14. Richard Thomas, *The Waltons*

15. Charlene Tilton, *Dallas*

11 Stars Who Shouldn't Have Become Talk Show Hosts

1. Tempestt Bledsoe

2. Danny Bonaduce

3. Gabrielle Carteris

4. Chevy Chase

5. Whoopi Goldberg

6. George Hamilton

7. Lauren Hutton

8. Vicki Lawrence

9. Alana Stewart

10. Alan Thicke

11. Carnie Wilson

Love & Romance

30 TV Personalities Married to Other TV Personalities

Celebrity couples have to work hard to make a marriage work, especially when one spouse's star is rising, and the other's is on its way down.

1. Gracie Allen and George Burns

2. Kirstie Alley and Parker Stevenson (in the process of being divorced)

3. Loni Anderson and Burt Reynolds (divorced)

4. Meredith Baxter and David Birney (divorced)

5. Lucille Ball and Desi Arnaz (divorced)

6. Bonnie Bartlett and William Daniels

7. Josie Bissett and Rob Estes

8. Delta Burke and Gerald McRaney

9. Dixie Carter and Hal Holbrook

10. Cher and Sonny Bono (divorced)

11. Connie Chung and Maury Povich

12. Pam Dawber and Mark Harmon

13. Jill Eikenberry and Michael Tucker

14. Farrah Fawcett and Lee Majors (divorced)

15. Melissa Gilbert and Bruce Boxleitner

16. Melanie Griffith and Don Johnson (divorced)

17. Teri Hatcher and Jon Tenney

18. Kathie Lee and Frank Gifford

19. Téa Leoni and David Duchovny

20. Daphne Maxwell Reid and Tim Reid

21. Jayne Meadows and Steve Allen

22. Anne Meara and Jerry Stiller

23. Rhea Perlman and Danny DeVito

24. Tracy Pollan and Michael J. Fox

25. Lisa Rinna and Harry Hamlin

26. Roseanne and Tom Arnold (divorced)

27. Connie Sellecca and John Tesh

28. Mary Steenburgen and Ted Danson

29. Marlo Thomas and Phil Donahue

30. Betty White and Allen Ludden

Six Unions Between TV Actresses and Rock Stars

TV/music marriages are the stuff of a tabloid reporter's dreams: always sexy, frequently tumultuous, occasionally short-lived.

1. Pamela Anderson and Tommy Lee (separated, then reunited)
2. Valerie Bertinelli and Eddie Van Halen
3. Donna D'Errico and Nikki Sixx
4. Heather Locklear and Tommy Lee (divorced)
5. Heather Locklear and Richie Sambora
6. Julianne Phillips and Bruce Springsteen (divorced)

13 Stars Who Appeared on The Dating Game

1. Farrah Fawcett
2. Sally Field
3. Mark Harmon
4. Pee-wee Herman (aka Paul Reubens)
5. Andy Kaufman
6. Steve Martin

7. Sal Mineo

8. Julie Newmar

9. Burt Reynolds

10. Nipsey Russell

11. Bobby Sherman

12. Marlo Thomas

13. Robert Vaughn

Nine Celebrities Reveal the Most Romantic Lines They've Ever Heard

1. Anthony Clark (*Boston Common*): "My favorite pickup line goes like this: 'Are those space pants you're wearing? Because your butt is out of this world!'"

2. Andy Dick (*NewsRadio*): "I was on a date with a girl, and she had a little bit too much to drink, threw up in my car, and said, "Oh, look, honey, it landed in the shape of a heart!'"

3. Joely Fisher (*Ellen*): "I heard this story years ago, and it's always stood out in my mind. I don't know what year it was, but Charles MacArthur, the playwright, spotted Helen Hayes, the actress, across the bar at the Algonquin Hotel, and, not knowing what to say, he walked over to her, grabbed a handful of peanuts, and said, 'I wish these were emeralds.'"

And on their twenty-fifth wedding anniversary, he gave her a handful of emeralds and said, 'I wish these were peanuts.'"

4. Jerry O'Connell (*Sliders*): "The most romantic line is from the movie *In a Lonely Place*. Humphrey Bogart says to Gloria Grahame, 'I was born when you kissed me. I died when you left, I lived a few weeks while you loved me.'"

5. Bobbie Phillips (*The Cape*): "I don't know about romantic, but my friend told me the funniest line I ever heard. She said, 'All I want for Valentine's Day is a pair of chocolate shoes, so at least when I put my foot in my mouth, it'll taste good.'"

6. Ray Romano (*Everybody Loves Raymond*): "The most romantic line I've ever heard came after a night of—how should we put this?—it was after a passionate interlude with my wife, a wife I had to convince to participate in the passionate interlude, and afterward she turned to me and said with a very loving tone, 'That wasn't as bad as I thought it was gonna be.'"

7. Shannon Sturges (*Savannah*): "The most romantic thing I ever heard was when my husband said 'I do,' on the day we got married. Because it's more than just a line, it's a commitment."

8. Holland Taylor (*The Naked Truth*): "I remember a very sweet moment when a lover and I were gazing into each other's eyes, and we

were just so newly together we didn't know what to say to each other and after a certain point, he said, 'Would you like a balloon?' I don't know why, but that went down really well with me."

9. Ally Walker (*Profiler*): "The most romantic thing I've ever heard is something said to me by my costar, Robert Davi: 'You're a hell of a guy, for a girl.'"

18 Celebrities Who Have Made Guest-Star Appearances as Loving Parents on Prime-Time Series

It's the current craze in stunt casting: bring in a familiar face to play a series regular's mom or dad. Occasionally, the casting is inspired—like when Tammy Faye Bakker Messner played Mimi's mom on *The Drew Carey Show*.

1. Tammy Faye Bakker Messner—Mimi's mom on *The Drew Carey Show*

2. Peter Boyle—Jonathan's dad on *The Single Guy*

3. Carol Burnett—Jamie's mom on *Mad About You*

4. Glenn Close—the voice of Homer's mom on *The Simpsons*

5. Tim Conway—Peg's dad on *Married . . . with Children*

6. Morgan Fairchild—Chandler's mom on *Friends*

7. James Farentino—Doug's dad on *ER*

8. Elliot Gould—Ross and Monica's dad on *Friends*

9. Florence Henderson—Beth's mom on *Dave's World*

10. Shirley Jones—Carly's mom on *Something So Right*

11. Carol Kane—Audrey's mom on *Ellen*

12. June Lockhart—Frank's mom on *Step by Step* and Leon's mom on *Roseanne*

13. Donna Mills—Jane's mom on *Melrose Place*

14. Carroll O'Connor—Jamie's dad on *Mad About You*

15. Suzanne Pleshette—Jonathan's mom on *The Single Guy*

16. Susan Saint James—Kate's mom on *The Drew Carey Show*

17. Connie Stevens—C.J.'s mom on *Baywatch*

18. Marlo Thomas—Rachel's mom on *Friends*

Big Screen, Little Screen

32 Movie Stars Who Got Their Big Breaks on Television

TV has been the launching pad to scores of successful film careers. Here's a sampling of some of the bigger success stories:

1. Tim Allen: *Home Improvement*

2. Alec Baldwin: *The Doctors*

3. Kim Basinger: *Dog and Cat; From Here to Eternity*

4. Warren Beatty: *Dobie Gillis*

5. Sandra Bullock: *Working Girl*

6. Jim Carrey: *In Living Color*

7. Cher: *The Sonny and Cher Show*

8. George Clooney: *Roseanne; ER*

9. Billy Crystal: *Soap; Saturday Night Live*

10. Geena Davis: *Buffalo Bill; Sara*

11. Johnny Depp: *21 Jump Street*

12. Danny DeVito: *Taxi*

13. Michael Douglas: *The Streets of San Francisco*

14. Clint Eastwood: *Rawhide*

15. Mia Farrow: *Peyton Place*

16. Sally Field: *Gidget; The Flying Nun*

17. Jodie Foster, *Bob & Carol & Ted & Alice; Paper Moon*

18. Tom Hanks: *Bosom Buddies*

19. Woody Harrelson: *Cheers*

20. Goldie Hawn: *Laugh-In*

21. Martin Landau: *Mission: Impossible*

22. Steve Martin: *The Smothers Brothers Comedy Hour*

23. Eddie Murphy: *Saturday Night Live*

24. Brad Pitt: *Glory Days*

25. Will Smith: *The Fresh Prince of Bel-Air*

26. Marisa Tomei: *A Different World*

27. Lily Tomlin, *Laugh-In*

28. John Travolta: *Welcome Back, Kotter*

29. Denzel Washington: *St. Elsewhere*

30. Robin Williams: *Mork & Mindy*

31. Bruce Willis: *Moonlighting*

32. Debra Winger: *Wonder Woman*

24 Movie Stars Who Worked in Soaps

Maybe it's not so bad having a day(time) job while you're waiting for your film career to take off. . . .

1. Armand Assante: *How to Survive a Marriage; The Doctors*

2. Kevin Bacon: *Search for Tomorrow; Guiding Light*

3. Alec Baldwin: *The Doctors*

4. Warren Beatty: *Love of Life*

5. Tom Berenger: *One Life to Live*

6. Robert De Niro: *Search for Tomorrow*

7. Olympia Dukakis: *Search for Tomorrow*

8. Laurence Fishburne: *One Life to Live*

9. Mark Hamill: *General Hospital*

10. Dustin Hoffman: *Search for Tomorrow*

11. James Earl Jones: *As the World Turns; Guiding Light*

12. Tommy Lee Jones: *One Life to Live*

13. Kevin Kline: *Search for Tomorrow*

14. Jack Lemmon: *The Brighter Day; The Road of Life*

15. Demi Moore: *General Hospital*

16. Christopher Reeve: *Love of Life*

17. Eric Roberts: *Another World*

18. Gena Rowlands: *The Way of the World*

19. Meg Ryan: *As the World Turns*

20. Susan Sarandon: *A World Apart; Search for Tomorrow*

21. Martin Sheen: *The Edge of Night*

22. Kathleen Turner: *The Doctors*

23. Christopher Walken: *Guiding Light*

24. Billy Dee Williams: *Another World; Guiding Light*

16 Movie Stars Who Tried to Make It on TV and Failed

Fame on the big screen is no guarantee of success on the small screen.

1. Ellen Burstyn: *The Ellen Burstyn Show*

2. Faye Dunaway: *It Had to Be You*

3. Henry Fonda: *The Smith Family*

4. Judy Garland: *The Judy Garland Show*

5. Betty Hutton: *The Betty Hutton Show*

6. Shirley MacLaine: *Shirley's World*

7. Elizabeth McGovern: *If Not for You*

8. Robert Mitchum: *A Family for Joe*

9. Dudley Moore: *Daddy's Girls; Dudley*

10. Anthony Quinn: *The Man and the City*

11. Debbie Reynolds: *The Debbie Reynolds Show*

12. Molly Ringwald: *Townies*

13. Frank Sinatra: *The Frank Sinatra Show*

14. Jimmy Stewart: *The Jimmy Stewart Show; Hawkins*

15. Lana Turner: *The Survivors*

16. Gene Wilder: *Something Wilder*

11 TV Stars Who Tried to Make It in the Movies but Failed

Likewise, fame on the small screen is no guarantee of success on the big screen. . . .

1. Pamela Anderson Lee: *Barb Wire*

2. David Caruso: *Kiss of Death; Jade*

3. Bill Cosby: *Leonard Part VI; Ghost Dad; Jack*

4. Ellen DeGeneres: *Mr. Wrong*

5. Kelsey Grammer: *Down Periscope*

6. Don Johnson: *Sweet Hearts Dance; Dead-Bang; The Hot Spot; Harley Davidson and the Marlboro Man; Paradise; Born Yesterday; Guilty as Sin*

7. Matt LeBlanc: *Ed*

8. Luke Perry: *Buffy the Vampire Slayer; 8 Seconds*

9. Jason Priestley: *Calendar Girl*

10. Roseanne: *She-Devil; Even Cowgirls Get the Blues; Blue in the Face*

11. David Schwimmer: *The Pallbearer*

Four TV Stars Who Gave Up Acting to Direct

Getting behind the camera seems to be the dream of every actor. Here are a handful who tried it—and never looked back (with the exception of the occasional cameo).

1. Ron Howard: *Grand Theft Auto* (1978); *Night Shift* (1982); *Splash* (1984); *Cocoon* (1985); *Gung Ho* (1986); *Willow* (1988); *Parenthood* (1989); *Backdraft* (1991); *Far and Away* (1992); *The Paper* (1994); *Apollo 13* (1995); *Ransom* (1996)

2. Penny Marshall: *Jumpin' Jack Flash* (1986); *Big* (1988); *Awakenings* (1990); *A League of*

Their Own (1992); *Renaissance Man* (1994); *The Preacher's Wife* (1996)

3. Rob Reiner: *This Is Spinal Tap* (1984); *The Sure Thing* (1985); *Stand by Me* (1986); *The Princess Bride* (1987); *When Harry Met Sally* (1989); *Misery* (1990); *A Few Good Men* (1992); *North* (1994); *The American President* (1995); *Ghosts of Mississippi* (1995)

4. Betty Thomas: *The Brady Bunch Movie* (1995); *Private Parts* (1997)

28 Feature Films Based on TV Shows

Hollywood has mined television so deeply that pretty soon we may see big-screen versions of shows like *Joanie Loves Chachi*. (We see Liv Tyler and Leonardo DiCaprio in the lead roles, if anyone's interested.)

1. *The Addams Family*

2. *The Avengers*

3. *Beavis and Butt-head Do America*

4. *The Beverly Hillbillies*

5. *The Brady Bunch Movie*

6. *Car 54, Where Are You?*

7. *Dennis the Menace*

8. *Dragnet*

9. *The Flintstones*

10. *Flipper*

11. *The Fugitive*

12. *George of the Jungle*

13. *Leave It to Beaver*

14. *The Little Rascals*

15. *Lost in Space*

16. *McHale's Navy*

17. *The Man From U.N.C.L.E.*

18. *Maverick*

19. *Mission: Impossible*

20. *Mr. Magoo*

21. *My Favorite Martian*

22. *Sea Hunt*

23. *Sgt. Bilko*

24. The *Star Trek* series of films

25. *The Twilight Zone*

26. *The Untouchables*

27. *The X-Files*

28. *Wanted: Dead or Alive*

23 Series Based on Feature Films

Television has also rifled through Hollywood's film archives and come up with the following series—some of them, like *M*A*S*H*, hugely successful.

1. *Alice* (*Alice Doesn't Live Here Any More*)
2. *Alien Nation*
3. *The Courtship of Eddie's Father*
4. *Dr. Kildare* (*Interns Can't Take Money*)
5. *Fame*
6. *Fast Times* (*Fast Times at Ridgemont High*)
7. *Flash Gordon*
8. *Freddy's Nightmares* (*Nightmare on Elm Street*)
9. *How the West Was Won*
10. *Lassie* (*Lassie Come Home*)
11. *Logan's Run*
12. *M*A*S*H*
13. *Mr. and Mrs. North*
14. *Mr. Belvedere* (*Sitting Pretty*)
15. *The Odd Couple*
16. *Operation Petticoat*
17. *Peyton Place*

18. *Planet of the Apes*

19. *RoboCop: The Series*

20. *The Saint* (*The Saint in New York*)

21. *Tarzan* (*Tarzan of the Apes*)

22. *Weird Science*

23. *Zorro* (*The Mark of Zorro*)

Nine MTV Talents Go to the Big Screen

1. Bill Bellamy: *Who's The Man* (1993); *Fled* (1996); *Love Jones* (1997); *How to Be a Player* (1997)

2. Chris Connelly: *The Bodyguard* (1992); *Last Action Hero* (1993)

3. Dan Cortese: *Demolition Man* (1993); *A Weekend in the Country* (1995); *Two Guys Talking About Girls* (1995)

4. & 5. Dre and Ed Lover: *Juice* (1992); *Who's the Man?* (1993)

6. Karen Duffy: *29th Street* (1991); *Malcolm X* (1992); *Who's the Man?* (1993); *Last Action Hero* (1993); *Reality Bites* (1994)

7. Denis Leary: *Strictly Business* (1991); *National Lampoon's Loaded Weapon 1* (1993); *The Sandlot* (1993); *Who's the Man?* (1993); *Gunmen* (1994); *Demolition Man* (1993);

Judgment Night (1993); *The Ref* (1994); *Operation Dumbo Drop* (1995); *The Neon Bible* (1996); *Two If by Sea* (1996)

8. Eric Nies: *Above the Rim* (1994)

9. Martha Quinn: *Eddie and the Cruisers II: Eddie Lives!* (1989); *Problem Child 2* (1991)

Noteworthy Films of Six Great Saturday Night Live *Veterans*

1. Dan Aykroyd: *1941* (1979); *The Blues Brothers* (1980); *Neighbors* (1981); *Doctor Detroit* (1983); *Trading Places* (1983); *Twilight Zone: The Movie* (1983); *Ghostbusters* (1984); *Nothing Lasts Forever* (1984); *Into the Night* (1985); *Spies Like Us* (1985); *Dragnet* (1987); *Driving Miss Daisy* (1989); *My Girl* (1991); *Coneheads* (1993)

2. John Belushi: *Goin' South* (1978); *National Lampoon's Animal House* (1978); *1941* (1979); *The Blues Brothers* (1980); *Neighbors* (1981)

3. Chevy Chase: *The Groove Tube* (1972); *Foul Play* (1978); *Caddyshack* (1980); *Oh, Heavenly Dog!* (1980); *Seems Like Old Times* (1980); *National Lampoon's Vacation* (1983); *Spies Like Us* (1985)

4. Billy Crystal: *The Princess Bride* (1987); *When Harry Met Sally* (1989); *Hamlet* (1990); *City Slickers* (1991)

5. Eddie Murphy: *48 Hrs.* (1982); *Trading Places* (1983); *Beverly Hills Cop* (1984); *Coming to America* (1988); *The Distinguished Gentleman* (1992); *The Nutty Professor* (1996)

6. Bill Murray: *Meatballs* (1979); *Caddyshack* (1980); *Tootsie* (1982); *Ghostbusters* (1984); *Little Shop of Horrors* (1986); *What About Bob?* (1991); *Groundhog Day* (1993); *Mad Dog and Glory* (1993); *Ed Wood* (1994)

And the
Winners Are . . .

Top 10 Multiple Emmy-winning Individuals

1. Dwight Hemion, producer/director (17)
2. Buz Kohan, writer/producer (13)
3. Ian Fraser, composer/music conductor (11)
4. Don Mischer, producer (11)
5. Jan Scott, art director/production designer (11)
6. Steven Bochco, producer/writer (10)
7. George Stevens, Jr., writer/narrator/producer (10)
8. Carl Reiner, actor/writer (9)
9. Mary Tyler Moore, actress (8)
10. Michael G. Westmore, makeup artist (8)

Three Series with the Most Emmy Nominations

1. *Cheers* (117)
2. *M*A*S*H* (109)
3. *Hill Street Blues* (98)

Three Series with the Most Emmy Wins

1. *The Mary Tyler Moore Show* (29)
2. *Cheers* (28)
3. *Hill Street Blues* (26)

Top 11 Male Performers with the Most Emmys

1. Ed Asner (7)
2. Art Carney (6)
3. Alan Alda (5)
4. Peter Falk (5)
5. Hal Holbrook (5)
6. Don Knotts (5)
7. Carroll O'Connor (5)
8. Laurence Olivier (5)
9. Dick Van Dyke (5)

10. Harvey Korman (4)
11. John Larroquette (4)

Top 11 Female Performers with the Most Emmys

1. Mary Tyler Moore (8)
2. Dinah Shore (8)
3. Candice Bergen (5)
4. Carol Burnett (5)
5. Cloris Leachman (5)
6. Lily Tomlin (5)
7. Tracey Ullman (5)
8. Tyne Daly (4)
9. Valerie Harper (4)
10. Michael Learned (4)
11. Rhea Perlman (4)

Seven Pairs of Emmy-winning Husbands and Wives

1. Bonnie Bartlett and William Daniels
2. Colleen Dewhurst and George C. Scott

3. Lynn Fontanne and Alfred Lunt

4. Rhea Perlman and Danny DeVito

5. Jessica Tandy and Hume Cronyn

6. Marlo Thomas and Phil Donahue

7. Lynn Whitfield and Brian Gibson

Three Sets of Emmy-winning Parents and Children

1. Danny and Marlo Thomas

2. James and Tyne Daly

3. Carl and Rob Reiner

Emmy Winners for Outstanding Drama, 1950 to Present

1950: *Pulitzer Prize Playhouse* (ABC)

1951: *Studio One* (CBS)

1952: *Robert Montgomery Presents* (NBC)

1953: *The U.S. Steel Hour* (ABC)

1954: *The U.S. Steel Hour* (ABC)

1955: *Producers' Showcase* (NBC)

1956: *Playhouse 90* (CBS)

1957: *Gunsmoke* (CBS)

1958: The Alcoa Hour/Goodyear Theatre (NBC); Playhouse 90 (CBS)

1959: Playhouse 90 (CBS)

1960: Macbeth (NBC)

1961: The Defenders (CBS)

1962: The Defenders (CBS)

1963: *The Defenders* (CBS)

1964: This category not included in 1964

1965: *The Fugitive* (ABC)

1966: *Mission: Impossible* (CBS)

1967: *Mission: Impossible* (CBS)

1968: *NET Playhouse* (NET)

1969: *Marcus Welby, M.D.* (ABC)

1970: *The Bold Ones: The Senator* (NBC)

1971: *Masterpiece Theater: Elizabeth R* (PBS)

1972: *The Waltons* (CBS)

1973: *Masterpiece Theater: Upstairs, Downstairs* (PBS)

1974: *Masterpiece Theater: Upstairs, Downstairs* (PBS)

1975: *Police Story* (NBC)

1976: *Masterpiece Theater: Upstairs, Downstairs* (PBS)

1977: *The Rockford Files* (NBC)

1978: *Lou Grant* (CBS)

1979: *Lou Grant* (CBS)

1980: *Hill Street Blues* (NBC)

1981: *Hill Street Blues* (NBC)

1982: *Hill Street Blues* (NBC)

1983: *Hill Street Blues* (NBC)

1984: *Cagney & Lacey* (CBS)

1985: *Cagney & Lacey* (CBS)

1986: *L.A. Law* (NBC)

1987: *thirtysomething* (ABC)

1988: *L.A. Law* (NBC)

1989: *L.A. Law* (NBC)

1990: *L.A. Law* (NBC)

1991: *Northern Exposure* (CBS)

1992: *Picket Fences* (CBS)

1993: *Picket Fences* (CBS)

1994: *NYPD Blue* (ABC)

1995: *NYPD Blue* (ABC)

1996: *ER* (NBC)

Emmy Winners for Outstanding Comedy Series, 1951 to Present

1951: *The Red Skelton Show* (NBC)

1952: *I Love Lucy* (CBS)

1953: *I Love Lucy* (CBS)

1954: *Make Room for Daddy* (ABC)

1955: *The Phil Silvers Show* (CBS)

1956: This category not included in 1956

1957: *The Phil Silvers Show* (CBS)

1958: *The Jack Benny Show* (CBS)

1959: *Art Carney Special* (NBC)

1960: *The Jack Benny Show* (CBS)

1961: *The Bob Newhart Show* (NBC)

1962: *The Dick Van Dyke Show* (CBS)

1963: *The Dick Van Dyke Show* (CBS)

1964: This category not included in 1964

1965: *The Dick Van Dyke Show* (CBS)

1966: *The Monkees* (NBC)

1967: *Get Smart* (NBC)

1968: *Get Smart* (NBC)

1969: *My World and Welcome to It* (NBC)

1970: *All in the Family* (CBS)

1971: *All in the Family* (CBS)

1972: *All in the Family* (CBS)

1973: *M*A*S*H* (CBS)

1974: *The Mary Tyler Moore Show* (CBS)

1975: *The Mary Tyler Moore Show* (CBS)

1976: *The Mary Tyler Moore Show* (CBS)

1977: *All in the Family* (CBS)

1978: *Taxi* (ABC)

1979: *Taxi* (ABC)

1980: *Taxi* (ABC)

1981: *Barney Miller* (ABC)

1982: *Cheers* (NBC)

1983: *Cheers* (NBC)

1984: *The Cosby Show* (NBC)

1985: *The Golden Girls* (NBC)

1986: *The Golden Girls* (NBC)

1987: *The Wonder Years* (ABC)

1988: *Cheers* (NBC)

1989: *Murphy Brown* (CBS)

1990: *Cheers* (NBC)

1991: *Murphy Brown* (CBS)

1992: *Seinfeld* (NBC)

1993: *Frasier* (NBC)

1994: *Frasier* (NBC)

1995: *Frasier* (NBC)

1996: *Frasier* (NBC)

Emmy Winners for Outstanding Lead Actor in a Drama Series, 1958 to present

1958: Raymond Burr, *Perry Mason* (CBS)

1959: Robert Stack, *The Untouchables* (ABC)

1960: Raymond Burr, *Perry Mason* (CBS)

1961: E. G. Marshall, *The Defenders* (CBS)

1962: E. G. Marshall, *The Defenders* (CBS)

1963: This category not included in 1963

1964: This category not included in 1964

1965: Bill Cosby, *I Spy* (NBC)

1966: Bill Cosby, *I Spy* (NBC)

1967: Bill Cosby, *I Spy* (NBC)

1968: Carl Betz, *Judd for the Defense* (ABC)

1969: Robert Young, *Marcus Welby, M.D.* (ABC)

1970: Hal Holbrook, *The Bold Ones: The Senator* (NBC)

1971: Peter Falk, *Columbo* (NBC)

1972: Richard Thomas, *The Waltons* (CBS)

1973: Telly Savalas, *Kojak* (CBS)

1974: Robert Blake, *Baretta* (ABC)

1975: Peter Falk, *Columbo* (NBC)

1976: James Garner, *The Rockford Files* (NBC)

1977: Edward Asner, *Lou Grant* (CBS)

1978: Ron Leibman, *Kaz* (CBS)

1979: Ed Asner, *Lou Grant* (CBS)

1980: Daniel J. Travanti, *Hill Street Blues* (NBC)

1981: Daniel J. Travanti, *Hill Street Blues* (NBC)

1982: Ed Flanders, *St. Elsewhere* (NBC)

1983: Tom Selleck, *Magnum, P.I.* (CBS)

1984: William Daniels, *St. Elsewhere* (NBC)

1985: William Daniels, *St. Elsewhere* (NBC)

1986: Bruce Willis, *Moonlighting* (ABC)

1987: Richard Kiley, *A Year in the Life* (NBC)

1988: Carroll O'Connor, *In the Heat of the Night* (NBC)

1989: Peter Falk, *Columbo* (ABC)

1990: James Earl Jones, *Gabriel's Fire* (ABC)

1991: Christopher Lloyd, *Avonlea* (DIS)

1992: Tom Skerritt, *Picket Fences* (CBS)

1993: Dennis Franz, *NYPD Blue* (ABC)

1994: Mandy Patinkin, *Chicago Hope*,(CBS)

1995: Mandy Patinkin, *Chicago Hope* (CBS)

1996: Dennis Franz, *NYPD Blue*(ABC)

Emmy Winners for Outstanding Lead Actress in a Drama Series, 1963 to Present

1963: Shelley Winters, *Two is the Number* (NBC)

1964: This category not included in 1964

1965: Barbara Stanwyck, *The Big Valley* (ABC)

1966: Barbara Bain, *Mission: Impossible* (CBS)

1967: Barbara Bain, *Mission: Impossible* (CBS)

1968: Barbara Bain, *Mission: Impossible* (CBS)

1969: Susan Hampshire, *The Forsyte Saga* (NET)

1970: Susan Hampshire, *The First Churchills* (PBS)

1971: Glenda Jackson, *Masterpiece Theater: Elizabeth R* (PBS)

1972: Michael Learned, *The Waltons* (CBS)

1973: Michael Learned, *The Waltons* (CBS)

1974: Jean Marsh, *Masterpiece Theater: Upstairs, Downstairs* (PBS)

1975: Michael Learned, *The Waltons* (CBS)

1976: Lindsay Wagner, *The Bionic Woman* (ABC)

1977: Sada Thomspon, *Family* (ABC)

1978: Mariette Hartley, *The Incredible Hulk* (CBS)

1979: Barbara Bel Geddes, *Dallas* (CBS)

1980: Barbara Babcock, *Hill Street Blues* (NBC)

1981: Michael Learned, *Nurse* (CBS)

1982: Tyne Daly, *Cagney & Lacey* (CBS)

1983: Tyne Daly, *Cagney & Lacey* (CBS)

1984: Tyne Daly, *Cagney & Lacey* (CBS)

1985: Sharon Gless, *Cagney & Lacey* (CBS)

1986: Sharon Gless, *Cagney & Lacey* (CBS)

1987: Tyne Daly, *Cagney & Lacey* (CBS)

1988: Dana Delany, *China Beach* (ABC)

1989: Patricia Wettig, *thirtysomething* (ABC)

1990: Patricia Wettig, *thirtysomething* (ABC)

1991: Dana Delany, *China Beach* (ABC)

1992: Kathy Baker, *Picket Fences* (CBS)

1993: Sela Ward, *Sisters* (NBC)

1994: Kathy Baker, *Picket Fences* (CBS)

1995: Kathy Baker, *Picket Fences* (CBS)

1996: Kathy Baker, *Picket Fences* (CBS)

Emmy Winners for Outstanding Lead Actor in a Comedy, 1963 to Present

1963: Dick Van Dyke, *The Dick Van Dyke Show* (CBS)

1964: This category not included in 1964

1965: Dick Van Dyke, *The Dick Van Dyke Show* (CBS)

1966: Don Adams, *Get Smart* (NBC)

1967: Don Adams, *Get Smart* (NBC)

1968: Don Adams, *Get Smart* (NBC)

1969: William Windom, *My World and Welcome to It* (NBC)

1970: Jack Klugman, *The Odd Couple* (ABC)

1971: Carroll O'Connor, *All in the Family* (CBS)

1972: Jack Klugman, *The Odd Couple* (ABC)

1973: Alan Alda, *M*A*S*H* (CBS)

1974: Tony Randall, *The Odd Couple* (ABC)

1975: Jack Albertson, *Chico and the Man* (NBC)

1976: Carroll O'Connor, *All in the Family* (CBS)

1977: Carroll O'Connor, *All in the Family* (CBS)

1978: Carroll O'Connor, *All in the Family* (CBS)

1979: Richard Mulligan, *Soap* (ABC)

1980: Judd Hirsch, *Taxi* (ABC)

1981: Alan Alda, *M*A*S*H* (CBS)

1982: Judd Hirsch, *Taxi* (NBC)

1983: John Ritter, *Three's Company* (ABC)

1984: Robert Guillaume, *Benson* (ABC)

1985: Michael J. Fox, *Family Ties* (NBC)

1986: Michael J. Fox, *Family Ties* (NBC)

1987: Michael J. Fox, *Family Ties* (NBC)

1988: Richard Mulligan, *Empty Nest* (NBC)

1989: Ted Danson, *Cheers* (NBC)

1990: Burt Reynolds, *Evening Shade* (CBS)

1991: Craig T. Nelson, *Coach* (ABC)

1992: Ted Danson, *Cheers* (NBC)

1993: Kelsey Grammer, *Frasier* (NBC)

1994: Kelsey Grammer, *Frasier* (NBC)

1995: Kelsey Grammer, *Frasier* (NBC)

1996: John Lithgow, *3rd Rock from the Sun* (NBC)

Emmy Winners for Outstanding Lead Actress in a Comedy, 1963 to Present

1963: Mary Tyler Moore, *The Dick Van Dyke Show* (CBS)

1964: This category not included in 1964

1965: Mary Tyler Moore, *The Dick Van Dyke Show* (CBS)

1966: Lucille Ball, *The Lucy Show* (CBS)

1967: Lucille Ball, *The Lucy Show* (CBS)

1968: Hope Lange, *The Ghost and Mrs. Muir* (NBC)

1969: Hope Lange, *The Ghost and Mrs. Muir* (ABC)

1970: Jean Stapleton, *All in the Family* (CBS)

1971: Jean Stapleton, *All in the Family* (CBS)

1972: Mary Tyler Moore, *The Mary Tyler Moore Show* (CBS)

1973: Mary Tyler Moore, *The Mary Tyler Moore Show* (CBS)

1974: Valerie Harper, *Rhoda* (CBS)

1975: Mary Tyler Moore, *The Mary Tyler Moore Show* (CBS)

1976: Beatrice Arthur, *Maude* (CBS)

1977: Jean Stapleton, *All in the Family* (CBS)

1978: Ruth Gordon (for the episode "Sugar Mama"), *Taxi* (ABC)

1979: Cathryn Damon, *Soap* (ABC)

1980: Isabel Sanford, *The Jeffersons* (CBS)

1981: Carol Kane, *Taxi* (ABC)

1982: Shelley Long, *Cheers* (NBC)

1983: Jane Curtin, *Kate & Allie* (CBS)

1984: Jane Curtin, *Kate & Allie* (CBS)

1985: Betty White, *The Golden Girls* (NBC)

1986: Rue McClanahan, *The Golden Girls* (NBC)

1987: Beatrice Arthur, *The Golden Girls* (NBC)

1988: Candice Bergen, *Murphy Brown* (CBS)

1989: Candice Bergen, *Murphy Brown* (CBS)

1990: Kirstie Alley, *Cheers* (NBC)

1991: Candice Bergen, *Murphy Brown* (CBS)

1992: Roseanne Arnold, *Roseanne* (ABC)

1993: Candice Bergen, *Murphy Brown* (CBS)

1994: Candice Bergen, *Murphy Brown* (CBS)

1995: Candice Bergen, *Murphy Brown* (CBS)

1996: Helen Hunt, *Mad About You* (NBC)

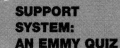

SUPPORT SYSTEM: AN EMMY QUIZ

Where would TV be without its tradition of great sidekicks and second bananas? We dedicate this test to those actors and actresses who did more than just support their series: they lifted them up to a higher level of greatness.

1. Who won the most Emmys for Outstanding Supporting Actor (and how many)?

A. John Larroquette   C. Don Knotts

B. Edward Asner   D. Art Carney

2. Who won the most Emmys for Outstanding Supporting Actress (and how many)?

A. Laurie Metcalf   C. Loretta Swit

B. Valerie Harper   D. Rhea Perlman

3. Name the two actresses who won for Outstanding Supporting Actress and Outstanding Lead Actress in a Comedy.

A. Valerie Harper   C. Betty White

B. Mary Tyler Moore   D. Beatrice Arthur

4. Who is the only actor to win for Outstanding Supporting Actor and Outstanding Lead Actor in a Comedy?

A. Edward Asner   C. Kelsey Grammer

B. Robert Guillaume   D. Peter Scolari

5. Name the only actress to win for Outstanding Supporting Actress and Outstanding Lead Actress in a Comedy for playing the same character in the same show.

A. Mary Tyler Moore   C. Rue McClanahan

B. Carol Kane   D. Vivian Vance

6. Among TV's most memorable scene-stealers were the guest villains on *Batman*. But only one was nominated for an Emmy for that role. Who was it?

A. Cesar Romero (the Joker)

B. Frank Gorshin (the Riddler)

C. Burgess Meredith (the Penguin)

D. Julie Newmar (Catwoman)

7. In 1968–69, the supporting category lumped comedy and drama together. Dramatic nominees Leonard Nimoy and Greg Morris lost to the only comedic actor nominated. Who was he?

A. Don Knotts   C. Gale Gordon

B. Werner Klemperer   D. Edward Platt

8. Who is the only Outstanding Supporting Actress winner to also win an Oscar?

A. Cloris Leachman   C. Agnes Moorehead

B. Candice Bergen   D. Elizabeth Ashley

9. Ann B. Davis was never nominated for *The Brady Bunch*, but more than a decade earlier she was a two-time winner for what show?

A. *Mr. Peepers*

B. *I Married Joan*

C. *The Bob Cummings Show*

D. *The Life of Riley*

10. Harry Morgan was nominated eight times for *M*A*S*H* (winning in 1979–80), nearly 20 years after he was nominated for another show. Name that show.

A. *Dragnet*   C. *Pete and Gladys*

B. *December Bride*   D. *Burns and Allen*

11. All three of the wonderful supporting actors in *Seinfeld* have been nominated, but only one has won. Which one?

A. Jason Alexander   C. Michael Richards

B. Julia Louis-Dreyfus

12. Which member of *The Mary Tyler Moore Show*'s cast was never nominated?

A. Georgia Engel   C. Ted Knight

B. Gavin MacLeod   D. Betty White

13. Which two great TV "aunts" won?

A. Frances Bavier (Aunt Bee, *Andy Griffith*)

B. Marion Lorne (Aunt Clara, *Bewitched*)

C. Madge Blake (Aunt Harriet, *Batman*)

D. LaWanda Page (Aunt Esther, *Sanford and Son*)

14. True or false: Game-show fixture Charles Nelson Reilly received an Outstanding Supporting Actor nomination.

15. True or false: William Frawley won as many Emmys as Vivian Vance.

ANSWERS

1. C (5). 2. D (4). 3. A and C: Harper for *The Mary Tyler Moore Show* and *Rhoda;* White for *The Mary Tyler Moore Show* and *The Golden Girls.* 4. B, for *Soap* and *Benson.* 5. B, for *Taxi.* 6. B. 7. B, for *Hogan's Heroes.* 8. A, for *The Mary Tyler Moore Show* and *The Last Picture Show.* 9. C: As Schultzy, Bob's devoted assistant, she won in 1957 and 1958–59. 10. B. 11. C. 12. B. 13. A and B. 14. True: for *The Ghost and Mrs. Muir,* 1969–70. 15. False: Frawley, nominated five times, never won; Vance, nominated four times, won once in 1953.

(From TV Guide, by Andy Edelstein)

Daytime Emmy Award Winners, 1971 to Present

1971: *The Doctors*

1972: *The Edge of Night*

1973: *The Doctors*

1974: *The Young and the Restless*

1975: *Another World*

1976: *Ryan's Hope*

1977: *Days of Our Lives*

1978: *Ryan's Hope*

1979: *Guiding Light*

1980: *General Hospital*

1981: *Guiding Light*

1982: *The Young and the Restless*

1983: *General Hospital*

1984: *The Young and the Restless*

1985: *The Young and the Restless*

1986: *As the World Turns*

1987: *Santa Barbara*

1988: *Santa Barbara*

1989: *Santa Barbara*

1990: *As the World Turns*

1991: *All My Children*

1992: *The Young and the Restless*

1993: *All My Children*

1994: *General Hospital*

1995: *General Hospital*

1996: *General Hospital*

1997: *General Hospital*

12 TV Stars Who Went on to Win Oscars

1. Cher: Best Actress for *Moonstruck* (1987)

2. Michael Douglas: Best Picture for *One Flew Over the Cuckoo's Nest* (1975), Best Actor for *Wall Street* (1987)

3. Olympia Dukakis: Best Supporting Actress for *Moonstruck* (1987)

4. Patty Duke: Best Actress for *The Miracle Worker* (1962)

5. Clint Eastwood: Best Director and Best Picture for *Unforgiven* (1992), Irving G. Thalberg Award (1995)

6. Sally Field: Best Actress for *Norma Rae* (1979), Best Actress for *Places in the Heart* (1984)

7. Jodie Foster: Best Actress for *The Accused* (1988), Best Actress for *Silence of the Lambs* (1991)

8. Tom Hanks: Best Actor for *Philadelphia* (1993), Best Actor for *Forrest Gump* (1994)

9. Kevin Kline: Best Supporting Actor for *A Fish Called Wanda* (1988)

10. Tommy Lee Jones: Best Supporting Actor for *The Fugitive* (1993)

11. Billy Bob Thornton: Best Screenplay Adaptation for *Sling Blade* (1996)

12. Marisa Tomei: Best Supporting Actress for *My Cousin Vinny* (1992)

42 Emmy Winners Who Also Won Oscars

1. Jack Albertson—Emmy: Outstanding Lead Actor in a Comedy Series for *Chico and the Man* (1976), Outstanding Single Performance by a Supporting Actor in Variety or Music for *Cher* (1975); Oscar: Best Supporting Actor for *The Subject Was Roses* (1968)

2. Ingrid Bergman—Emmy: Outstanding Single Performance by an Actress for *The Turn of the Screw* (1960), Outstanding Lead Actress in a Limited Series or a Special for *A Woman Called Golda* (1982); Oscar: Best Actress for *Gaslight* (1944), *Anastasia* (1956), Best Supporting Actress for *Murder on the Orient Express* (1974)

3. Shirley Booth—Emmy: Outstanding Performance by an Actress in a Series for *Hazel* (1962

and 1963); Oscar: Best Actress for *Come Back, Little Sheba* (1952)

4. Marlon Brando—Emmy: Outstanding Supporting Actor in a Limited Series or Special for *Roots: The Next Generations* (1979); Oscar: Best Actor for *On the Waterfront* (1954), *The Godfather* (1972)

5. Art Carney—Emmy: Best Series Supporting Actor for *The Jackie Gleason Show* (1953 and 1954), Best Actor in a Supporting Role for *The Honeymooners* (1955), Individual Achievement for *The Jackie Gleason Show* (1967 and 1968), Outstanding Supporting Actor in a Limited Series or Special for *Terrible Joe Moran* (1984); Oscar: Best Actor for *Harry and Tonto* (1974)

6. Bette Davis—Emmy: Outstanding Lead Actress in a Limited Series or Special for *Strangers: the Story of a Mother and Daughter* (1979); Oscar: Best Actress for *Dangerous* (1935), *Jezebel* (1938)

7. Melvyn Douglas—Emmy: Outstanding Single Performance by an Actor in a Leading Role in a Drama for *Do Not Go Gentle into That Good Night* (1968); Oscar: Best Supporting Actor for *Hud* (1963), *Being There* (1979)

8. Patty Duke—Emmy: Outstanding Single Performance by an Actress in a Leading Role for *My Sweet Charlie* (1970), Outstanding Lead Actress in a Limited Series for *Captains and the Kings* (1977); Outstanding Lead Actress in a Limited Series or Special for *The Miracle*

Worker (1980); Oscar: Best Supporting Actress for *The Miracle Worker* (1962)

9. Sally Field—Emmy: Outstanding Lead Actress in a Drama or Comedy Special for *Sybil* (1977); Oscar: Best Actress for *Norma Rae* (1979), *Places in the Heart* (1984)

10. Jane Fonda—Emmy: Outstanding Lead Actress in a Limited Series or Special for *The Dollmaker* (1984); Oscar: Best Actress for *Klute* (1971), *Coming Home* (1978)

11. Ruth Gordon—Emmy: Outstanding Lead Actress in a Comedy Series for the *Taxi* episode "Sugar Mama" (1979); Oscar: Best Actress for *Rosemary's Baby* (1968)

12. Louis Gossett, Jr.—Emmy: Outstanding Lead Actor for a Single Appearance in a Drama or Comedy Series for *Roots* (1977); Oscar: Best Supporting Actor for *An Officer and a Gentleman* (1982)

13. Lee Grant—Emmy: Outstanding Performance by an Actress in a Supporting role in a Drama for *Peyton Place* (1966), Outstanding Single Performance by an Actress in a Leading Role for *The Neon Ceiling* (1971); Oscar: Best Supporting Actress for *Shampoo* (1975)

14. Helen Hayes—Emmy: Best Actress (1952); Oscar: Best Actress for *The Sin of Madelon Claudet* (1931), Best Supporting Actress for *Airport* (1970)

15. Katharine Hepburn—Emmy: Outstanding Lead Actress in a Special Program for *Love Among the Ruins* (1975); Oscar: Best Actress for *Morning Glory* (1932), *Guess Who's Coming to Dinner* (1967), *The Lion in Winter* (1968); *On Golden Pond* (1981)

16. Dustin Hoffman—Emmy: Outstanding Lead Actor on a Miniseries or Special for *Death of a Salesman* (1986); Oscar: Best Actor for *Kramer vs. Kramer* (1980), *Rain Man* (1989)

17. William Holden—Emmy: Best Lead Actor in a Limited Series for *The Blue Knight* (1974); Oscar: Best Actor for *Stalag 17* (1953)

18. Holly Hunter—Emmy: Outstanding Lead Actress in a Miniseries or Special for *Roe vs. Wade* (1989), *The Positively True Adventures of the Alleged Texas Cheerleader-Murdering Mom* (1993); Oscar: Best Actress for *The Piano* (1993)

19. Glenda Jackson—Emmy: Outstanding Continued Performance by an Actress in a Leading Role in a Dramatic Series for *Elizabeth R* (1972), Outstanding Single Performance by an Actress in a Leading Role for *Elizabeth R* (1972); Oscar: Best Actress for *Women in Love* (1970), *A Touch of Class* (1973)

20. Cloris Leachman—Emmy: Outstanding Single Performance by an Actress in a Leading Role for *A Brand New Life* (1973), Best Supporting Actress in a Comedy for *The Mary Tyler Moore Show* (1974), Outstanding Continuing or

Single Performance by a Supporting Actress in a Variety or Music Program for *Cher* (1975), Outstanding Performer in Children's Programming for *The Woman Who Willed a Miracle* (1983), Outstanding Individual Performance in a Variety or Music Program for *Screen Actors Guild 50th Anniversary Celebration* (1984); Oscar: Best Supporting Actress for *The Last Picture Show* (1971)

21. Karl Malden—Emmy: Outstanding Supporting Actor in a Limited Series or Special for *Fatal Vision* (1985); Oscar: Best Supporting Actor for *A Streetcar Named Desire* (1951)

22. Thomas Mitchell—Emmy: Best Actor (1952); Oscar: Best Supporting Actor for *Stagecoach* (1939)

23. Rita Moreno—Emmy: Outstanding Continuing or Single Performance by a Supporting Actress in Variety or Musical for *The Muppet Show* (1977), Outstanding Lead Actress for a Single appearance in a Drama or Comedy Series for *The Rockford Files* (1978); Oscar: Best Supporting Actress for *West Side Story* (1961)

24. Laurence Olivier—Emmy: Outstanding Single Performance by an Actor for *The Moon and Sixpence* (1960), *Long Day's Journey into Night* (1973), Outstanding Lead Actor in a Special Program for *Love Among the Ruins* (1975), Outstanding Supporting Actor in a Limited Series or Special for *Brideshead Revisited*

(1982), Outstanding Lead Actor in a Limited Series or Special for *Laurence Olivier's King Lear* (1984); Oscar: Best Actor for *Hamlet* (1948)

25. Geraldine Page—Emmy: Outstanding Single Performance by an Actress in a Leading Role in a Drama for *A Christmas Memory* (1967), *The Thanksgiving Visitor* (1969); Oscar: Best Actress for *The Trip to Bountiful* (1985)

26. Jack Palance—Emmy: Best Single Performance (Actor) for *Requiem for a Heavyweight* (1956); Oscar: Best Supporting Actor for *City Slickers* (1991)

27. Vanessa Redgrave—Emmy: Outstanding Lead Actress in a Limited Series or Special for *Playing for Time* (1981); Oscar: Best Supporting Actress for *Julia* (1977)

28. Jason Robards—Emmy: Outstanding Lead Actor in a Miniseries or Special for *Inherit the Wind* (1988); Oscar: Best Supporting Actor for *All the President's Men* (1976), *Julia* (1977)

29. Cliff Robertson—Emmy: Outstanding Single Performance by an Actor in a Leading Role in a Drama for *The Game* (1966); Oscar: Best Actor for *Charly* (1968)

30. Eva Marie Saint—Emmy: Outstanding Supporting Actress in a Miniseries or Special for *People Like Us* (1990); Oscar: Best Supporting Actress for *On the Waterfront* (1954)

31. Paul Scofield—Emmy: Outstanding Single

Performance by an Actor in a Leading Role for *Male of the Species* (1969); Oscar: Best Actor for *A Man for All Seasons* (1966)

32. George C. Scott—Emmy: Outstanding Single Performance by an Actor in a Leading Role for *The Price* (1971); Oscar: Best Actor for *Patton* (1970)

33. Simone Signoret—Emmy: Outstanding Single Performance by an Actress in a Leading Role in a Drama for *A Small Rebellion* (1966); Oscar: Best Actress for *Room at the Top* (1959)

34. Maureen Stapleton—Emmy: Outstanding Single Performance by an Actress in a Leading Role in a Drama for *Among the Paths to Eden* (1968); Oscar: Best Supporting Actress for *Reds* (1981)

35. Meryl Streep—Emmy: Outstanding Lead Actress in a Limited Series for *Holocaust* (1978); Oscar: Best Supporting Actress for *Kramer vs. Kramer* (1979), Best Actress for *Sophie's Choice* (1982)

36. Barbra Streisand—Emmy: Outstanding Individual Achievement in Entertainment for *My Name is Barbra* (1965), Outstanding Music Special for *Barbra Streisand: The Concert* (1995), Outstanding Individual Performance in a Variety or Music Program for *Barbra Streisand: The Concert* (1995); Oscar: Best Actress for *Funny Girl* (1968), Best Song for *Evergreen* (1976)

37. Jessica Tandy—Emmy: Outstanding Lead Actress in a Miniseries or Special for *Foxfire* (1988); Oscar: Best Actress for *Driving Miss Daisy* (1989)

38. Claire Trevor—Emmy: Best Single Performance (Actress) for *Dodsworth* (1956); Oscar: Best Supporting Actress for *Key Largo* (1948)

39. Peter Ustinov—Emmy: Best Single Performance by an Actor for *Life of Samuel Johnson* (1957), *Barefoot in Athens* (1967), *A Storm in Summer* (1970); Oscar: Best Supporting Actor for *Spartacus* (1960), *Topkapi* (1964)

40. Shelley Winters—Emmy: Outstanding Single Performance by an Actress in a Leading Role for *Two Is the Number* (1964); Oscar: Best Supporting Actress for *The Diary of Anne Frank* (1959), *A Patch of Blue* (1965)

41. Joanne Woodward—Emmy: Outstanding Lead Actress in a Drama or Comedy Special for *See How She Runs* (1978), Outstanding Lead Actress in a Limited Series or Special for *Do You Remember Love* (1985), Outstanding Informational Special for *Broadway's Dreamers: The Legacy of the Group Theater* (1990); Oscar: Best Actress for *The Three Faces of Eve* (1957)

42. Loretta Young—Emmy: Best Actress Starring in a Regular Series for *The Loretta Young Show* (1954), Best Continuing Performance in a Dramatic Series (Actress) for *The Loretta*

Young Show (1956), Best Actress in a Leading Role in a Dramatic Series for *The Loretta Young Show* (1959); Oscar: Best Actress for *The Farmer's Daughter* (1947)

Oscar Emcees, 1953 to Present

1953: Bob Hope and Conrad Nagel

1954: Donald O'Connor and Fredric March

1955: Bob Hope and Thelma Ritter

1956: Jerry Lewis, Claudette Colbert, and Joseph L. Mankiewicz

1957: Jerry Lewis and Celeste Holm

1958: Bob Hope, Jack Lemmon, David Niven, Rosalind Russell, James Stewart, and Donald Duck

1959: Bob Hope, Jerry Lewis, David Niven, Sir Laurence Olivier, Tony Randall, and Mort Sahl

1960: Bob Hope

1961: Bob Hope

1962: Bob Hope

1963: Frank Sinatra

1964: Jack Lemmon

1965: Bob Hope

1966: Bob Hope

1967: Bob Hope

1968: Bob Hope

1969: No emcee

1970: No emcee

1971: No emcee

1972: Helen Hayes, Alan King, Sammy Davis, Jr., and Jack Lemmon

1973: Carol Burnett, Michael Caine, Charlton Heston, and Rock Hudson

1974: John Huston, Diana Ross, Burt Reynolds, and David Niven

1975: Sammy Davis, Jr., Bob Hope, Shirley MacLaine, and Frank Sinatra

1976: Walter Matthau, Robert Shaw, George Segal, Goldie Hawn, and Gene Kelly

1977: Richard Pryor, Jane Fonda, Ellen Burstyn, and Warren Beatty

1978: Bob Hope

1979: Johnny Carson

1980: Johnny Carson

1981: Johnny Carson

1982: Johnny Carson

1983: Liza Minnelli and Dudley Moore

1984: Johnny Carson

1985: Jack Lemmon

1986: Alan Alda, Jane Fonda, and Robin Williams

1987: Chevy Chase, Goldie Hawn, and Paul Hogan

1988: Chevy Chase

1989: No emcee

1990: Billy Crystal

1991: Billy Crystal

1992: Billy Crystal

1993: Billy Crystal

1994: Whoopi Goldberg

1995: David Letterman

1996: Whoopi Goldberg

1997: Billy Crystal

14 Memorable Oscar Night Acceptance Speeches

1. F. Murray Abraham (Best Actor for *Amadeus,* 1984): "It would be a lie if I told you I didn't know what to say. I've been working on this speech for about twenty-five years."

2. Cher (Best Actress for *Moonstruck,* 1987); "I don't think this means I am somebody, but I guess I'm on my way."

3. Sally Field (Best Actress for *Places in the Heart,* 1984): "The first time [for *Norma Rae*] I didn't feel it, but this time I feel it, and I can't deny the fact that you like me. Right now, you like me!"

4. Louise Fletcher (Best Actress for *One Flew Over the Cuckoo's Nest,* 1975): "It looks like you all hated me so much as coldhearted Nurse Ratched that you are giving me this award for it. All I can say is I've loved being hated by you."

5. Whoopi Goldberg (Best Supporting Actress for *Ghost,* 1990): "Ever since I was a kid, I wanted this!"

6. Sir Alec Guiness (Honorary Oscar, 1979): "I feel very fraudulent taking this. But, I'm grabbing this while the going's good."

7. Dustin Hoffman (Best Actor for *Kramer vs. Kramer,* 1979): "I'd like to thank my parents for not practicing birth control."

8. John Wayne (Best Actor for *True Grit,* 1969): "If I'd known, I'd have put the eye patch on thirty-five years earlier."

9. Shirley MacLaine (Best Actress for *Terms of Endearment,* 1983): "I deserve this! This show has been as long as my career."

10. Paul Newman (Honorary Oscar, 1985): "I am especially grateful that this did not come wrapped in a gift certificate to Forest Lawn. I hope that my best work is down the pike and not behind."

11. Barbara Stanwyck (Honorary Oscar, 1981): "A few years ago, I stood on this stage with William Holden as presenter. I loved him very much and I miss him. He always wished that I would get an Oscar. And so tonight, my golden boy, you've got your wish."

12. Oliver Stone (Best Director and Best Picture for *Platoon,* 1986): "I think through this award you're really acknowledging that for the first time you really understand what happened over there [in Vietnam]. And I think what you're saying is that it should never in our lifetime happen again."

13. Dianne Wiest (Best Supporting Actress for *Hannah and Her Sisters,* 1986): "Gee, this isn't what I imagined it would be like in the bathtub."

14. Paul Williams (Best Original Song for "Evergreen," 1976): "I was going to thank all the little people, then I remembered I *am* the little people."

Switch Hits

19 Cases of Stolen Identities

When an actor wants out of a show, it doesn't mean that you have to kill off his character. Just hire a new actor, stick him in the old actor's shoes, and try to convince yourself that the viewers won't notice the difference.

1. Elvia Allman replaced Virginia Sale as Selma Plout on *Petticoat Junction.*

2. Michael Ansaras replaced Henry Silva as evil Kane on *Buck Rogers in the 25th Century.*

3. Jessica Bowman replaced Erika Flores as Colleen on *Dr. Quinn, Medicine Woman.*

4. Sarah Chalke replaced Lecy Goranson as Becky on *Roseanne* (for two seasons).

5. Jack Coleman replaced Al Corley as Steven Carrington on *Dynasty.*

6. Joan Crawford replaced her daughter, Christina Crawford, as Joann Kane on *The Secret Storm* (for four episodes, when Christina was ill).

7. Richard Deacon replaced Roger Carmel as Roger Buell on *The Mothers-in-Law*.

8. Brian Forster replaced Jeremy Gelbawks as Christopher Partridge on *The Partridge Family*.

9. June Lockhart and Hugh Reilly replaced Cloris Leachman and Jon Shepodd as Ruth and Paul Martin on *Lassie*.

10. Meredith MacRae replaced Gunilla Hutton, who replaced Jeannine Riley as Billie Jo Bradley on *Petticoat Junction*

11. Daphne Maxwell Reid replaced Janet Hubert-Whitten as Vivian Banks on *The Fresh Prince of Bel-Air*.

12. Patricia Driscoll replaced Bernadette O'Farrell as Maid Marion on *The Adventures of Robin Hood*.

13. Donna Reed replaced Barbara Bel Geddes as Miss Ellie on *Dallas* (for one season).

14. Kasey Rogers replaced Irene Vernon as Louise Tate on *Bewitched*.

15. Emma Samms replaced Pamela Sue Martin as Fallon Carrington on *Dynasty*.

16. Dick Sargent replaced Dick York as Darrin Stephens on *Bewitched*.

17. Lori Saunders replaced Pat Woodell as Bobbie Jo Bradley on *Petticoat Junction*.

18. Mark Stevens replaced Patrick McVey as Steve Wilson on *Big Town*.

19. Lynette Winter replaced Susan Walther as Henrietta Plout on *Petticoat Junction*.

13 Who Played Different Characters on the Same Show

Patty Duke isn't the only star who can play cousins—identical cousins—on TV. Here are thirteen who have played cousins, twins, and assorted lookalikes.

1. David Canary played twins Adam and Stuart Chandler on *All My Children*.

2. Patty Duke played cousins Patty and Cathy Lane on *The Patty Duke Show*.

3. Stacy Galina played cousins Mary-Frances Sumner and Kate Whittaker on *Knots Landing*.

4. Tony Geary played cousins Luke Spencer and Bill Eckert on *General Hospital*.

5. Anne Heche played twins Victoria Love and Marley McKinnon on *Another World*.

6. Carolyn Jones played cousins Morticia Addams and Ophelia on *The Addams Family*.

7. Lisa Kudrow played twins Phoebe and Ursula on *Friends* (Ursula originally appeared as a waitress on *Mad About You*).

8. Martin Lawrence played Martin Payne, his mother, and Sheneneh on *Martin*.

9. Sheryl Lee played cousins Laura Palmer and Maddie Ferguson on *Twin Peaks*.

10. Elizabeth Montgomery played Samantha Stephens and her cousin Serina on *Bewitched*.

11. Julianne Moore played half sisters/cousins Frannie Hughes and Sabrina Fullerton on *As the World Turns*.

12. David Schwimmer played Ross and his looka-like Russ on *Friends*.

13. Jaleel White played nerd Steve Urkel and urbane Stefan Urquelle on *Family Matters*.

22 TV Shows That Started as Radio Shows

1. *The Adventures of Ellery Queen*
2. *Amos 'n' Andy*
3. *Arthur Godfrey's Talent Scouts*
4. *Beat the Clock*
5. *Blind Date*
6. *The Bob Hope Show*
7. *Buck Rogers*
8. *The Dave Garroway Show*
9. *Dragnet*
10. *Father Knows Best*
11. *Gunsmoke*
12. *The Jack Benny Show*
13. *Lassie*
14. *The Lone Ranger*
15. *Meet the Press*
16. *My Favorite Husband*
17. *Perry Mason*
18. *Space Patrol*
19. *Tarzan*
20. *This Is Your Life*
21. *Twenty Questions*
22. *What's My Line*

20 Successful Spinoffs

1. *Benson* from *Soap*
2. *The Bionic Woman* from *The Six Million Dollar Man*
3. *The Colbys* from *Dynasty*
4. *A Different World* from *The Cosby Show*
5. *Empty Nest* from *The Golden Girls*
6. *Family Matters* from *Perfect Strangers*
7. *Frasier* from *Cheers*
8. *Gomer Pyle, U.S.M.C.* from *The Andy Griffith Show*
9. *Good Times* from *Maude*
10. *The Jeffersons* from *All in the Family*
11. *Knots Landing* from *Dallas*
12. *Laverne and Shirley* from *Happy Days*
13. *Lou Grant* from *The Mary Tyler Moore Show*
14. *Maude* from *All in the Family*
15. *Melrose Place* from *Beverly Hills, 90210*
16. *Phyllis* from *The Mary Tyler Moore Show*
17. *Rhoda* from *The Mary Tyler Moore Show*
18. *The Simpsons* from *The Tracey Ullman Show*
19. *Star Trek: Deep Space Nine* from *Star Trek: The Next Generation*
20. *Xena: Warrior Princess* from *Hercules: The Legendary Journeys*

Scandals

12 Actors Who Have Been Arrested

Some were arrested for little more than harmless mischief, others for much worse. Here, then, rap sheets of the rich and famous.

1. Tim Allen (*Home Improvement*): Arrested for selling cocaine to an undercover cop in 1978.

2. Johnny Depp (*21 Jump Street*): Charged with criminal mischief after trashing his suite at New York's Mark Hotel in 1994.

3. Robert Downey, Jr. (*Saturday Night Live*): Arrested for cocaine, heroin, and weapons possession and driving under the influence in July 1996.

4. Charles Dutton (*Roc*): Served seven and a half years in prison on a manslaughter conviction for stabbing another man to death in a fight. Was paroled in 1976.

5. Farrah Fawcett (*Charlie's Angels*): Arrested twice in 1970 for stealing clothes from boutiques.

6. Woody Harrelson (*Cheers*): Arrested in Ohio in 1982 and charged with disorderly conduct. Arrested for planting four hemp seeds in Kentucky in 1996. Also arrested in 1996 for trespassing, after climbing the Golden Gate Bridge's tower to protest a redwood forest sale.

7. Stacy Keach (*Mike Hammer*): Arrested at London's Heathrow Airport in 1984 for smuggling cocaine.

8. Ricki Lake (*Ricki Lake*): Arrested at an antifur protest in 1994 in Karl Lagerfeld's offices for criminal mischief and trespassing.

9. Martin Lawrence (*Martin*): Arrested in 1996 for carrying a concealed weapon as he was about to board a flight to Phoenix. Arrested in 1997 for punching a nightclub patron.

10. Paul Reubens (*Pee-wee's Playhouse*): Arrested for indecent exposure at an adult theater on July 26, 1991.

11. Suzanne Somers (*Three's Company, Step By Step*): Arrested for writing bad checks in 1970.

12. Ken Wahl (*Wiseguy*) Arrested for vandalism and disturbing the peace at a bar at the Beverly Hills Plaza Hotel in December 1996.

Eight TV Stars Arrested for Driving Under the Influence

1. Tim Allen (1997)

2. Brett Butler (1981)

3. Johnny Carson (1992)

4. Chevy Chase (1995)

5. Tyne Daly (1992)

6. Amanda Donohoe (1994)

7. Kelsey Grammer (1987)

8. Jan-Michael Vincent (1983, 1986)

Seven Former Child Stars Who Were Very, Very Naughty

Child actors don't always grow gracefully into adult actors. But they do grow up fast, and, in some cases, they grow up without a moral compass. Here are some who went astray.

1. Danny Bonaduce (*The Partridge Family*): Arrested for possession of cocaine in 1985. Arrested for trying to purchase crack in 1990. Arrested for assaulting a transvestite prostitute in 1991.

2. Todd Bridges (*Diff'rent Strokes*): Arrested for threatening to blow up cars in 1986. Arrested

in 1989 for shooting a drug dealer (he was later acquitted). Arrested in 1990 for cocaine possession. Arrested in 1993 for possession of a loaded gun and possession of drugs.

3. Butch Patrick (*The Munsters*) Arrested for possession of Quaaludes in 1979. Arrested for robbing and beating a limousine driver in 1990.

4. Mackenzie Phillips (*One Day at a Time*): Arrested for cocaine possession and public intoxication in 1978.

5. Dana Plato (*Diff'rent Strokes*): Arrested for the armed robbery of a Las Vegas video store in February 1991. Arrested again in 1992 for forging a Valium prescription.

6. Tommy Rettig (*Lassie*): Arrested for growing marijuana in 1972. Arrested for conspiracy to smuggle cocaine in 1975.

7. Adam Rich (*Eight is Enough*) Arrested for marijuana possesion in 1983. Arrested three times in 1991: for shoplifting, for breaking a pharmacy window, and for trying to steal a syringe half-full of Demerol.

10 Infamous TV Star Faux Pas

Models of sophistication and self-restraint were few and far between in recent years. From an embarrassment of riches, here are our top ten moments of extreme tackiness.

1. Ted Danson wore blackface at a Friars Club roast of his then-girlfriend Whoopi Goldberg in 1993.

2. Paul Reubens behaved lewdly at a porn theater in 1991 (the movie playing was called *Nancy Nurse Turns Up the Heat*).

3. *Roseanne*'s Tom Arnold left a very nasty note on *Seinfeld* star Julia Louis-Dreyfus's car when she parked in his spot at the studio lot in 1993. Louis-Dreyfus called him on it, then later returned to her car to find a picture of a man's derriere sitting on her windshield.

4. Roseanne grabbed her crotch and spat while singing the national anthem at a baseball game in San Diego in 1990.

5. During a 1994 *Tonight Show* interview with Jay Leno, Bobcat Goldthwait set a chair on fire.

6. Howard Stern arrived at the 1992 MTV Video Music Awards in full Fartman regalia, baring his not-quite-firm buns for all the world to see.

7. Madonna cursed like a sailor—she said the

"F" word at least 13 times—during an interview with David Letterman in 1994.

8. An indignant Zsa Zsa Gabor slapped a police officer who pulled her over for a traffic violation in 1989—even though she was driving without her license and registration (and *with* an open container of alcohol).

9. In 1995, Drew Barrymore stood on David Letterman's desk and flashed her breasts as a birthday present for the *Late Show* host.

10. At the 1996 MTV Video Music Awards, cohost Janeane Garofalo approached Mel Gibson for a quick interview, then asked him, "Do you think I look fat in this dress?" Mel was not amused.

21 Stars Who Have Gone to See the Strippers at Scores

The scantily clad women who dance at New York City's upscale strip joint have been ogled by some of the biggest names in television.

1. Jason Alexander

2. Tom Arnold

3. Dean Cain

4. George Clooney

5. John Cusack

6. John Goodman
7. Keith Hamilton Cobb
8. Bill Maher
9. Tim Meadows
10. Judd Nelson
11. Chuck Norris
12. John Ratzenberger
13. Michael Richards
14. Dennis Rodman
15. Antonio Sabato, Jr.
16. Pauly Shore
17. Jerry Seinfeld
18. John Stamos
19. Howard Stern
20. Rolonda Watts
21. Steven Weber

Songs in the Key of TV

39 TV Stars Who Had Songs on the Billboard Top 40

Some had multiple hits, others only had one—but where would we be without such one-hit wonders as Vicki Lawrence's "The Night the Lights Went Out in Georgia" or Sheb Wooley's "The Purple People Eater"?

1. Steve Allen, *The Tonight Show* and *The Steve Allen Show:* 1962's "Don't Go Near the Indians" (17)

2. Ed Ames, *Daniel Boone:* 1967's "My Cup Runneth Over" (8) and "Who Will Answer" (19)

3. Jim Backus, *Gilligan's Island:* 1958's "Delicious!" (40)

4. Walter Brennan, *The Real McCoys:* three hits, including 1962's "Old Rivers" (5)

5. Edd Byrnes, *77 Sunset Strip:* 1959's "Kookie, Kookie (Lend Me Your Comb)" (4)

6. David Cassidy, *The Partridge Family:* five hits, including 1971's "Cherish" (9) and 1972's "How Can I Be Sure" (25)

7. Shaun Cassidy, *The Hardy Boys:* three hits, including 1977's "Da Doo Ron Ron" (1)

8. Richard Chamberlain, *Dr. Kildare:* three hits, including "Three Stars Will Shine Tonight (Theme from *Dr. Kildare*)" (10)

9. Bill Cosby, *I Spy, The Cosby Show,* and *Cosby:* 1967's "Little Old Man (Uptight—Everything's Alright)" (4)

10. Johnny Crawford, *The Rifleman:* four hits, including 1962's "Cindy's Birthday" (8)

11. Michael Damien, *The Young and The Restless:* three hits, including 1989's "Rock On" (1)

12. Patty Duke, *The Patty Duke Show:* 1965's "Don't Just Stand There" (8) and "Say Something Funny" (22)

13. Shelly Fabares, *Donna Reed* and *Coach:* 1962's "Johnny Angel" (1) and "Johnny Loves Me" (21)

14. Lorne Greene, *Bonanza* and *Battlestar Galactica:* 1964's "Ringo" (1)

15. Andy Griffith, *The Andy Griffith Show* and *Matlock*: 1955's "Make Yourself Comfortable" (26)

16. Janet Jackson, *Good Times*, *Diff'rent Strokes:* A string of number-one hits, including 1986's "When I Think of You" and 1990's "Escapade"

17. Don Johnson, *Miami Vice* and *Nash Bridges:* 1986's "Heartbeat" (5) and 1988's "Till I Loved You," with Barbra Streisand (25)

18. Cheryl Ladd, *Charlie's Angels:* 1978's "Think It Over" (34)

19. Vicki Lawrence, *The Carol Burnett Show* and *Mama's Family:* 1973's "The Night the Lights Went Out in Georgia" (1)

20. LL Cool J, *In the House:* five hits, including 1991's "Around the Way Girl" (9)

21. Julie London, *Emergency!:* 1955's "Cry Me a River" (9)

22. Gloria Loring, *Days of Our Lives:* 1986's "Friends and Lovers" (2)

23. George Maharis, *Route 66:* 1962's "Teach Me Tonight" (25)

24. Wink Martindale, game show host: 1959's "Deck of Cards" (7)

25. Eddie Murphy, *Saturday Night Live:* 1985's "Party All the Time (2) and 1989's "Put Your Mouth on Me" (27)

26. Fess Parker, *Disneyland*'s "Davy Crockett" and *Daniel Boone*: 1955's "The Ballad of Davy Crockett" (5) and 1957's "Wringle, Wrangle" (12)

27. Suzi Quatro, *Happy Days*: 1979's "Stumblin' In" (4)

28. Della Reese, *Chico and the Man* and *Touched by an Angel*: three hits, including 1959's "Don't You Know" (2)

29. John Schneider, *The Dukes of Hazzard*: 1981's "It's Now or Never" (14)

30. Bobby Sherman, *Here Come the Brides*: five hits, including 1969's "Little Woman" (3)

31. Will Smith, *The Fresh Prince of Bel-Air*: four hits, including 1991's "Summertime," with D.J. Jazzy Jeff (4)

32. David Soul, *Starsky and Hutch*: 1977's "Don't Give Up on Us" (1)

33. Rick Springfield, *General Hospital*: 17 hits, including 1981's "Jessie's Girl" (1)

34. Connie Stevens, *Hawaiian Eye*: 1959's "Kookie, Kookie (Lend Me Your Comb)" with Edd Byrnes (4) and 1960's "Sixteen Reasons" (3)

35. Gale Storm, *My Little Margie*: six hits, including 1955's "I Hear You Knocking" (2) and 1957's Dark Moon" (4)

36. John Travolta, *Welcome Back, Kotter*: four hits, including 1978's "You're the One That I Want" (1)

37. Jack Wagner, *General Hospital:* 1994's "All I Need" (2)

38. Bruce Willis, *Moonlighting:* 1987's "Respect Yourself" (5)

39. Sheb Wooley, *Rawhide:* 1958's "The Purple People Eater" (1)

17 TV Theme Songs That Became Billboard Hits

1. *Another World:* "Another World (You Take Me Away To)" (Crystal Gayle and Gary Morris)

2. *Baretta:* "Keep Your Eye on the Sparrow" (Rhythm Heritage)

3. *The Dukes of Hazzard:* "Good Ol' Boys" (Waylon Jennings)

4. *Friends:* "I'll Be There For You" (The Rembrandts)

5. *Happy Days:* "Happy Days" (Pratt and McClain)

6. *Hawaii Five-O:* "Hawaii Five-O" (the Ventures)

7. *The Heights:* "How Do You Talk to an Angel" (*The Heights* cast)

8. *Hill Street Blues:* "Theme from *Hill Street Blues*" (Mike Post)

9. *I Love Lucy:* "Disco Lucy" (Wilton Place Street Band)

10. *Laverne & Shirley:* "Making Our Dreams Come True" (Cyndi Grecco)

11. *Magnum, P.I.:* "Theme from *Magnum, P.I.*" (Mike Post)

12. *Miami Vice:* "Theme from *Miami Vice*" (Jan Hammer)

13. *Moonlighting:* "Theme from *Moonlighting*" (Al Jarreau)

14. *Party of Five:* "Close to Free" (the Bodeans)

15. *Welcome Back, Kotter:* "Welcome Back" (John Sebastian)

16. *The X-Files:* "Theme from *The X-Files*" (Mark Snow)

17. *The Young and the Restless:* "Nadia's Theme" (Barry DeVorzon and Perry Botkin, Jr.)

14 Recording Stars Who Sang TV Theme Songs

1. The Beach Boys, *Karen*

2. Johnny Cash, *The Rebel*

3. Roberta Flack, *The Hogan Family*

4. Amy Grant, *Sister Kate*

5. Al Jarreau, *Moonlighting*

6. Waylon Jennings, *The Dukes of Hazzard*

7. Naomi and Wynonna Judd, *The Torkelsons*

8. King, *Teech*

9. Patti LaBelle, *The Oprah Winfrey Show*

10. Ziggy Marley and the Melody Makers, *Arthur*

11. Reba McEntire, *Delta*

12. Linda Ronstadt, *Headmaster*

13. Paul Simon, *The Oprah Winfrey Show*

14. Phoebe Snow, *9 to 5*

21 Classic Songs That Were Used as TV Theme Songs

1. "Georgia on My Mind," sung by Ray Charles, *Designing Women*

2. "Ob-La-Di, Ob-La-Da," sung by Patti LuPone, *Life Goes On*

3. "Reflections," by Diana Ross and the Supremes, *China Beach*

4. "Stand," by R.E.M., *Get a Life*

5. "One Hand in My Pocket," by Alanis Morrisette, *Townies*

6. "Amazing Grace," sung by Rev. John Newton, *Amazing Grace*

7. "Moon River," by Henry Mancini and Johnny Mercer, *The Andy Williams Show*

8. "Blue Skies," by Irving Berlin, *Blue Skies*

9. "Hot in the City," sung by Billy Idol, *Booker*

10. "You May Be Right," sung by Southside Johnny, *Dave's World*

11. "Day by Day," sung by Clydine Jackson, *Day by Day*

12. "Easy Street," *Easy Street*

13. "What a Wonderful World," by Louis Armstrong, *Family Matters*

14. "And She Was," by David Byrne, sung by the Talking Heads, *Flying Blind*

15. "Do You Know What It Means to Miss New Orleans?" by Louis Armstrong, *Frank's Place*

16. "Lady Madonna," sung by Aretha Franklin, *Grace Under Fire*

17. "Rock Around the Clock," by Bill Haley and the Comets, *Happy Days*

18. "Princes of the Universe," by Queen, *Highlander*

19. "William Tell Overture" by G. Rossini, *The Lone Ranger*

20. "Love and Marriage," sung by Frank Sinatra, *Married . . . with Children*

21. "Paint it Black," by the Rolling Stones, *Tour of Duty*

20 TV Stars Who Sang the Theme Songs to Their Own Shows

1. Eddie Albert, *Green Acres*

2. Richard Chamberlain, *Dr. Kildare*

3. Christine Ebersole, *Rachel Gunn, R.N.*

4. Dale Evans, *The Roy Rogers Show*

5. Greg Evigan, *B.J. and the Bear* and *P.S. I Luv U* (with Suzanne Fountain)

6. Eva Gabor, *Green Acres*

7. Erica Gimpel, *Fame*

8. Kelsey Grammer, *Frasier*

9. Lisa Hartman, *Tabitha*

10. David Hasselhoff, *Baywatch*

11. Queen Latifah, *Living Single*

12. Patti LuPone, *Life Goes On*

13. Lee Majors, *The Fall Guy*

14. David Naughton, *Makin' It*

15. Carroll O'Connor, *All in the Family*

16. Fess Parker, *Disneyland*'s "Davy Crockett"

17. Jerry Reed, *Concrete Cowbo*

18. Holly Robinson, *21 Jump Street* and *Hangin' with Mr. Cooper*

19. Cybill Shepherd, *Cybill*

20. Jean Stapleton, *All in the Family*

Two Fictional Music Groups That Went on to Become Recording Sensations

1. The Monkees: The rock-and-roll foursome barely performed on their first two best-selling albums—studio musicians did the bulk of the work. In 1967, they fought for—and won—the right to play their own music.

2. The Partridge Family: Only two "members" of the Partridge Family—David Cassidy and Shirley Jones—actually ever performed on any of the groups' best-selling records.

Rosie O'Donnell Picks Ten Shows with the Best Theme Songs

Daytime's favorite new talk show host has an encyclopedic knowlege of TV theme songs (which she shares with her talk show audience on a daily basis). Of the hundreds that she knows and loves, these are the ones that move her the most.

1. *The Brady Bunch*
2. *The Courtship of Eddie's Father*
3. *Spider-Man*
4. *The Partridge Family*
5. *Gigantor*
6. *Good Times*

7. *Maude*

8. *American Bandstand*

9. *The Flintstones*

10. *Laverne & Shirley*

Danny Elfman Picks 10 Shows with the Best Theme Songs

Danny Elfman knows a thing or two about theme music: He has scored the themes for such TV series as *The Simpsons*, *Tales from the Crypt*, and *Pee-wee's Playhouse*, and such movies as *Mars Attacks!*, *To Die For*, *Batman*, *Edward Scissorhands*, and *Beetlejuice*. His favorites are:

1. *Route 66*

2. *The Twilight Zone*

3. *The Outer Limits*

4. *Mission: Impossible*

5. *The Addams Family*

6. *Gilligan's Island*

7. *The Munsters*

8. *Peter Gunn*

9. *I Married Joan*

10. *One Step Beyond*

R.I.P.

25 Celebrities Who Died While Their Series Were Still on the Air

1. Bea Benaderet, *Petticoat Junction*, 1968

2. Dan Blocker, *Bonanza*, 1972

3. George Cleveland, *Lassie*, 1957

4. Nicholas Colasanto, *Cheers*, 1985

5. Ray Collins, *Perry Mason*, 1965

6. Michael Conrad, *Hill Street Blues*, 1983

7. Jim Davis, *Dallas*, 1981

8. Colleen Dewhurst, *Murphy Brown* and *Avon-lea*, 1991

9. Selma Diamond, *Night Court*, 1985

10. Peter Duel, *Alias Smith and Jones*, 1971

11. Redd Foxx, *The Royal Family*, 1991

12. Will Geer, *The Waltons*, 1978

13. Florence Halop, *Night Court*, 1986

14. John Hancock, *Love & War*, 1992

15. Richard Hart, *The Adventures of Ellery Queen*, 1951

16. Jon-Erik Hexum, *Cover Up*, 1984

17. Diana Hyland, *Eight is Enough*, 1977

18. Joseph Kearns, *Dennis the Menace,* 1962

19. Dorothy Kilgallen, *What's My Line?*, 1965

20. Ted Knight, *Too Close for Comfort*, 1986

21. Michael Landon, *Us* (a pilot for CBS), 1991

22. Will Lee, *Sesame Street*, 1983

23. Alice Pearce, *Bewitched*, 1972

24. Freddie Prinze, *Chico and the Man*, 1977

25. Larry Riley, *Knots Landing*, 1992

13 Stars Who Comitted Suicide

1. Brenda Benet, *Days of Our Lives*, 1982

2. Ray Combs, *Family Feud*, 1996

3. Peter Duel, *Alias Smith and Jones*, 1971

4. Ed Flanders, *St. Elsewhere*, 1995

5. Dave Garroway, *Today*, 1982

6. Rusty Hamer, *Make Room for Daddy*, 1990

7. Hugh O'Connor, *In the Heat of the Night*, 1995

8. Tara Preston, *The Guiding Light*, 1985

9. Freddie Prinze, *Chico and the Man*, 1977

10. George Reeves, *Superman*, 1959

11. Will Rogers, Jr., *The Will Rogers, Jr. Show*, 1993

12. Inger Stevens, *The Farmer's Daughter*, 1970

13. Herve Villechaize, *Fantasy Island*, 1993

Three Stars Who Died of a Drug Overdose

1. John Belushi, *Saturday Night Live*, 1982

2. Judy Garland, *The Judy Garland Show*, 1969

3. Anissa Jones, *Family Affair*, 1976

Comic Relief

14 Stand-Up Comics Turned Sitcom Stars

Stand-up comics in situation comedies are nothing new (think Newhart or Cosby), but in 1988 a stand-up named Roseanne Barr hit the small screen and suddenly television was bombarded by a whole new generation of comic talent.

1. Tim Allen

2. Brett Butler

3. Drew Carey

4. Bill Cosby

5. Ellen DeGeneres

6. Jamie Foxx

7. Redd Foxx

8. Martin Lawrence

9. Bob Newhart

10. Freddie Prinze

11. Paul Reiser

12. Roseanne

13. Jerry Seinfeld

14. Garry Shandling

28 Famous Folks Who Have Called Dr. Frasier Crane's Radio Show for Advice

Those head-cases who call Frasier each week have more than just their neuroses in common: Most of their voices belong to someone famous.

1. Ed Begley, Jr.

2. Mel Brooks

3. Rosemary Clooney

4. Jeff Daniels

5. Dominick Dunne

6. Patty Hearst

7. Tommy Hilfiger

8. Bruno Kirby

9. Robert Klein

10. Christine Lahti

11. Piper Laurie

12. Timothy Leary

13. Jay Leno

14. Patti LuPone

15. John Malkovich

16. Henry Mancini

17. Joe Mantegna

18. Reba McEntire

19. Mary Tyler Moore

20. Christopher Reeve

21. Carl Reiner

22. Ben Stiller

23. Eric Stoltz

24. Garry Trudeau

25. Eddie Van Halen

26. JoBeth Williams

27. Elijah Wood

28. Steve Young

Bill Maher Picks Five Dream Panels of Guests for Politically Incorrect

Every night, *Politically Incorrect* host Bill Maher assembles an eclectic panel of guests to talk about politics and current events. The discussions are frequently lively, illuminating, and always irreverent. We asked Maher to give us his dream panel—instead he gave us five (some more twisted than others).

1. John, Paul, George, and one of the Spice Girls

2. Simone De Beauvoir, Bertrand Russell, Winston Churchill, and Tim Conway

3. Charlie Chaplin, Fatty Arbuckle, Roman Polanski, and Liv Tyler

4. David Keith (*High Incident*), Keith David (*Clockers*), David Carradine, and Keith Carradine

5. Robert J. Oppenheimer, Enrico Fermi, Werner Heisenberg, and Morgan Fox (*Playboy*'s Miss December 1990)

Top 10 Ways David Letterman Has Kept His Cool After All These Years

Why do we still love Dave? Let us count the ways:

10. The perfect mix. Example: The September 20, 1996, episode featured Drew Barrymore, Pearl Jam, an octogenarian shoe-shine man, and Bob Borden's Four-State Burrito Bonanza.

9. The ever-popular "remote cam" sketches, which have included "Can a Guy in a Bear Suit Get a Free Hot Dog?" and "Can a Dog Walker Get into Friday's?"

8. Mom. On Thanksgiving, Dave called Dorothy and played "Guess the Pie." (She had baked three pies, and Dave had to guess what kind they were.)

7. Kids. Dave often smirks when he says, "You know, I'm good with the kids." But he actually is. Recently, during a "Kids Tell Jokes" sketch, he let a curly-haired tot twirl around and model her new jumper. Her joke: "Knock, knock." "Who's there?" "Olive." "Olive who?" "Olive you, David Letterman."

6. His no-holds-barred interviews. When Sarah Ferguson, the Duchess of York, came for a visit, he put her at ease by flirting with her, then asked her pointed questions like "What is York?" and "Do you like wrestling?"

5. The "Fun with Rupert and Leonard" sketches. Dave hides in a curbside van with a walkie-talkie and feeds instructions to his pals Rupert Jee and Leonard Tepper, who have receivers hidden in their glasses. Recently Dave had them telling puzzled store clerks, "Don't call me Veronica."

4. Superstar guests. "You're both very unusual-looking," Dave told guests Beavis and Butt-head. "Yeah, well, you look kinda old," Butt-head replied. Beavis picked his nose and talked about the TV show he wants to do: *Big Boobs and Fire*.

3. His ability to make complicated issues accessible to Everyman. During a candid conversation with Diane Sawyer about Michael Jackson, Dave boiled it down to one question: "Is this a guy that I would feel comfortable with in a car driving to Newark?"

2. His power of persuasion. During the sketch "Dave Interviews CBS Job Applicants," he got one guy to stand on his head while singing songs from *Guys and Dolls,* then brought him into the studio to sing "The Oldest Established" with *Guys and Dolls* star Nathan Lane.

1. The element of surprise. Who'd have thought that Dave and Bob Dole would get on so famously? On the November 8, 1996, show, Dole made his first postelection talk-show appearance. He and Dave chatted about serious

matters for a while, then Dave lightened things up a bit by joking about Bill Clinton. "He is fat. He's huge! He's got to be close to 300 pounds, Bob." Replied Dole, "I never tried to lift him; I just tried to beat him."

The *Brady Bunch*/ *Friends* Connection

Friends is not the first hit sitcom to focus on the growing pains of a half dozen well-scrubbed young people; in many ways, *Friends* is simply the *Brady Bunch* kids grown a few years older and transplanted from the '70s to the '90s. Consider these eerie parallels:

RACHEL

- Class president and prom queen

- Was engaged to an orthodontist; nearly married him

- Had a nose job

- First job: waitress at Central Perk

MARCIA

- Class president; got Monkee Davy Jones to appear at prom

- Had a crush on a dentist; fantasized about marrying him

- Had a swollen nose after getting hit by a football

- First job: server at Haskell's Ice Cream Hut

CHANDLER

- Loved scale models in high school

- Wisecracker

- Had hat stolen by bully at Central Perk

- Shares apartment with Joey

PETER

- Built scale-model volcano in high school

- Wisecracker

- Got black eye from bully at school

- Shared bedroom with Bobby

PHOEBE

- Most childlike Friend

- Plays guitar at Central Perk

- Got chicken pox

- Sang "Smelly Cat" to audition for music video

CINDY

- Youngest Brady

- Played fairy princess in school play

- Got measles

- Sang "On the Good Ship Lollipop" to audition for supposed Hollywood agent

ROSS

- Has girlfriend named Rachel

- Doctor (Ph.D. in paleontology)

- Played keyboards in college

GREG

- Had girlfriend named Rachel

- Doctor (became an obstetrician)

- Played guitar in a high school rock band

MONICA

- Envies overachieving elder sibling (Ross)

- Worried about her looks in high school (she was overweight)

- To change her hair, got bad haircut from Phoebe

- Took job as dancing waitress

JAN

- Envied overachieving elder sibling (Marcia)

- Worried about her looks in high school (she wore glasses)

- To change her hair, got brunette wig

- Took up tap dancing

JOEY

- Actor who played Sigmund Freud and a TV-soap neurosurgeon

- Plays with Foosball table

- Sold men's fragrance in a department store

BOBBY

- Active fantasy life in which he played football with Joe Namath and played Jesse James

- Played with pool table

- Sold hair tonic door-to-door

MARCEL

- Disappeared, spurring frantic search by all six Friends

TIGER

- Disappeared, spurring frantic search by all six Brady kids

(From TV Guide, *by Rick Schindler)*

10 Shows Don Rickles Has Watched When He Needed a Good Laugh Over the Years

1. *The Tonight Show* starring Johnny Carson

2. Any Bob Newhart series

3. *The Jackie Gleason Show*

4. *The Jack Benny Show*

5. *M*A*S*H*

6. *All in the Family*

7. *Golden Girls*

8. *The Larry Sanders Show*

9. *Mad About You*

10. *C.P.O. Sharkey*

Jay Thomas's List of Hollywood Myths and Truths

Radio and TV star Jay Thomas (*Murphy Brown, Love & War, Ink*) illustrates just how easy it is to make it in showbiz with this illuminating list that separates Hollywood myths from Hollywood truths.

1. Hollywood Myth: Runaways in Hollywood get involved with drugs and pimps, living on the streets, hungry and in squalor . . .

Hollywood Truth: Most runaways get off the bus and hook up with a movie-of-the-week producer, end up playing themselves on TV, and sometimes even receive the coveted "Created By" credit.

2. Hollywood Myth: With all the incredibly talented people in Hollywood already, you really don't stand a chance of making it. . . .

   Hollywood Truth: There is a massive shortage of actors, writers, directors and producers in Hollywood, and that's why you keep seeing the same names and faces over and over again. They keep having to recycle the limited number of folks in the business.

3. Hollywood Myth: Only the best stand-up comics get their own sitcom. . . .

   Hollywood Truth: Two words: "Pauly Shore" . . . 'nuff said.

4. Hollywood Myth: You need an incredible amount of theatrical and technical training to make it to the big time. . . .

   Hollywood Truth: You just need a nice car.

5. Hollywood Myth: The only way for a woman to make it in Hollywood is to sleep her way to the top. . . .

   Hollywood Truth: Another way to make it is to get yourself a good sexual harassment attorney.

11 Famous Fans of Seinfeld Say Why They Love the Show

1. Jackie Collins: "*Seinfeld* is like a great lover— you know you're going to have a satisfying half hour every time."

2. New York Mayor Rudolph Giuliani: "It makes sense for *Seinfeld* to be one of the best sitcoms ever, because it takes place in New York City and is about New Yorkers. From *I Love Lucy* to *The Odd Couple* to *Seinfeld*, any sitcom about New York City and about New Yorkers tends to be great."

3. Mary Hart: "The humor is something that strikes a chord all across America and makes it one of the best sitcoms of all time. There is always something each and every one of us can relate to—from the barking dog to the smelly valet service. Not to mention the fact that every episode is highly orchestrated. And by George if there isn't a completely humorous finale to the medley of predicaments these characters find themselves in week after week!"

4. Jay Leno: "The thing that made Jerry such a successful comedian is the same thing that has made the show so incredibly successful: finding the small bits of everyday life we all go through and putting them on the screen."

5. Bill Maher: "I would say that I probably haven't missed a dozen episodes over the years. For me it's probably because I've known Jerry since I was so young. We started out together. It's just funny because those of us who knew Jerry then and knew his apartment and knew his life, well, that's the show. I read things in the paper that say, 'Oh, such-and-such a show is ripping off *Friends*.' Ripping off *Friends?!* Excuse me, but *Friends* is ripping off Jerry, lock, stock, and tomahawk. Down to the camera angles and the shots—everything. Hey, if you're going to do it, at least put a crawl at the bottom of the screen thanking the guy. There's not a lot of people who can be consistently funny over time, and Jerry's one of them. The other thing I think it tapped into sociologically is the idea that there are a lot of single people in America, and TV sitcoms have always sort of been built around families. I'm forty and never been married. I think at one point in our history, if you were forty and never married they would have thought you were three feet off the ground or just a weirdo. Now, it's just not that odd. People choose to be single in life, and this show sort of said, 'You know, that's okay.'"

6. Regis Philbin: "When they talk about television in the nineties, the *Seinfeld* show is the one they'll remember. It's so good it's spawned a bunch of copycats, and most of

them are hits. But no show can duplicate its spirit, its writing, or its talent."

7. Miss Piggy: "Moi just loves *Seinfeld*—it's one of my favorite shows. I especially like its star, that comedian Jerry what's-his-name. . . ."

8. Mary Tyler Moore: "The unexpected turns, the complete dedication to the multiple layers of the characters, the chances that each actor takes . . . It's like watching each one of them on the high wire, and when they make it to the end, you cheer."

9. Neil Simon: "It's a terrific show. It's just funny. They come up with very odd scenes, and yet they're very recognizable. I mean, they go to a Chinese restaurant and have trouble getting a table. And you say, "I've gone through that." And they break all the rules of regular living. Like, nobody just opens a door and comes in the way Elaine walks into the apartment without a key. But they made the rules, and we accept them. I'm much more literal than that, you know? I would have somebody ring a doorbell."

10. Geraldo Rivera: "I love *Seinfeld* because it is the only show that captures all the wonderful eccentricities of New York, the most eccentric city in the world, in such an honest and hilarious way."

11. Barbara Walters: "Why is *Seinfeld* one of the best sitcoms ever? Two reasons, I believe:

One, because he is himself in great part. The show is so close to real life that we can all identify with it. And two, he genuinely has an offbeat way of looking at everything. When I interviewed him, I laughed through most of the interview. Because he just sees things differently from the rest of us. This magical, unknown, intrinsically funny man with this straight expression is just hilarious."

TV Guide's Top 10 All-time Favorite Seinfeld Episodes

10. "The Pen"—Jerry puts his parents' condo in an uproar simply by accepting a pen as a gift. A perfect example of how tiny events assume inordinate significance on *Seinfeld* (as in life), this one also has Julia Louis-Dreyfus's funniest scene, when a blotto Elaine, upon meeting Jerry's Aunt Stella, does her Stanley Kowalski impression.

9. "The Bubble Boy"— George and Susan visit a boy in a plastic bubble, but John Travolta was never like this ("How about taking your top off? he asks Susan). *Seinfeld* breaks a boundary as it pokes fun (and a hole) in a situation other shows would milk for sentiment.

8. "The Pick"—Another subject no other show would dare to do: nosepicking. But we're also fond of Elaine's new nickname after her

Christmas-card photo reveals too much ("Hi, Nip!") and Kramer's hilarious turn as a Calvin Klein underwear model.

7. "The Parking Garage"—"Six Characters in Search of an Author" is an absurdist classic; so is this episode, which might be called "Four Characters in Search of Their Car." *Seinfeld* proves it can truly be "a show about nothing"—and still be funny.

6. "The Junior Mint"—Only Jerry would forget the name of the woman he's dating ("it rhymes with a female body part"); only Kramer would take Junior Mints to an operating theater. Seinfeld himself calls this episode a turning point.

5. "The Subway"—Jerry's going to Coney Island; George has a job interview; Kramer has to pay off his parking tickets; Elaine's off to a lesbian wedding. But their plans derail on the subway. Note the elegant symmetry of this episode as it splits into four stories that reconverge at the end.

4. "The Outing"—*Friends* has a running gag about how people mistakenly think Chandler is gay, but *Seinfeld* did it first. Because Jerry is "single, thin, and neat," a reporter assumes he and George are a couple—"not that there's anything wrong with that."

3. "The Soup Nazi"—An example of one of the show's strongest suits: accurate observation.

Yes, Virginia, there is a real Soup Nazi in New York. We hear his soup is delicious (but we're too afraid to try it).

2. "The Rye"—George's parents are outraged when their gift of a marble rye isn't served by their in-laws-to-be. Jerry mugs a little old lady. Kramer feeds a horse too much Beef-a-Reeno. Elaine ruins her boyfriend's jazz audition for reasons we can't go into here.

1. "The Contest"—*Seinfeld*'s ne plus ultra. Part of this episode's brilliance is in how it fearlessly tackles a taboo topic without ever referring to it by name (we won't either; suffice it to say that George gets caught at it by his mom when he thinks he's alone in the house with an issue of *Glamour*). The four friends compete to see who can remain "master of your domain" the longest—and the results put each character into razor-sharp focus.

(From TV Guide, *by Rick Schindler)*

Kid Stuff

12 Former Child TV Stars Who Found Fame as Adults

You could write an entire *Where Are They Now?* book about Hollywood's forgotten child stars. Here are a dozen who managed to survive their early fame, then went on to find it all over again.

1. Scott Baio: child—*Happy Days;* adult—*Charles in Charge*

2. Valerie Bertinelli: child—*One Day at a Time;* adult—made-for-TV movies

3. Susan Dey: child—*The Partridge Family;* adult—*L.A. Law, Love & War*

4. Micky Dolenz: child—*Circus Boy;* adult—*The Monkees*

5. Patty Duke: child—*The Patty Duke Show;* adult—made-for-TV movies

6. Nicole Eggert: child—*Charles in Charge;* adult—*Baywatch*

7. Shelly Fabares: child—*The Donna Reed Show;* adult—*Coach*

8. Michael J. Fox: child—*Family Ties;* adult—*Spin City*

9. Melissa Gilbert: child—*Little House on the Prairie;* adult—made-for-TV movies

10. Ron Howard: child—*The Andy Griffith Show;* adult—*Happy Days*, feature film director

11. Billy Mumy: child—*Lost in Space;* adult—*Babylon 5*

12. Kristy McNichol: child—*Family;* adult—*Empty Nest*

Herb Scannell, President, Nickelodeon/Nick at Nite, Picks the TV Shows He Wishes He Had Been on as a Kid

1. *Wonderama:* It was a New York kids' show with lots of prizes.

2. *Birthday Party:* Every day was someone's birthday . . . on TV! More toys!

3. *Man From U.N.C.L.E.:* Illya was cool.

4. *Supermarket Sweep:* They came to my home-

town. Greed and fame in one show. What a concept!

5. *Hullabaloo:* I always wanted to be a groovy teenager . . . even as a kid.

6. *Batman:* They needed a kid villain.

7. *Please Don't Eat the Daisies:* Cool dog. Loads of kids, one more wouldn't hurt.

8. *Honey West:* Cool spy stuff and karate too.

9. *The Avengers:* England swings, especially Mrs. Peel. As a kid, I never knew any "Mrs." like her.

10. *The White Shadow:* It was on when I was a teen—I wanted to play basketball with Carver High.

Maureen McCormick's Favorite TV Families

McCormick was part of TV's most famous family: *The Brady Bunch.* Now, she has grown up into a lovely lady, who is bringing up one very lovely girl, seven-year-old Natalie. Together, they watch reruns of the series that McCormick watched when she was a child. Her favorite TV families are:

1. The Taylors from *The Andy Griffith Show*

2. The Ricardos from *I Love Lucy*

3. The Petries from *The Dick Van Dyke Show*

4. The Stevenses from *Bewitched*
5. The Bunkers from *All In the Family*
6. The Jetsons from *The Jetsons*
7. The Clampetts from *The Beverly Hillbillies*

Animal Magnetism

TV's 10 Most Precious Pooches

When TV goes to the dogs, viewers sit up and beg for more. Each of these 10 has its own special canine quality: some, like Lassie are courageous, some, like Murray, are cuddly, and some, like Scooby-Doo, are cowardly.

1. Astro (*The Jetsons*)

2. Buck (*Married . . . with Children*)

3. Dreyfuss (*Empty Nest*)

4. Eddie (*Frasier*)

5. Lassie (*Lassie*)

6. Murray (*Mad About You*)

7. Rin Tin Tin (*Rin Tin Tin*)

8. Scooby-Doo (*Scooby-Doo*)

9. Tiger (*The Brady Bunch*)

10. Wishbone (*Wishbone*)

And Seven Other Beloved Beasts

Dog may be man's *best* friend, but there are several other scene-stealing species that have also managed to capture our hearts.

1. Arnold the pig (*Green Acres*)

2. Clarence the cross-eyed lion (*Daktari*)

3. Dino the dinosaur (*The Flintstones*)

4. Fred the cockatoo (*Baretta*)

5. Marcel the monkey (*Friends*)

6. Salem the talking cat (*Sabrina the Teenage Witch*)

7. Skippy the Australian kangaroo (*Skippy*)

Real Names of Nine TV Dogs

1. Bear (Dreyfuss, *Empty Nest*)

2. Buck (Buck, *Married . . . with Children*)

3. Buck (Neil, *Topper*)

4. Comet (Comet, *Full House*)

5. Lincoln (Diefenbacher, *Due South*)

6. Lord Nelson (Ladadog, *Please Don't Eat the Daisies*)

7. Maui (Murray, *Mad About You*)

8. Moose (Eddie, *Frasier*)

9. Soccer (Wishbone, *Wishbone*)

12 Shows in Which Animals Rule

1. *B.J. and the Bear* (1979–81): A chimp and his trucker friend

2. *Flipper* (1964–67): A dolphin and his human friends

3. *Gentle Ben* (1967–69): A bear and a boy

4. *Lancelot Link, Secret Chimp* (1970–72): Secret agent monkeys

5. *Lassie* (1954–74): An intelligent collie and her less intelligent human keepers

6. *Maya* (1967–1968): Pet elephant to an Indian boy who befriends an American boy searching for his dad

7. *Me and the Chimp* (1972): A runaway chimp and a dentist

8. *Mr. Ed* (1961–66): A talking horse who befriends an architect

9. *Mr. Smith* (1983): A talking orangutan with an IQ of 256

10. *Rin Tin Tin* (1954–59): A heroic German shepherd in the old West

11. *Salty* (1974): A seal who befriends two orphaned brothers

12. *Wishbone:* (1995–): A Jack Russell terrier reenacts great works of literature

Animals? No, Not Really

They're neither fish nor fowl. (Actually, they may be part fish, part fowl, or part vegetable.)

1. The Beast (*Beauty and the Beast*): half man, half beast

2. Harry (*Harry and the Hendersons*): Bigfoot

3. Lucan: a boy who was raised by wolves

4. The Man from Atlantis: a survivor of Atlantis, complete with webbed hands and feet

5. Manimal: a human who can transform himself into any kind of animal

6. The Monkees: four mop-top rockers

7. Swamp Thing: half human, half plant

8. Teenage Mutant Ninja Turtles: half human, half turtle "heroes on the half shell"

12 Shows That Sound Like They Might Be About Animals—But They're Not

1. *Baa Baa Black Sheep* (an adventure series about a squadron of Marine misfits)

2. *Blackadder* (a satire about British history)

3. *Branded* (a drama about a court-martialed Army officer)

4. *The Bronx Zoo* (a drama about a New York City high school)

5. *Crazy Like a Fox* (a humorous detective series)

6. *Empty Nest* (a comedy about a widowed dad with three grown daughters)

7. *Falcon Crest* (a prime-time soap set in a vineyard)

8. *The Partridge Family* (a comedy about a musical family)

9. *Rawhide* (a western)

10. *Trapper John, M.D.* (a medical drama)

11. *Wings* (a comedy about a Nantucket airport)

12. *Wolf* (a drama about a private eye named Tony Wolf)

15—Count 'em!—15 Fishing Shows

1. *Bassmasters*
2. *Fishing North America*
3. *Fishing University*
4. *Fishing with Roland Martin*
5. *Fishin' Hole*
6. *Fishin' with Orlando Wilson*
7. *Fly Fishing the World*
8. *Good Fishing*
9. *In-Fisherman*
10. *North American Fisherman*
11. *Reel Guys*
12. *Saltwater Journal*
13. *Saltwater Sportsman*
14. *Spanish Fly*
15. *Walker's Cay Chronicles*

10 Things You Never Knew About Lassie

1. Seven Lassies are descended from the star of 1943's *Lassie Come Home*. All are male.
2. The first Lassie made his movie debut only months after being abandoned by his owners for chasing motorcycles.

3. MGM mogul Louis B. Mayer posted a sign on the lot permitting Lassie to lift his leg anywhere he pleased.

4. Lassie grew so attached to Tommy Rettig (who played Lassie's first owner on the CBS series launched in 1954) that he looked to Rettig to confirm his trainer's instructions. Dog and boy had to be separated.

5. In the mid-'50s, when a lion got loose on the CBS set during filming, Lassie II diverted the big cat—and saved the day.

6. Lassie's special roast-beef treats were so tempting, Jon Provost (who played Lassie's second TV owner, Timmy) often snitched 'em.

7. Lassie IV was honored for his show's environmental message at a Senate lunch, and even "met" Lady Bird Johnson.

8. Actors who auditioned for a role on *Lassie* were only hired if Lassie liked them. That's why Jed Allan (who played Ranger Scott Turner on the series in the late '60s) snuggled up to a female collie before his audition.

9. Lassie's dogfights were actually friendly frolics, with vicious snarls and other sound effects dubbed in.

10. Lassie V, who starred during the syndicated years (1971–74), refused to perform if his trainer was late with his morning doughnut.

(from TV Guide*, by Penelope Patsuris)*

Aliens Among Us

21 Kinds of Aliens That Have Appeared on the Star Trek Series

Once upon a time, if you could tell the difference between a Vulcan and a Klingon, you could pretty much navigate your way around the *Star Trek* universe. But these days, with all the various *Star Trek* spinoffs, there are all manner of strange alien life forms and, frankly, we can't always remember the difference between the Betazoids and the Benzites. Here, then, a quick refresher on just some of the hundreds of known species.

1. Bajorans: a spiritual race from the planet Bajor; most wear a decorative earring on their right ear; all are enemies of the Cardassians.

2. Benzites: blue-skinned humanoids from the Federation planet Benzar.

3. Betazoids: humanoids from the Federation planet Betazed who develop telepathic capa-

bilities in adolescence (although they can't read the minds of aliens like the Ferengi).

4. Borg: a predatory cyborg race from the Delta Quadrant. Each is equipped with different technological capabilities to perform certain tasks. They are all linked by the Borg collective, sharing a single consciousness.

5. Cardassian: a humanoid race with snakelike features; they enjoy torture and are hostile to the Federation.

6. Deltan: a sexually charged race from the planet Delta IV. All are hairless except for their eyebrows.

7. Ferengi: a sophisticated humanoid capitalist species with big ears; they are sinister and untrustworthy and sexist.

8. The Horta: silicon-based rock-dwelling creatures who live underground on the planet Janus VI.

9. The Kazon Nistrum: a sinister race who try to invade the tunnels leading to the Ocampa. They have also attacked the *Voyager*.

10. Klingon: fearless humanoid warriors from the planet Qo'noS who value honor. They used to be aggressive enemies of the Federation, but are now are uneasy allies.

11. Ocampa: alien species with a life span of nine years who live in a below-the-surface habitat.

12. Rigelians: humanoid race similar to the Vulcans.

13. Romulans: offshoots of the Vulcans, they are fierce warrior enemies of the Federation who tried to split the alliance between the Federation and Klingons.

14. Talarian: a warrior race identifiable by a hairless enlargement on their skulls.

15. Talaxian: a race of spotty-skinned scavengers whose home planet was destroyed by a bomb.

16. Talosians: one of the first alien races encountered in the original *Star Trek* series pilot. These bald, bulbous-headed creatures from planet Talos IV were nearly wiped out by nuclear war, after which they became dependent upon their illusion-creating technology.

17. Tellarites: an easily angered, aggressive species with piglike facial features.

18. Tholians: an intelligent, territorial race that entraps enemies with an energy field known as the Tholian Web.

19. Tribbles: a cute, furry, gentle species kept as a pet (albeit a pesky one, which reproduces at the speed of light).

20. Trill: a joined species—human on the outside, sluglike on the inside.

21. Vulcans: logical, unemotional, pointy-eared aliens from the planet Vulcan.

Actors Who Have Appeared on Both the Star Trek *Series and* Babylon 5

Actor	*Trek* Character	*Babylon* Character
Michael Ansara	Klingon Cmdr. Kang	Technoc Mage Eric
Majel Barrett	Christine Chapel	Centauri Lady Morella
Dwight Schultz	Lt. Barclay	Earth force soldier Amis
Andreas Katsulas	Romulan Cmdr. Tomalak	G'Kar
Paul Winfield	Captain Dathon	General Richard Franklin
Malachi Throne	Commodore Mendez	Centauri Prime Minister Malachi
Patricia Tallman	Federation Terrorist Kiros	Telepath Lytsa Alexander
Caitlin Brown	Vekor	Na'Toth
Ron Canada	Martin Benbeck	Captain Ellis Pierce
Bernie Casey	Lt. Commander Cal Hudson	Derek Cranston
Brad Dourif	Ensign Suder	Brother Edward
Carel Struycken	Mr. Homn	unnamed Trader
David Warner	Gul Madred	Aldous Gajic

Chris Carter Picks the Five Scariest Monsters Ever Seen on The X-Files

The creator of *The X-Files* has come up with some pretty creepy creatures—from space invaders to sewer dwellers. Here are five that even he finds frightening.

1. The Flukeman (the sewer monster from season two's "The Host")

2. The Peacock Brothers (murderous inbreds from season four's "Home")

3. Donnie Faster (the death fetishist from season two's "Irresistible")

4. Eugene Tooms (the serial killer who eats human livers from season one's "Squeeze" and "Tooms")

5. Always, aliens—especially scary ones

TV's Five Funniest Space Cases

1. The Coneheads: Beldar (Dan Aykroyd), Prymaat (Jane Curtin), and their daughter, Connie (Laraine Newman), *Saturday Night Live*

   Home planet: Remulak (they say they're from France)

   You know they're aliens because they don't have French accents, but do have large pointy heads

2. Gordon Shumway, aka ALF (Alien Life Form), *Alf*

   Home planet: Melmac

   You know he's an alien because he is a short, furry, long-snouted creature who likes to eat cats

3. Martin O'Hara (Ray Walston), *My Favorite Martian*

   Home planet: Mars

   You know he's an alien because he occasionally sprouts antennae

4. Mork (Robin Williams), *Mork & Mindy*

   Home planet: Ork

   You know he's an alien because he sleeps on his head, curses in his native Orkan tongue ("Shazbat!"), and has a shiny red space suit

5. The Solomons: Dick (John Lithgow), Sally (Kristen Johnston), Harry (French Stewart), and Tommy (Joseph Gordon-Levitt), *3rd Rock from the Sun*

   Home planet: undetermined

   You know they're aliens because they think Jell-O is an alien life form.

10 Truly Stellar Episodes of Star Trek

1. **"The City on the Edge of Forever"** Hands down, the best of the best: Bones trips out on an experimental drug and disappears into a time machine. Kirk and Spock follow and land in 1930s New York (when locals stare at the slanty-browed, pointy-eared Vulcan, Kirk tries to pass him off as Asian, claiming his ears got caught in a Chinese rice picker). Kirk falls deeply in love with a social worker (Joan Collins) only to learn, via Spock's jerry-built tricorder, that she has two possible futures: She'll either head a pacifist movement that delays U.S. entry into WWII (allowing Hitler to develop the bomb and take over the planet) or get hit by a truck and die. Kirk could prevent her death but, in a shattering denouement, he doesn't. And by the way, Shatner can act.

2. **"Amok Time"** The *Enterprise* is in a big uproar over Spock: He's crabby, he's got the shakes, he throws his soup at sexy Nurse Chapel and squashes his computer monitor with his fist like it's made of cardboard (considering the show's puny props budget, it probably was). Most illogical. What's bugging our favorite science officer? He's entering the Vulcan mating cycle, Pon farr—and he must return home to mate or die! This spectacular, sprawling second-season opener is a primer in Vulcan sexology. (We even get to see Spock do an orgasmic eyeball roll as he goes deep into Plak-tow—in earthling terms,

the Blood Fever!) Trekkers also got their first gander at Spock's home planet (which, eagle-eyed blooper lovers will notice, has pesky over-head lights just like they do on a Hollywood soundstage—ooops!). It's also the first time we hear the "Live long and prosper!" motto and see the famous Nimoy-invented Vulcan greeting. Hey, what more do you want?

3. **"Mirror, Mirror"** See Chekov try to kill Kirk! See Kirk head-butt Spock! See Spock do the sieg heil! See Sulu turn into a dirty lech and put the make on Uhura! Anything can happen in this episode—and does. Due to a transporter mal-function, Kirk, Bones, Scotty, and Uhura wind up on a parallel-universe *Enterprise* where the mirror images of Spock, Chekov, and Sulu are acting like neo-Nazis. Swell script by *Twilight Zone* regular Jerome Bixby, establishing a richly imagined alternate reality. Swell 20-cent goatee on Spock. And really swell whoopee between Shatner (who had a cute little beer belly the week they shot this episode) and the exquisite Barbara Luna as Kirk's all-time best space chick, Marlena Moreau, a seductress whose libido is even bigger than her hair.

4. **"The Doomsday Machine"** Chilling! The *Enter-prise* encounters a planet-munching mega-weapon created by a long-dead alien race. When mad-as-a-hatter Commodore Decker (the bug-eyed, brilliant William Windom) leads a one-man suicide mission into the weapon's

maw, Kirk rigs Decker's starship to self-destruct. But as the vessel hurtles toward the techno-monster, Kirk finds himself stuck on board due to a transporter malfunction. Of course, we know he'll survive. Of course, we know the doomsday machine (which looks like a papier-mâché gefilte fish) wouldn't scare your grandma. But every time we watch this episode we have no fingernails left.

5. **"Journey to Babel"** Spock has a mommy and daddy? You bet—and they're played with indescribable deliciousness by Mark Lenard and Jane (*Father Knows Best*) Wyatt. Written by Roddenberry's beloved gal Friday, D.C. Fontana, this is part whodunit (there's a murder en route to an interplanetary conference and Dad is the prime suspect) and part *General Hospital* (Dad has a bad ticker and only the estranged Spock—who hasn't spoken to him in 18 years—can save him). Plus, there's a wild Aliens "R" Us cocktail party with Day-Glo hors d'oeuvres. Guess where George Lucas got that bar scene in *Star Wars*.

6. **"11001001"** The first time *The Next Generation* really made us sit up and take notice. The Bynars—little silver computer nerds who travel in twos and sound like rewinding tape machines—board the *Enterprise D*, ostensibly to upgrade the ship's computer system. Instead, they fake a magnetic containment shield leak and, after the ship is evacuated, hijack it to their

home planet (the computer that runs their world has crashed and they need the *Enterprise*'s system to reactivate it). Tons o' fun and great Bynar makeup by the legendary Michael Westmore. Added bonus: Riker, played by Jonathan Frakes (who delivers some real old-time movie-star magic in this episode), takes a holodeck trip to a 1950s Bourbon Street jazz club, falls for a beautiful barfly named Minuet, and utters the best come-on (sorry, Kirk) in all of *Trek* history: "What's a knockout like you doing in a computer-generated gin joint like this?"

7. **"Yesterday's Enterprise"** A space rift puts the *Enterprise D* into an alternate time line and face-to-face with the ghost ship *Enterprise C*. The destruction of the C, with all hands on deck, led the way to a Federation/Klingon detente. But in this new time line, that detente never happened and the two factions are now waging a war that has cost four billion lives. Guinan (Whoopi Goldberg) wants Picard to send the C and its 500-member crew back through the rift—and to certain death—so that there will be peace in the quadrant. No way, says Picard. Way, says Guinan. Fan favorite Tasha Yar (Denise Crosby), who had been snuffed by a grotesque oil monster in season one, is also alive in this new time line—and volunteers to go back with the doomed C crew for a more dignified death.

8. **"Best of Both Worlds (Part I)"** Warning! Warning! Hotshot, kick-butt Federation officer approaching!

And she's got her eye on Riker's job! Played with smarty-pants bitchery by the splendid Elizabeth Dennehy (Brian's daughter), Lieutenant Commander Shelby not only wants to be Number One but is also a Borg expert. So, of course, she's got an opinion (or 12) when those cybernetic creepazoids invade the *Enterprise* and kidnap Picard. Shelby leads an away team into Borg headquarters and discovers they have Borgified Picard and named him Locutus. With no choice but to destroy his beloved Captain, Riker issues the command: "Mr. Worf, fire!" and the screen goes black. Wow! This is the ultimate summer cliffhanger—good enough for the big screen: gorgeous cinematography, fist-pumping direction, and a smart 'n' scary script by Michael Piller, one of *TNG*'s exec producers and the unsung genius of the franchise.

9. **"Tapestry"** It's a wonderful life? Yeah, right. In critical condition on the operating table, Picard has an out-of-body experience and runs smack-dab into the omnipotent show-off Q (usually played with ham and lots of relish by John de Lancie, who, this round, is darn serious). "Welcome to the afterlife, Jean-Luc," he says. "I'm God . . . and you're dead." Q gives the captain a chance to return to his hell-raising, womanizing cadet days and, this time, not be stabbed through the heart in that notorious bar brawl. Picard jumps at the chance but sadly discovers that life without his artificial heart is quite artificial indeed: He is a pathetic sham of a man. No

passion, no courage, and no pals. Worse yet, he doesn't get to be captain of the fabulous starship *Enterprise* (actually, we take that back—worse yet, he winds up in bed with Q . . . but we digress). Picard begs the all-powerful pooh-bah for his old life back—violence, wicked ways, and all—which many Trekkers see as a direct affront to everything Roddenberry stood for. But this episode is so good, why Q-uibble?

10. **"The Visitor"** Easily *Deep Space Nine*'s finest hour and the most haunting, heartfelt Trek installment ever: Sisko seemingly dies in a warp-core accident, a tragedy that not only puts the Feds on the brink of war with the Klingons but sets Sisko's distraught 18-year-old son, Jake, on a collision course through life. After materializing to Jake over the years like Hamlet's father, Sisko makes one last visit to his aged son—who is lonely, divorced, professionally washed up, chronically ill, and ready to kill himself. After three years of lethargic performances, Avery Brooks finally comes to the party with this episode and he, as well as Cirroc Lofton and Tony Todd (as the two Jakes) are glorious. Anyone who has lost loved ones and dreamed they are alive—only to awaken to harsh reality—will find this episode painful yet totally unforgettable.

(From TV Guide, by Michael Logan)

14

What's in a Name?

First Names of 12 TV Characters Known Mostly by Their Last Names

No introduction necessary—at least not anymore.

1. Lynn (Belvedere, *Mr. Belvedere*)

2. Giles (French, *Family Affair*)

3. Ken (Hutch, *Starsky and Hutch*)

4. Theo (Kojak, *Kojak*)

5. Cosmo (Kramer, *Seinfeld*)

6. Stace (MacGyver, *MacGyver*)

7. Quincy (Magoo, *Mr. Magoo*)

8. Alexander (Scott, better known as Scotty, *I Spy*)

9. Montgomery (Scott, better known as Scotty, *Star Trek*)

10. Waylon (Smithers, *The Simpsons*)

11. Dave (Starsky, *Starsky and Hutch*)

12. Wilson (Wilson, *Home Improvement*)

Four Characters Whose First Names Have Yet to Be Revealed

1. The Chief *(Get Smart)*

2. Detective Columbo *(Columbo)*

3. Newman *(Seinfeld)*

4. Mr. Spock *(Star Trek)*

33 Celebrities with Unusual Names

1. Khandi Alexander

2. Billie Jean Beanblossom

3. Buzz Belmondo

4. Taurean Blacque

5. Hart Bochner

6. Delta Burke

7. LeVar Burton

8. Sid Caesar

9. Charisma Carpenter

10. Scatman Crothers

11. Farrah Fawcett

12. Fyvush Finkel

13. Darlanne Flugel

14. Bryant Gumbel

15. Dorian Harewood

16. Marg Helgenberger

17. Dwayne Hickman

18. Season Hubley

19. T'Keyah "Crystal" Keymah

20. Tawny Kitaen

21. Swoosie Kurtz

22. Lash LaRue

23. Wink Martindale

24. Groucho Marx

25. Soleil Moon Frye

26. Nia Peeples

27. Stone Phillips

28. Puck

29. Keshia Knight Pulliam

30. Mr. T

31. Malcolm-Jamal Warner

32. Flip Wilson

33. Daphne Zuniga

17 Stars Whose Names Are Frequently Mispronounced

Is there any faux pas (that's fo-pa, not fox-pass) worse than mispronouncing a celebrity's name? Probably, but just to set the record straight:

1. Madchen Amick: may-chen ah-mik

2. Rene Auberjonois: ren-ay oh-bare-zhun-wah

3. Scott Baio: bye-oh

4. Mayim Bialik: my-um bee-ah-lik

5. Yasmine Bleeth: yaz-mean

6. Neve Campbell: nev (not neev or nev-ee)

7. Chevy Chase: chevy (not shevy)

8. David Duchovny: du-kuv-nee

9. Janeane Garofalo: ja-neen ga-roff-alo

10. Robert Guillaume: gee-yome

11. Mariska Hargitay: ma-rish-ka har-ge-tay

12. Téa Leoni: tay-uh lay-oh-nee

13. Jared Leto: let-o (not lee-to)

14. Julia Louis-Dreyfus: loo-wee dry-fus

15. Tiffani-Amber Thiessen: thee-sin

16. Sela Ward: see-la

17. Noah Wyle: while-ee

53 Stars Who Changed Their Names

They all had their reasons: Some names were too plain, some were too long, and some were just about impossible to pronounce.

1. David Adkins to Sinbad

2. Alfred Alistair to Alistair Cooke

3. Milton Berlinger to Milton Berle

4. Nathan Birnbaum to George Burns

5. Joan Blunden to Joan Lunden

6. Angeline Brown to Angie Dickinson

7. James Brunderlin to James Brolin

8. James Scott Bumgarner to James Garner

9. Sarah Ophelia Cannon to Minnie Pearl

10. Raymond Cranton to Chad Everett

11. Dino Crocetti to Dean Martin

12. Suzanne Cupito to Morgan Brittany

13. Alphonse D'Abruzzo to Alan Alda

14. Tim Dick to Tim Allen

15. Linda Evanstad to Linda Evans

16. Stefania Federkiewicz to Stefanie Powers

17. Bernice Frankel to Bea Arthur

18. Joyce Penelope Frankenberg to Jane Seymour

19. Sarah Jane Fulks to Jane Wyman

20. Bert John Gervis, Jr., to Burt Ward

21. Michael Gubitosi to Robert Blake

22. Mary Hohanna Harum to Mary Hart

23. Milton Hines to Soupy Sales

24. Barbara Huffman to Barbara Eden

25. Carol Diahann Johnson to Diahann Carroll

26. Vivian Roberta Jones to Vivian Vance

27. Arthur Kelm to Tab Hunter

28. Tadewurz Wladyzui Konopka to Ted Knight

29. Benjamin Kubelsky to Jack Benny

30. Walter Matuschanskayasky to Walter Matthau

31. Patsy Ann McClenny to Morgan Fairchild

32. Susie Jane Miller to Susan Saint James

33. Joan Molinsky to Joan Rivers

34. Donna Mullenger to Donna Reed

35. Beverly Louise Neill to Amanda Blake

36. George Newhart to Bob Newhart

37. Krekor Ohanian to Mike Connors

38. Jill Oppenheim to Jill St. John

39. Eugene Maurice Orowitz to Michael Landon

40. Margaret Elizabeth McLarty to Eileen Fulton

41. Téa Pantleoni to Téa Leoni

42. Eunice Quedens to Eve Arden

43. Leonard Rosenberg to Tony Randall

44. Emma Samuelson to Emma Samms

45. John Elroy Sanford to Redd Foxx

46. Fannie Rose Shore to Dinah Shore

47. Ruby Stevens to Barbara Stanwyck

48. Cheryl Jean Stoppelmoor to Cheryl Ladd

49. Lawrence Tureaud to Mr. T

50. Doris von Kappelhoff to Doris Day

51. Robert Williams to Robert Guillaume

52. Muzyad Yakhoob to Danny Thomas

53. Donald Yarmy to Don Adams

Four Who Changed Their Names—After They Became Famous

1. Pamela Anderson to Pamela Lee
2. Phylicia Ayers-Allen to Phylicia Rashad
3. Roseanne Barr to Roseanne Arnold to Roseanne
4. Larry "Bud" Melman to Calvert De Forrest (which is actually his real name)

26 TV Terms of Endearment

Nicknames and pet names. Some given in affection (or annoyance).

1. Beaver—Theodore Cleaver, *Leave It to Beaver*
2. Bones—Dr. Leonard McCoy, *Star Trek*
3. Bud—James Anderson, Jr., *Father Knows Best*
4. Buddy—Letitia Lawrence, *Family*
5. Coach—Ernie Pantusso, *Cheers*
6. Dingbat—Edith Bunker, *All in the Family*
7. Doogie—Douglas Howser, *Doogie Howser, M.D.*
8. Fonzie—Arthur Fonzarelli, *Happy Days*
9. Gidget—Frances Lawrence, *Gidget*
10. Gopher—Yeoman-Purser Burl Smith, *The Love Boat*

11. Grasshopper—Kwai Chang Caine, *Kung Fu*

12. Half Pint—Laura Ingalls, *Little House on the Prairie*

13. Hawkeye—Benjamin Franklin Pierce, *M*A*S*H*

14. Hoss—Eric Cartwright, *Bonanza*

15. Hot Lips—Margaret Houlihan, *M*A*S*H*

16. Kitten—Kathy Anderson, *Father Knows Best*

17. Little Buddy—Gilligan, *Gilligan's Island*

18. Lovey—Mrs. Thurston Howell III, *Gilligan's Island*

19. Meathead—Michael Stivic, *All in the Family*

20. Mr. Eddie's Father—Tom Corbett, *The Courtship of Eddie's Father*

21. Princess—Betty Anderson, *Father Knows Best*

22. The Professor—Roy Hinkley, *Gilligan's Island*

23. Radar—Walter O'Reilly, *M*A*S*H*

24. The Skipper—Jonas Grumby, *Gilligan's Island*

25. Squiggy—Andrew Squiggman, *Laverne & Shirley*

26. Trapper—John McIntyre, *M*A*S*H*

20 Shows That Originated with Different Titles

How would their fates have changed if they had kept their original names? Would *Dynasty* have shot to number one in the Nielsen ratings with a name like *Oil?* Would the *Brady Bunch* have stuck together if they had been the *Brady Brood?* And who would have sung along with a theme song that went, "Flagstones, meet the Flagstones . . ."?

1. *All in the Family: Those Were the Days*

2. *Beverly Hills, 90210: The Class of Beverly Hills*

3. *The Bold and the Beautiful: Rags*

4. *The Brady Bunch: The Brady Brood*

5. *Charlie's Angels: The Alley Cats*

6. *Diff'rent Strokes: 45 Minutes from Harlem*

7. *Dynasty: Oil*

8. *Falcon Crest: The Vintage Years*

9. *The Flintstones: The Flagstones*

10. *Homefront: 1945*

11. *I Spy: Danny Doyle*

12. *Leave It to Beaver: Wally and Beaver*

13. *McHale's Navy: McHale's Men*

14. *One Life to Live: Between Heaven and Hell*

15. *The Partridge Family: Family Business*

16. *Ryan's Hope: A Rage to Love*

17. *Search for Tomorrow: Search for Happiness*

18. *Seinfeld: The Seinfeld Chronicles*

19. *The Waltons: Spencer's Mountain*

20. *The Young and the Restless: The Innocent Years*

16 Cooking Shows with Interesting Names

As the nation's waistline expands, so does its interest in shows that feature food. And as our taste in food gets more exotic, so do the titles of our cooking shows.

1. *Cooking Secrets of the CIA*

2. *Dinner and a Movie*

3. *Floyd's Food Frontier*

4. *The Frugal Gourmet*

5. *Gourmet Getaways*

6. *Grillin' and Chillin'*

7. *How to Boil Water*

8. *Mediterranean Mario*

9. *Molto Mario*

10. *Ready . . . Set . . . Cook!*

11. *The Surreal Gourmet*

12. *Taste of the Orient*

13. *Three Dog Bakery*

14. *Two Fat Ladies*

15. *Two Hot Tamales*

16. *Yan Can Cook*

12 Shows with the Name "Bob" in Them

1. *Bob*

2. *Bob & Carol & Ted & Alice*

3. *The Bob and Ray Show*

4. *The Bob Considine Show*

5. *The Bob Crane Show*

6. *The Bob Crosby Show*

7. *The Bob Cummings Show*

8. *Bob Hope Presents the Chrysler Theater*

9. *The Bob Hope Show*

10. *The Bob Newhart Show*

11. *The Bob Smith Show*

12. *Love That Bob*

Four Shows Named for One Man

In a 1997 *TV Guide* interview, Bob Newhart admitted that he had used his name one time too often and might call his prospective series *George and Leo* (which he indeed did): "We just finally ran out of names. The only things left were *The* or *Show*."

1. *The Bob Newhart Show* (1961–62)

2. *The Bob Newhart Show* (1972–78)

3. *Newhart* (1982–1990)

4. *Bob* (1992–93)

Three Cars with Names

When the car is the star of the show, it deserves its own name.

1. General Lee: The 1969 Dodge Charger owned by the Duke cousins on *The Dukes of Hazard*

2. Gladys: The 1928 Porter belonging to Dave Crabtree (and possessed by the spirit of his mother) on *My Mother the Car*

3. KITT: An acronym (Knight Industries Two Thousand) for the computerized Pontiac Trans Am driven by crime fighter Michael Knight on *Knight Rider*

Television Land

12 TV Inventions That We Wish Really Existed

Wouldn't it be nice to come home from work in the Batmobile and have Thing hand you a cold bottle of Buzz beer?

1. A *Saturday Night Live* bass-o-matic

2. Batman's Batmobile

3. Buzz beer from *The Drew Carey Show*

4. Captain Video's Cosmic Ray Vibrator

5. The Flintstones' vacuum cleaner (a baby elephant with a suction trunk)

6. Mork's egg bed

7. *Star Trek* phasers

8. The Robot from *Lost in Space*

9. Maxwell Smart's shoe phone

10. Thing from *The Addams Family*

11. Tribbles

12. Vitameatavegamin

12 Memorable TV Characters We've Never Actually Seen

How can 12 who were nearly invisible leave such an indelible impression?

1. Carlton the doorman from *Rhoda*

2. Charlie from *Charlie's Angels*

3. Dr. Dick, Maryann's husband, from *Cybill*

4. Jeffrey, Jerry Seinfeld's cousin, from *Seinfeld*

5. Lars, Phyllis's husband, from *The Mary Tyler Moore Show*

6. Maris, Niles' wife, from *Frasier*

7. Robin Masters, Magnum's employer, from *Magnum, P.I.*

8. The missus, Columbo's wife, from *Columbo*

9. John Beresford Tipton, the millionaire, from *The Millionaire*

10. Ugly Naked Guy from *Friends*

Our 10 Favorite Drinking Joints

A little something for every taste, from homey Cheers to slimy Moe's.

1. The bar aboard the *Pacific Princess* (*The Love Boat*)

2. The Brick (*Northern Exposure*)

3. Cheers (*Cheers*)

4. Jacky's 33 (*Dr. Katz, Professional Therapist*)

5. King Kamehameha Club (*Magnum, P.I.*)

6. Long Branch Saloon (*Gunsmoke*)

7. Moe's Tavern (*The Simpsons*)

8. Shooters (*Melrose Place*)

9. Ten-Forward Lounge (*Star Trek: The Next Generation*)

10. Warsaw Tavern (*The Drew Carey Show*)

Seven Places to Go for a Good Cup of Coffee

Get your double decaf skinny latte at Cafe Nervosa, your cup of joe at the Double R.

1. Buy the Book (*Ellen*)

2. Cafe Nervosa (*Frasier*)

3. Central Perk (*Friends*)

4. The Coffee House (*Party of Five*)

5. Double R Diner (*Twin Peaks*)

6. Mel's Diner (*Alice*)

7. Monk's (*Seinfeld*)

10 TV Deaths That Made Us Cry

They were fictional characters, yet our sense of loss felt so real, so final.

1. Andy Sipowicz, Jr., gets shot on *NYPD Blue* (1996)

2. Colonel Henry Blake is killed in a plane crash on *M*A*S*H* (1975)

3. Gary's bike gets hit by a car on *thirtysomething* (1991)

4. Jesse dies of AIDS on *Life Goes On* (1993)

5. James Evans gets killed in a car wreck on *Good Times* (1976)

6. Catherine gets kidnapped and killed on *Beauty and the Beast* (1989)

7. Coach dies after a long vacation on *Cheers* (1985)

8. Sergeant Esterhaus dies of a heart attack in

the arms of Grace Gardner on *Hill Street Blues* (1984)

9. Det. Steve Crosetti fills himself with drugs and booze and jumps into the river on *Homicide* (1994)

10. Edith dies of a stroke on *All in the Family* (1980)

Two Who Returned from the Dead

Miracles do happen—especially in the world of prime-time television.

1. Bobby Ewing, *Dallas:* After being killed in a hit-and-run accident at the end of the 1984–85 season, Bobby reappeared on *Dallas* in the fall of 1986, lathering up in his wife Pam's shower. It turned out that the whole previous season had just been Pam's dream.

2. Thomas Magnum, *Magnum, P.I.:* After being shot and killed (and then ascending to heaven!) at the end of the 1986–87 season, Magnum was resurrected the following fall when the series was unexpectedly renewed. Again, his death had only been a dream.

16

TV 'Toons

10 Things You Never Knew About
The Flintstones

The Flintstones has been a cartoon favorite since
its 1960 debut. In 1994, *TV Guide* readers voted
The Flintstones TV's all-time best 'toon. Here, 10
fascinating Flintstones factoids:

1. Fred Flintstone's gang seems a lot like Ralph
   Kramden's because creators William Hanna
   and Joseph Barbera wanted to take advantage
   of *The Honeymooners*' popularity. Fred never
   threatened to send Wilma to the moon, but . . .

2. Apollo 7 Cmdr. Walter Schirra did exclaim,
   "Yabba-dabba-doo!" to NASA's mission control
   when he saw the earth from space in 1968.

3. The catchy "Meet the Flintstones" song wasn't
   introduced until two years into the series' six-
   year run. It was tacked on to earlier episodes
   when the show was syndicated.

4. Fred met Dino (the *first* purple dinosaur) while snorkosaurus hunting. Dino, who spoke only in his first episode, returned to the Flintstones' home as their wiseacre (but wordless) companion.

5. The Flintstones' baby, Pebbles, was almost a boy named Rocky. Her birth—the first in animated history—gave the show its highest rated episode.

6. More than 100 babies born during the same half hour as Pebbles were sent a $25 savings bond and a Pebbles doll. Their mothers each got a dozen roses.

7. Jean Vander Pyl, voice of Wilma and Pebbles, gave birth to a son the same day Pebbles was born on the air.

8. When Barney and Betty decided to start a family, they wished upon a star, and the next morning they found Bamm-Bamm, presumed to be orphaned, on their front stoop.

9. John Stephenson, the voice of Mr. Slate (Fred and Barney's boss at the quarry), is also heard at the end of each *Dragnet* episode intoning, "In a moment, the results of the trial."

10. Ann-Margret did a cameo as Ann-Margrock and Tony Curtis as Stony Curtis. Curtis was originally animated with an ascot, but the actor requested that it be removed so he'd look more like a caveman.

(from TV Guide, *by Penelope Patsuris)*

43 Famous Folks Who Have Lent Their Voices to The Simpsons

Being a "guest voice" on *The Simpsons* is probably the coolest gig on TV. Rock stars, sports stars, movie stars, and even a few superstars have given the show some very vocal support.

1. Gillian Anderson as her character from *The X-Files*, FBI Special Agent Dana Scully

2. Anne Bancroft as Dr. Zweig, the shrink Marge consults about her fear of flying

3. Albert Brooks as Homer's psycho new boss Hank at a nuclear plant in a "planned community." Also as Jacques, the bowling instructor with the hots for Marge, and as a used-car salesman

4. Johnny Cash as a coyote who appears to Homer during a chili-induced hallucination

5. Glenn Close as Homer's mother

6. Beverly D'Angelo as Lurleen Lumpkin, waitress and singer

7. Rodney Dangerfield as Mr. Burns' illegitimate son Larry

8. Ted Danson, Woody Harrelson, Rhea Perlman, George Wendt, and John Ratzenberger as the gang that hangs out at a Cheers-like bar where Homer goes after he is banned from Moe's

9. Danny DeVito as Herb Powell, Homer's rich half brother

10. Kirk Douglas as a homeless man named Chester who claims to have invented Itchy and Scratchy

11. David Duchovny as his character from *The X-Files*, FBI Special Agent Fox Mulder

12. Harvey Fierstein as Karl, Homer's effiminate secretary

13. Sara Gilbert as Laura Powers, Bart's neighbor and his first female object of affection

14. Jeff Goldblum as Troy McClure's agent, MacArthur Parker

15. Kelsey Grammer as Sideshow Bob, Krusty the Clown's sidekick-turned-criminal

16. Phil Hartman as attorney Lionel Hutz, a barfly, Moses, and bad actor Troy McClure

17. Dustin Hoffman as Mr. Bergstrom, Lisa's substitute teacher

18. David Hyde Pierce as Sideshow Bob's brother Cecil

19. Michael Jackson as a nutcase who thought he was Michael Jackson

20. James Earl Jones as the narrator for the Halloween episode entitled "The Raven"

21. Cloris Leachman as comic book proprietor Mrs. Glick

22. Jack Lemmon as the Pretzel Man who sells Marge a franchise

23. Jon Lovitz as Artie Ziff (Marge's date to her high school prom) Professor Lombardo, Sinclair (director of Marge's play), and critic Jay Sherman

24. Joe Mantegna as Fat Tony

25. Penny Marshall as Ms. Botz, the babysitter from hell

26. Jackie Mason as Krusty's father, Rabbi Krustofsky

27. Audrey Meadows as Grampa's girlfriend Beatrice

28. Mandy Patinkin as Hugh Parkfield, Lisa's future husband

29. Luke Perry filling in for Sideshow Bob

30. Michelle Pfeiffer as Mindy Simmons, the new worker at Homer's plant that he falls for.

31. Pamela Reed as Ruth Powers, Marge's neighbor and partner in crime

32. Christina Ricci as Erion, a friend Lisa meets during her beach vacation

33. Alex Rocco as Roger Myers, creator of Itchy and Scratchy

34. Winona Ryder as the new student in Lisa's class who does everything better than Lisa

35. Susan Sarandon as Bart's Russian ballet teacher

36. Daniel Stern as an older version of Bart

37. Patrick Stewart as Number One, the leader of Stonecutters, a secret club that Homer joins

38. Meryl Streep as Jessica, Rev. Lovejoy's daughter, who is trouble and falls for Bart

39. Donald Sutherland as Mr. Hollis Hurlbut, the curator of the Springfield Historical Society

40. Elizabeth Taylor as baby Maggie when she spoke her first word: Daddy.

41. Kathleen Turner as Stacy Lovell, creator of a Barbie-like doll called Malibu Stacy

42. Tracey Ullman as British dog trainer Mrs. Winfield

43. John Waters as John, a gay antiques dealer

And 49 More Who Played Themselves on The Simpsons

1. Buzz Aldrin

2. Steve Allen

3. Paul Anka

4. Tony Bennett

5. Wade Boggs

6. Ernest Borgnine
7. Mel Brooks
8. Dr. Joyce Brothers
9. James Brown
10. José Canseco
11. Johnny Carson
12. Roger Clemens
13. David Crosby
14. Dennis Franz
15. Smokin' Joe Frazier
16. Ken Griffey, Jr.
17. George Hamilton
18. Neil Patrick Harris
19. George Harrison
20. Chick Hearn
21. Hugh Hefner
22. Bob Hope
23. Magic Johnson
24. Tom Jones
25. Tom Kite
26. Don Mattingly
27. Linda McCartney

28. Paul McCartney

29. Bette Midler

30. Bob Newhart

31. Leonard Nimoy

32. Conan O'Brien

33. Luke Perry

34. Tito Puente

35. Linda Ronstadt

36. Mickey Rooney

37. Steve Sax

38. Mike Scioscia

39. Brooke Shields

40. Ozzie Smith

41. Suzanne Somers

42. Ringo Starr

43. Sting

44. Darryl Strawberry

45. Elizabeth Taylor

46. James Taylor

47. Adam West

48. Barry White

49. James Woods

Seven Rock Groups That Have Appeared on The Simpsons

1. Aerosmith

2. Cypress Hill

3. The Ramones

4. The Red Hot Chili Peppers

5. Smashing Pumpkins

6. Sonic Youth

7. Spinal Tap

26 Famous Folks Who Have Played Recurring Roles in Cartoon Series

1. Don Adams as Inspector Gadget, *Inspector Gadget*

2. Jason Alexander as Duckman, *Duckman*

3. Louie Anderson as Louie, *Life with Louie*

4. Hank Azaria as Moe, Apu, Police Chief Wiggum, Lou, Dr. Nick Riviera, Carl Smith, Professor Frink, Akira, and Jailbird, *The Simpsons*

5. Jim Backus as Quincy Magoo, *Mr. Magoo*

6. Jim Belushi as the team's business manager, *The Mighty Ducks*

7. LeVar Burton as Kwame, *Captain Planet and the Planeteers*

8. Dan Castellaneta as Homer, Krusty the Clown, Grampa Simpson, Barney Gumble, Itchy, Mayor Quimby, Grounds Keeper Willy, Scott Christian, Mole man, Arnie Pie, and Sideshow Mel, *The Simpsons*

9. Tim Curry as King Chicken, *Duckman*

10. Tim Daly as Superman, *Superman*

11. Dana Delany as Lois Lane, *Superman*

12. Lou Ferrigno as the Hulk, *The Incredible Hulk*

13. Dennis Franz as police officer Klegghorn, *The Mighty Ducks*

14. Whoopi Goldberg as Gaia, *Captain Planet and the Planeteers*

15. Phil Hartman as Lionel Hutz, Moses, and Troy McClure, *The Simpsons*

16. Julie Kavner as Marge Simpson, Patty, Selma, and Grandma Bouvier, *The Simpsons*

17. Jon Lovitz as Jay Sherman, *The Critic*

18. Howie Mandel as Bobby and Bobby's father, *Bobby's World*

19. Kathy Najimy as Peggy Hill, *King of the Hill*

20. Roseanne as little Rosey, *Little Rosey*

21. George Segal as Jonny's dad, *The Real Adventures of Jonny Quest*

22. Harry Shearer as Montgomery Burns, Smithers, Principal Skinner, Dr. Marvin Monroe, Otto, Reverend Lovejoy, Ned Flanders, Dr. Julius Hibbert, Kent Brockman, Dr. Pryor, Eddie, Herman, Mr. Largo, Jasper, McBain, Lenny, Dave Sutton, Scratchy, Jebediah Springfield, etc., *The Simpsons*

23. Lily Tomlin as Ms. Frizzle, *The Magic School Bus*

24. Nancy Travis as Bernice, *Duckman*

25. Damon Wayons as Waynehead, *Waynehead*

26. Ian Ziering as Wildwing, *The Mighty Ducks*

Dilbert's Favorite TV Shows

You probably know Dilbert even if you're not an engineer trapped in a bland cubicle from nine to five like he is. The comic strip that bears his name appears daily in 1,400 newspapers in 35 countries. His Web site is one of the Internet's most popular. His newsletter has about 60,000 subscribers. And his recent book, *The Dilbert Future* (Harper Business), is a bestseller. Even though we rarely see this workplace wonk leave his desk, *TV Guide* was sure that, like the rest of us, he likes to go home after a long, aggravating day, kick back, relax, and watch some TV. What does he turn to? We wanted to know. Here Dilbert tells us—with the help of creator Scott Adams—exactly what he likes and why.

The X-Files I enjoy this show, but it makes me paranoid for about two days. I usually run through the house during commercials flushing all the toilets to slow down anything that might be crawling through the pipes to get me.

Friends I love science fiction, so I was naturally drawn to this show about guys who hang around with stunningly attractive women and act like they don't notice.

ER This is a fine television show, but it's difficult to watch while having a snack. Every time I turn it on there's a picture of someone with a telephone pole through their torso or something similarly hideous. Television isn't very useful to me if I can't eat a pizza while watching it.

Good Morning America This is the best morning television show because of the babe factor. (And I'm not referring to that talking pig in the movie who was pretty neat in his own right.) This show has Joan Lunden, Elizabeth Vargas, Amy Atkins, and—if we're lucky enough to have a serious epidemic this week—even Dr. Nancy Snyderman. Sometimes the show is enjoyable with the sound turned on too, or so I'm told.

The Drew Carey Show This is one of my favorite shows because the main character—I forget his name—is so good looking.

60 Minutes I appreciate this show due to its truth in labeling. I've timed it and it's almost always 60 minutes long. A lot of shows have inflated claims in their titles, like *America's Funniest Home Videos*. But *60 Minutes* gives you exactly what they promise, unlike that show *48 Hours*. As an engineer, I don't like surprises.

Star Trek: Voyager I enjoy all things Star Trek, but I am bothered by the fact that they are lost in a sector of space that has no Klingons, Romulans, or Vulcans. That's like moving *Beverly Hills, 90210* to a trailer park. This has "management decision" written all over it.

The Simpsons This is a well-written documentary. But the people are strange-looking. Nobody has hair like those people.

Babylon 5 This is the best television show ever made. It's too complicated for the average viewer to understand without reading the *Babylon 5* Web pages first, and I respect that in a show. Plus the stars get to have sex with aliens. That really opens up your options.

NewsRadio This is a fantasy about an office where there are no cubicle walls, the boss knows the employees by name, the secretary is scantily clad, and there are no Quality Initiatives. That's where I want to go when I die.

(from TV Guide, *by Scott Adams)*

Daria Morgendorffer's Top Five Reasons to Turn Off the TV and Read a Damn Book

Daria is one of TV's few intelligent teen 'toons. She began life on *Beavis and Butt-head*—where she raised the IQ substantially—and is now the star of her own MTV cartoon series.

5. Books don't suck your soul out through your nostrils while you sleep.

4. It'll give you an idea of the cruel hardships faced by our pioneer ancestors before cable.

3. Barbara Walters.

2. Maybe if you change position, those bedsores will start to heal.

1. *Daria* is in reruns again.

Six Bad Ideas from Dr. Katz: Professional Therapist

Before he found his true calling, Comedy Central's Dr Katz: Professional Therapist was Dr. Katz: Amateur Inventor. Some of his more notable failures:

1. A cure for penicillin

2. Serious putty

3. Nonalcoholic root beer

4. The artificial appendix

5. The rectal barometer

6. He also developed a time machine that could take passengers into the future, but only one day at a time.

17

The 50 Greatest TV Stars of All Time

What makes a TV star immortal? It's a question we pondered as we set about selecting and ranking (from number 50 to number one) television's greatest stars. In the half century that television has been with us, countless thousands of performers have been beamed into our living rooms. Most of them have faded into obscurity. Others we remember fondly—if something triggers a memory of them. And then there are those extraordinary few—stars who spring to mind again and again, always with astonishing clarity and admiration.

All of these elite performers are important innovators. But what really makes them stand head and shoulders above the TV throng is personality. Television is a uniquely intimate medium.

It burns through charisma and cleverness to reveal a person's essential nature. That's the X-factor that makes some performers such enduring favorites.

In *TV Guide*'s pantheon of television's 50 greatest stars, you will find enormous talent, beauty, and charm. But you will find something else: a quality of character that makes these people truly great.

50. Ed Sullivan "Ed Sullivan will be around as long as someone else has talent," Fred Allen once quipped, and certainly no TV star has ever been less prepossessing than this unlikely master of ceremonies. Sullivan's puckered syntax was an impressionist's delight, and his body language was so tense and herky-jerky he made Richard Nixon seem like Nureyev. Nevertheless, his variety hour was the only place on TV where you could see dramatic scenes and musical excerpts from currently running Broadway shows, ballet and opera stars, Bo Diddley, Topo Gigio, and Wayne and Shuster—often on the same show. In 1956, Ed booked Elvis Presley (and tried unsuccessfully to tame Presley's raw carnality by photographing him from the waist up). In 1964 the Beatles made their U.S. TV debut "right here on stage." Where else? Sullivan was a consummate showman with an unerring instinct about popular tastes. His legacy is just this: For 23 seasons—Sunday nights on CBS from 1948 until 1971—this former newspaper gossip columnist was, for all intents and purposes, nothing less than America's minister of culture.

49. **Ricky Nelson** Ricky was TV's first real teenager, but he wasn't the troublemaking sort. Rebellion was definitely out—the close-knit and loving Nelsons on *The Adventures of Ozzie and Harriet* made the Waltons look like the Bundys. But rock 'n' roll was most decidedly in. For parents in rock shock and puberty panic, Ricky (soon to be just Rick) was a palatable alternative: a safe Elvis. From the moment he sang Fats Domino's "I'm Walking" in an episode in 1957, Nelson became a chart-topping teen idol—the numbers he sang on the show sold millions of records and can legitimately be called TV's first music videos. He strummed the electric chords that reverberated into MTV and broke the ground on which *Beverly Hills, 90210* was built. TV's first teen is the grandfather of them all.

48. **Bart Simpson** He's a puny, smart-alecky, disrespectful fourth-grader with bad hair and an even worse attitude: a mocker, a prankster, a working-class kid whose chances of graduating from Harvard Medical School are about the same as his chances of becoming Miss America. Ever since the debut of the dysfunctional family sitcom *The Simpsons* in 1989, social scientists have been moaning about what a bad role model he is for America's preteens. To them we say (as Bart would), "Hey, man. Don't have a cow." This little guy isn't

evil—he's refreshingly iconoclastic, a Bowery Boy for the '90s who knows humbug when he sees it and isn't afraid to tell you so. And, of course, he isn't even real: he's a cartoon character. But he is going to go down in broadcasting history. Almost single-handedly, he sustained the fledgling Fox network, winning it audience acceptance as well as critical applause. First seen on *The Tracey Ullman Show*, he also helped revive an entire art form—animation, which had been largely unseen in prime time since *The Flintstones*. Hey, who says this jaundiced juvenile is an underachiever? He's Bart Simpson. Who the hell are you?

47. **Howard Cosell** Inexorably intelligent, preternaturally polysyllabic, irredeemably irritating, Cosell was the maestro of the microphone, an unathletic man who was unbeatable at one sport: running on at the mouth. Born Howard William Cohen, Cosell was a lawyer by training, a reporter by inclination, and a gadfly by instinct. In the previously sanitized profession of sportscasting, he was an anomaly: brash, opinionated, so eager, in his famous words, to "tell it like it is" that he unhesitatingly savaged his colleagues and tackled such taboo subjects as drug use among athletes and racism in sports. But he was also rigorously principled. At the height of Cosell's career, he announced he would no longer cover his métier, boxing, because the sport

had become too corrupt and brutal. Cosell's words may have poured out in a torrent, but he stood behind every one.

46. **Julia Child** The ingredients for a great French meal? Voilà: half a pound of butter (okay, a pound of butter), a cup of cream, and a generous portion of Julia Child. Think back 30-some years, when Cuisinarts weren't as common as can openers, when what many called dinner was more cordon blah than cordon bleu. With *The French Chef*, which ran for 14 years on PBS, the deliciously down-to-earth Child, she of the high-pitched piping voice so scathingly parodied by Dan Aykroyd on *Saturday Night Live*, made the world safe for soufflés (to say nothing of béarnaise and hollandaise). Food played no part in her Southern California upbringing ("My mother could cook some kind of a cheese dish and make baking-powder biscuits, but that's about it," she has said). But after Pearl Harbor, Julia signed on with the Office of Strategic Services, a forerunner of the CIA, and married Paul Child, an OSS staffer. When he was posted in Paris after the war, Julia enrolled at the Cordon Bleu, where she more than measured up. At 84, she has, thank goodness, not yet seen fit to beat it, in the past few years launching two PBS series: *In Julia's Kitchen with Master Chefs* and *Baking with Julia*. Clearly, she's always known the way to our hearts—right through our stomachs.

45. David Letterman There's something about David Letterman and gaps. There's the one between his two front teeth. And the generation gap, which he bridges with astonishing ease: College kids think he's cool, even though at 49 he may be older than their parents. But the most important gap is the one he's put between himself and other TV hosts with his irreverent showmanship. He wanted to be Carson's heir, but he's more the direct descendant of Steve Allen and Ernie Kovacs. His loopy mix of comedy bits, on-location shoots, and wacky stunts (dressing in Velcro and leaping at a Velcro wall, wearing an Alka-Seltzer suit and being lowered into a tank of water, dreaming up gizmos like the Monkey Cam) earned him an armful of Emmys (and 55 nominations for his shows) and moved the talk show closer to being an art form. It also made it sillier. And more watched and more important than ever before. Between Letterman and the stuff of TV legends, there's hardly a gap at all.

44. Raymond Burr Raymond Burr was 40 years old and best known for his creepy supporting role in Alfred Hitchcock's *Rear Window* by the time he became a TV star. But oh, what a star he became. Burr fleshed out Perry Mason, writer Erle Stanley Gardner's upright lawyer who had been a staple of novels, movies, and radio since the 1930s, imbuing him with the qualities we wish all litigators had: integrity, diligence, perseverance. They were qualities that Burr himself also seemed to possess. During the show's nine-year run he lived in a bungalow on the studio lot, rising many days at 3:30 A.M. to memorize his courtroom monologue. You can't think of Burr without hearing the series' doleful theme music in your head or seeing him in your mind's eye, extracting the often painful truth from a reluctant witness. In the crowded pantheon of prime-time lawyers, Burr's Mason is the only barrister we would put on permanent retainer.

43. **Lawrence Welk** An' a one, an' a two . . ." Necessity is often the mother of success. Lawrence Welk developed his dance band's trademark light, breezy, staccato style because the local musicians he often hired as sidemen in the 1930s simply weren't accomplished enough to sustain the long notes. By 1955, Lawrence Welk and his orchestra had parlayed their "Champagne Music" into a hit show on local TV in Los Angeles. On July 2 of that year, Welk and the boys launched a weekly series that would run on ABC for 16 years. People made fun of the bandleader's German accent, his schmaltzy music, his bubble machine, and even his Champagne Lady. No matter. This former North Dakota farm boy had found a formula that clicked. And the band played on—after ABC canceled the show in 1971, Welk himself syndicated new episodes for 11 more years. The reruns still

air today, on PBS of all places. As the maestro himself would have put it, "Wunnerful, wunnerful."

42. **Phil Donahue** In the beginning, there was Phillip John Donahue, the patriarch of the audience-participation, single-topic talk show, the inquisitive, exuberant fellow who begat Oprah and Jenny and Maury and Ricki. Donahue, whose show began in 1967, dealt routinely with issues that had previously been swept under the rug: marital rape, incest, sexual dysfunction, all the while running up and down studio aisles hollering, "Caller, are you there?" It was on his show, winner of 20 Emmy awards, that we saw two men exchange wedding vows and Nelson Mandela reflect on his years in prison. Ultimately, Donahue became a victim of his own creation. There were younger, hipper hosts taking on raunchier subjects. But they all acknowledge their debt to the titan of talk. "There isn't anyone on television," noted Sally Jessy Raphaël, "who isn't doing Phil Donahue."

41. **Alan Alda** "Hawkeye represented the one quality that held the whole family together, the quality of fundamental decency," wrote Alistair Cooke for *TV Guide* in 1983, just before the final episode of the 11th and final season of *M*A*S*H* became the most-watched show in TV history. "Played less

well, by an actor less high-strung, less deeply forlorn, the whole series could have expired in its infancy." High-strung and forlorn was "Hawkeye" Pierce; the fundamental decency was all Alan Alda's. The only person ever to win Emmys as performer, writer, and director, he took home a total of five, as well as 28 nominations, seven People's Choice awards, two Writer's Guild of America awards, three Director's Guild awards, and six Golden Globes. But the image of him—gangly in greens and bathrobe, the cackling laugh, the Groucho delivery of one-liners that punctured pretense while deadening the pain of war—is his real legacy. Alda once told a med school graduating class: "The head bone is connected to the heart bone—and don't let them come apart." As the head and heart of the 4077th, he never did.

40. **Patty Duke** "Meet Cathy, who's lived most everywhere/ From Zanzibar to Berkeley Square/ But Patty's only seen the sights/ A girl can see from Brooklyn Heights/ What a crazy pair!" Anyone old enough to have reached a TV's "on" button in the mid-60s knew all the words to the theme song of *The Patty Duke Show*. The comedy's petite but hugely talented star played both roles: refined Cathy, with the delicate Scottish burr, and rock-'n'-roll Patty, whose native tongue was slang. Of course, this wasn't exactly Duke's debut. At age 12, she had vaulted to fame on Broadway as

Helen Keller in *The Miracle Worker*, at 16 she'd won an Oscar for the movie adaptation. Duke went on to appear in 39 TV movies—including playing teacher Anne Sullivan to Melissa Gilbert's Keller in the 1979 TV remake of the movie that had put her name in lights—and four miniseries in the last 20 years. In every project, she displayed a fierce commitment to her craft. Performers who find fame as children rarely hold on to their success as teenagers. Still fewer manage to continue on as grown-up stars. Duke has done it all.

39. **Michael J. Fox** In 1982, it barely made a ripple when a young Canadian named Michael J. Fox signed on to play an obnoxious young political conservative named Alex P. Keaton in a generation-gap comedy called *Family Ties*. He wasn't even the star, just one of the kids in an ensemble cast. Now, hop in the DeLorean and go back to the future: Five years later, Fox had won three Emmys, the show was being written around his quicksilver ability to fashion uproarious moments from nothing but a stammer or a nervous swipe of a hand through his hair, and he was starring in some of the biggest box-office movies of the decade. Leap ahead again, and he's back at it, carrying the ABC hit *Spin City* on those shrugging shoulders. Timing is everything—especially classic, polished timing, and Fox has better timing than just about anyone else. Past, present, or future.

38. **Carroll O'Connor** Like a turnip with a stogie stuffed in it—that was Archie Bunker's face. Like a squawking radio stuck between stations—that was his voice. And the blue-collar New Yorker was so politically incorrect he was practically his own party. In 1971, Bunker may have been a stretch for the cultured, liberal Carroll O'Connor, but given the role of his life, he gave TV the performance of its life. He made us love a bigot, and held a mirror up to the Archie Bunker in all of us. And then, in 1988, he made a screeching 180-degree turn, and became the rational, racially tolerant Southern cop Bill Gillespie in *In the Heat of the Night*. Again the show dealt with social issues, and again O'Connor triumphed. In a medium often accused of lacking a conscience, O'Connor has always reminded us that despite our differences, we're all in the same family.

37. **Susan Lucci** Okay, so she hasn't won an Emmy . . . 16 times. But look at it this way: Consider the achievement of having been nominated over and over, of being so sublime at what she does—playing Erica Kane Martin Brent Cudahy Chandler Montgomery Montgomery Chandler Marick Marick on ABC's *All My Children*—that her name has almost automatically made the list of the best in her business for more than two decades. Don't feel too bad for Susan Lucci: She's got loads of other awards, devoted fans, and a line of

beauty products that keeps home-shopping operators working overtime. But what Lucci has the most of, something rarer than talent or statuettes, is glamour. She is the queen of daytime TV, and her crown is more than secure—it's permanently attached. Who remembers who won last year's Emmy, anyway?

36. David Janssen Even after the success of the 1993 Harrison Ford big-screen remake, one thing remains clear: David Janssen is, was, and always will be The Fugitive. Seldom have an actor and a character merged in the public mind so completely. It wasn't Janssen's first series—in *Richard Diamond, Private Detective*, he helped define the tough TV gumshoe—and it wouldn't be his last. But something magical happened to Janssen when he debuted in 1963 as the falsely accused Dr. Richard Kimble: He became him, and we believed it. We ached for him as he searched, alone and afraid, for the murderous one-armed man. Women wanted to hug him and everybody wanted to help him hide from the relentless Lieutenant Gerard (Barry Morse). Now, 16 years after the actor's death at age 49, nearly three decades since his character proved his innocence, Janssen/Kimble remains one of the most cherished of TV personas.

35. Fred Rogers For almost 30 years now, Fred Rogers—that's Mister Rogers to you—has entered his house and performed the same ritual: shedding the garments of the outside world, covered, as they are, with the soot of worry, fear, and other harsh realities. In their place, he puts on a well-worn cardigan and those comfy sneakers . . . and we slip into them, too. The soothing star of PBS's *Mister Rogers' Neighborhood* makes us, young and old alike, feel safe, cared for, and valued, while he teaches us about what's good, and gives us support in handling all the bad that takes place beyond his door. Nothing fancy, no hyperkinetic cartoons, no pressure on us to achieve amazing feats. His simple home might not be a wacky playhouse, and the puppets might sound remarkably like him, but wherever Mister Rogers is, so is sanctuary.

34. **Barbara Walters** Here's how to know when you're really famous: Barbara Walters wants to interview you. For two decades on ABC's *Barbara Walters Specials* she has been sitting down with the very biggest names and getting them to open up like they never have before. (One such extraordinary moment came in 1980, when Richard Pryor confessed to her that he had been freebasing cocaine on the night he was horribly burned.) But that's only the glitzier half of Walters's résumé. She spent 15 years with NBC's *Today* before becoming the first woman to coanchor a nightly network newscast when, in 1976, she jumped networks to join Harry Reasoner on

ABC's evening news. Since 1984, she has been coanchor (with Hugh Downs) of ABC's *20/20*—contributing hard-hitting interviews with newsmakers from Colin Powell to members of O.J. Simpson's defense team. Simply put, no one has ever combined the entertainment and public-affairs aspects of TV as successfully as Walters. Seems like the only VIP Barbara Walters hasn't interviewed is . . . Barbara Walters.

33. **Telly Savalas** In the '70s, a decade known for hard-bitten, cynical loners, NYPD Lieutenant Theo Kojak went them all one better. He was hard-bitten, cynical, and bald. Telly Savalas, however, did have hair. Lots of wavy, brown hair. It's just that audiences never saw it, because he began shaving his head in 1965, when director George Stevens suggested a clean pate would add to Savalas's impact as Pontius Pilate in *The Greatest Story Ever Told*. The New York–born son of Greek immigrants went on to more than 30 film roles, playing mostly heavies. "I'm always thought of as tough and sinister, and I've been unable to get away from a police badge or killer's knife," he said of his career. It was, of course, a gold shield that made him a household name. In 1973, he created the nattily dressed Kojak in the classic TV movie *The Marcus-Nelson Murders*. That fall, Savalas's streetwise alter ego began an unforgettable five-year run on CBS that would earn him an Emmy and

bequeath to TV history two indelible trade-marks: Kojak's ever-present lollipops and his catchphrase, "Who loves ya, baby?"

32. **Rocky and Bullwinkle** The top-secret orders from cold-war villain Fearless Leader to master spies Boris Badenov and Natasha Fatale were always the same: "Get Moose and Squirrel." But they never did, and neither did a sizable chunk of the cartoon's intended audience—from 1959 to 1973, Rocky and Bullwinkle were the hippest, punniest pen-and-ink creatures on TV. It's no coincidence that Rocky was a flying squirrel, because much of the duo's material went over people's heads—to the glee of the show's subversive creator, Jay Ward. On weekdays, Saturday mornings, and, for one season, in a nighttime slot, manic Rocket J. Squirrel (voice by June Foray) and slow-witted Bullwinkle J. Moose (Bill Scott) saved the world and defended the honor of good ol' Wossamotta U—and paved the way for future cutting-edge comedies like *The Simpsons*. The humor was so silly, the satire so zippy, we didn't mind the rough, flat animation. Each week they pulled a rabbit out of the hat—and despite what Bullwinkle said, it was always the right hat.

31. **Phil Silvers** People who think of the '50s as a bland era of cheerful conformity and automatic respect for authority have obviously never seen *The Phil Silvers Show*. Running for

just four seasons on CBS, the show served up one of the greatest rebels of them all—that con man in khaki, Master Sergeant Ernie Bilko. As played with fast-talking relish and impeccable timing by Silvers, a onetime vaudeville and burlesque comic, Bilko was a schemer, a swindler, and an absolute laugh riot. Aided and abetted by an extraordinary troupe of second bananas, Bilko ran roughshod over peacetime Fort Baxter, Kansas, with one scam after another, constantly frustrating anyone in command, especially poor Colonel Hall (Paul Ford). In the real Army, a guy like Bilko would have spent 1955 to 1959 in the stockade. The fictional Bilko and his happy platoon spent those years garnering nine major Emmys while creating a master (sergeant) of anarchy who's been often copied, but never equaled.

30. **Jerry Seinfeld** He wasn't the first stand-up comic to bring his act to television, but this acute 43-year-old Brooklyn-born observer has been far and away the most successful and influential. "I guess I came out of the 'me decade,'" Jerry Seinfeld has said of his 1980s comedy roots, "so I did me." His format-bending sitcom—it's known as the "show about nothing"—slipped almost unannounced into the NBC schedule in 1990 and began a slow climb up the Nielsen ranks. By the 1992–93 season—which included the notorious "Master of His Domain" episode, a hilarious, double-entendre-

laced half hour—*Seinfeld* had vaulted into the top 10. The show's quirky take on big-city life, with all its anxieties and inconveniences, perfectly showcased its star's charming, low-key exasperation. In June 1996, *Time* anointed Seinfeld one of the 25 most influential Americans. Not bad for a guy who modestly describes his comedy as "reality with a twist of lemon."

29. **Sid Caesar** *Your Show of Shows* was a TV milestone: It proved the new medium could present 90 minutes of live entertainment every Saturday night, crammed with quality humor that could parody foreign movies and operas as easily as popular culture. Its manic epicenter was Sid Caesar, a master of double-talk, dialects, ad-libbing, and pantomime. Whether alone or with his most frequent skit partner, Imogene Coca, he could take a basic gag and stretch it to the point of absurdity. Yet, as fellow cast member Carl Reiner pointed out, "The basis of Sid's humor came from an internal source: pain." Indeed, TV's most transcendent comic was also its most tortured. Caesar suffered through a 20-year addiction to liquor and pills. "I know of no other comedian who could have done nearly 10 years of live TV," Caesar's writer Mel Brooks once said. "Nobody's talent was ever more used up than Sid's over a period of years. TV ground him into sausages—one sausage a week." Sadly, little of the comic's best work has been preserved. But anyone who saw him in his radi-

ant prime knows that Sid remains the master. Hail, Caesar!

28. **Roseanne** Growing up Jewish and working-class in Mormon Utah fueled her outsider's perspective. "I was just a weird woman from the day I was born," she once explained. But from her hardscrabble life, the former Roseanne Barr crafted a persona not previously seen in stand-up comedy: the angry, caustic housewife who didn't take any guff from the men in her life (most of whom were jerks, anyway). She successfully transformed that persona into a hit sitcom that captured the resentments, frustrations, and even the occasional joys of being a less-than-perfect blue-collar wife and mother in a glamour-obsessed world. For the most part, she managed to maintain that vision, even as her success propelled her into the financial stratosphere she ridiculed and her off-camera antics became front-page fodder. Years from now, when the turmoil and scandals are forgotten, the incomparable *Roseanne* reruns will remain her true legacy.

27. **Don Knotts** He was thin as half a rail, all bulgy eyes, puffy lips, and Adam's apple. He exhibited tics and lurches and arm-flailings that registered on the Richter scale. Let's face it: Knotts was a nervous wreck. At least, that was his comic signature—first as Mr. Morrison, the twitchy bundle of bones caught in the

headlights of Steve Allen's classic man-on-the-street comedy sketches; years later as landlord to Jack, Janet, and Chrissy on *Three's Company*. But best of all was his turn as the Chicken Little of Mayberry: Barney Fife, *The Andy Griffith Show*'s hypervigilant, overofficious deputy who was allowed to pack a service revolver but had to keep his bullet in his pocket. Knotts' flawless timing as Griffith's comic foil and his ability to take an annoying character and make him endearing was a monumental achievement that won him five Emmys in as many nominations—and set the tone for generations of manic TV sidekicks to come.

26. **Farrah Fawcett** Hers was the smile that blinded. Hers was the face that reduced men to gawking fools, the bod that launched millions of swimsuit posters, the cascading hairdo that inspired countless ghastly imitations. But most of all, hers was the jiggle. She came seemingly out of nowhere, with the unlikely name of Farrah Fawcett-Majors, and starred as the blond third of a girl gang of detectives—Charlie's Angels, in every episode putting her life and virtue on the line, but never, ever putting on a bra. In the blink of a kohl-rimmed eye, she sparked a merchandising mania that included T-shirts, lunch boxes, dolls, and a signature line of shampoo, among other Farrah-phernalia. Twenty years later, no female TV star has even come close to creating

the sensation Fawcett did in her single season on *Charlie's Angels*. Eventually she would triumph in gritty TV-movies such as *Murder in Texas* and *The Burning Bed*, proving—to our amazement and delight—that there was ample substance beneath that seductive facade.

25. **Bob Hope** It is impossible to imagine television without him. If Milton Berle was television's Columbus, Bob Hope was its Lewis and Clark. Berle put the fledgling medium on the map; Hope charted the territory, going just about everywhere a person could go (although, ironically, he never starred in a sitcom). In the process, he staked his rightful claim as America's Comedian. His NBC specials—he's made nearly 300 of them—titillated as well as entertained Middle America. He decorated his specials with beautiful young women, but for every leering remark he lobbed, he received a snappy comeback. ("The peacock," he once said about the NBC symbol, "was hatched from an egg I laid.") His hosting turns at the Academy Awards set the standard. His televised visits to entertain U.S. troops in war zones showed him to be our most patriotic and passionate funnyman. And when he would stride onto *The Tonight Show* set unannounced—ski-jump nose in the air, loose arms swinging as the band struck up his theme song—it was quite evident: Royalty had arrived. Thanks for the memories.

24. **Robert Young** In the early 1950s, movie star Robert Young had the lead role in a radio serial called *Father Knows Best*. "I feel myself being drawn to television," he said, "like a man in a canoe heading toward Niagara Falls." He took the plunge in 1954, and his radio show went with him. *Father Knows Best* ran for nine years, during which Young made his mark as America's quintessential '50s dad. At the height of the comedy's popularity, Young simply walked away; he was tired and wanted to do something else. In 1969 (at age 62), he found that something else, and ended a self-imposed five-year hiatus to star as Marcus Welby, M.D., the kind of caring general practitioner we all wish we had. That year, he won the Emmy for best actor in a drama series, a nice counterpoint to the two he won during his sitcom years—and a double-genre feat that only one other person in TV history (Carroll O'Connor) has been able to duplicate. If that's going over Niagara Falls in a canoe, no one's ever done it with more aplomb.

23. **Miss Piggy** This shocking-pink hybrid of Alexis Carrington and Scarlett O'Hara burst onto *The Muppet Show* in 1976 as spokespig for the moi generation, and she hasn't stopped bursting ever since. With Muppeteer extraordinaire Frank Oz at her right hand, Miss Piggy has shown two decades of TV and movie audiences that she is caring and heartfelt,

and if you disagree she will make time in her busy schedule to trounce you into the dirt. One of Jim Henson's finest, fullest, funniest creations, Miss Piggy strikes a chord in all of us because she's so much like what we try to hide about ourselves: Bluster covers insecurity, sweetness covers envy, star behavior covers career frustration, and yards of material cover midswine bulge. "I always knew," she once told *TV Guide* in an exclusive interview, "that I was destined for le top." From barnyard to penthouse, you've come a long way, bacon . . . er, baby.

22. **Edward R. Murrow** In an eerily darkened TV control room, he would sit and look directly at us and talk directly to us, and we knew he was the most intensely honest creature we would ever meet in this medium. He interviewed movie stars and pop-culture icons on *Person to Person*. In 1954 he took on Senator Joseph McCarthy and brought him to his knees on *See It Now*. His 1960 "Harvest of Shame," about the plight of migrant workers, is the most influential documentary in TV history. Even 31 years after his death, he is a major presence: When we watch *Nightline*, we are watching Murrow; when we watch *60 Minutes* or *Frontline*, we are watching Murrow. He is TV news's model, benchmark, and ultimate goal—the first that remains to this day the best.

21. Peter Falk *Columbo*'s creators first offered the part of the dumpy detective to Bing Crosby. But der Bingle prided himself on his nattiness and wanted no part of a production that would cast him as a slob. So Falk, who'd previously played a DA on the short-lived '60s series *The Trials of O'Brien*, got called in on the case. He had no problem with his character's sartorial malfeasance. In fact, he took it upon himself to hand-select Columbo's wardrobe. While most TV detectives of the era were suave and articulate, Falk's Columbo always looked and sounded like he'd just gotten out of bed. But beneath that rumpled exterior there existed a crisp mind, as the bad guys would discover each week. The cagey cop with the lopsided squint was a bit of a mystery—we never learned his first name, never saw his oft-mentioned wife—but Falk imbued him with an innocent and irrepressible charm. His performance? Call it a tour de (police) force.

20. James Arness He looked and acted the way a frontier marshal should: tall (6'6"), lean, and taciturn. (Offscreen, the press-averse Arness was just as stingy with his words.) But *Gunsmoke*, the longest running drama (635 episodes) in TV history, was no cookie-cutter Western. Arness added unparalleled depth and authenticity to one of pop culture's most common characters. Dillon never fired unless he was shot at, and he often agonized over the brutality he was embroiled in. For two decades, we watched Arness grow craggier and more weathered, even if the year in Dodge City always remained 1873. By the end of the show's run in 1975, Arness had molded Dillon into a kind of composite of the screen's greatest lawmen: a bit of Wyatt Earp, a touch of the Duke, a dollop of Shane. "A lot of actors can't hardly wait to get out and do some other characters, like they don't like the one they're doing," he once said. "I never had any feeling of that whatsoever. To me, it was a joy playing the role all the way from beginning to end."

19. **Tom Selleck** He is prime time's most magnetic leading man, the Clark Gable of the small screen. Women melt at Selleck's rugged good looks. But men like him, too. Why isn't he threatening? Perhaps it's his easy athleticism or the ready sparkle in his eye that indicates he doesn't take himself too seriously. Either way, from 1980 to 1988, Selleck had the cushiest job in television. As former Navy Intelligence officer turned sometime sleuth Thomas Magnum, he got to tool around Oahu in a fiery-red Ferrari. But Selleck delivered the show's fluffy private-eye and romantic plots with flair. And *Magnum, P.I.* supplied us with something that had been missing on TV: a hero who was also a Vietnam veteran. In guest roles, Selleck shone just as brightly—as the annoyingly perfect rival detective Lance White on *The Rockford Files* or as Monica's

charming suitor on *Friends*. Whether he's the star or a supporting actor, Tom is always terrific.

18. Richard Chamberlain Ben Casey vs. Dr. Kildare? It was an either/O.R. proposition. Actually, it really wasn't much of a contest. Chamberlain, as the ravishingly handsome, shamelessly sincere intern (later resident) James Kildare, got three times as much fan mail as his neurosurgeon rival. It really came down to bedside manner. While Vince Edwards's Ben Casey was surly, Chamberlain's Kildare was kind and caring. In fact, Dr. Kildare so thoroughly typecast Chamberlain that he had trouble finding work when the series ended in 1966. But in the late '70s and early '80s, he resuscitated his career. By playing a rugged frontiers-man in *Centennial*, a 17th-century sailor turned samurai in *Shogun*, and a lovelorn priest in *The Thorn Birds*, the erstwhile doc carved out a new niche as the dashing king of the miniseries.

17. Bob Newhart Of all the shows that have been on the air, how many are true classics and how many performers have based their reputations on having been involved in just one of them? Well, Bob Newhart has starred in two, *The Bob Newhart Show* and *Newhart:* back-to-back gems that tickled America for a total of 14 seasons. In fact, Newhart has been the star of his own series in each of the last four decades, an unmatched achievement in TV. He's done it by seeming like both the dullest and hippest guy in the room, no matter whether it was a psychologist's office or a New England inn. This unassuming, practically nondescript former accountant first took TV by storm in 1961 as a polite, stammering stand-up comic pretending to have frustrating phone conversations with annoying dullards. With perfect timing, a lovable mix of befuddlement and crankiness, and a talent for choosing brilliant costars, Newhart is this generation's George Burns: the funny straight man, the straight funnyman—the calm eye of a comic hurricane.

16. **Dinah Shore** Another gracious *Dinah Shore Show* comes to an end, and the hostess rears back like a baseball pitcher going into his motion, turns, and throws the audience a great big—Mmmmmm-wah!—kiss. "I don't know how to be afraid of that old red eye," Shore once said of the TV camera. "It's one person to me. . . . I'm comfortable with it." Comfortable? That's an understatement. From 1951, when she debuted on NBC with a 15-minute music show, until 1963, when the hour-long *Dinah Shore Chevy Show* left the air, this Tennessee-born songbird was the sovereign female performer on TV. Between 1954 and 1958, she won an Emmy every year, charming audiences with her natural effervescence, and making "See the U.S.A. in your

Chevrolet" a national catchphrase. The silken-voiced Shore returned to TV in 1970 to star in a series of daytime talk shows that would last until 1980. Her direct, unpretentious interviewing style gave Shore a second career in TV—and a new generation of fans eager to catch her kisses.

15. **Walter Cronkite** Walter Cronkite was making $37.50 a week as a United Press reporter when CBS's Edward R. Murrow came calling with an offer of $120 in 1945. Cronkite didn't bite, but when the Korean War broke out in 1950, CBS renewed its courtship, and wooed itself a legend. A new term, anchor, was coined to describe Cronkite's role during the 1952 conventions. It fit him like a glove, perhaps because, as humorist Art Buchwald later observed, Cronkite had the only honest face in TV. His appearance was donnish, his voice gravelly, his diction oddly syncopated. As anchors began to seem machine-stamped, he stayed determinedly out of sync. That was fine with America. If we had to hear bad news—and in his 46-year tenure at CBS, Cronkite has had to deliver plenty—Uncle Walter was who we wanted to hear it from. And that's the way it was.

14. **Milton Berle** TV's first star dished out a raucous brand of humor that may seem a bit primitive today, but in 1948, America caught Tuesday-night fever for Berle's unruly antics

on *Texaco Star Theater*. Restaurants closed, bars darkened, one Brooklyn laundromat installed sets and advertised, "Watch Berle while your clothes whirl." Primarily a nightclub and radio comic, Berle was the perfect pioneer for the infant medium. By filling the seven-inch screen with nonstop nonsense—he'd blacken his teeth, wear women's dresses, insult the audience, and burst onstage in the middle of a guest's act—Berle became a serious star. His exuberant burlesque soon yielded to more sophisticated humor and homey sitcoms; by 1960, he'd be hosting *Jackpot Bowling*. Yet he has never left the tube, popping up in such unlikely venues as the *MTV Video Music Awards* and *Beverly Hills, 90210*. "Waiting for me to retire," he said, "is like leaving the porch light on for Jimmy Hoffa."

13. **George Burns and Gracie Allen** They were already huge audience favorites when they transferred their radio act to TV in 1950. After all, George and Gracie had been honing their onstage personae for nearly 30 years: the bemused, detached husband and his scatter-brained wife. But now audiences could see George's raised eyebrow and contemplative cigar-puffing, Gracie's eyes shining with childlike enthusiasm as she wreaked havoc with logic. Despite Allen's initial hesitancy about leaving radio, she and Burns made a smooth transition, understanding fully how to exploit the new medium's intimacy. Taking a cue from

Thornton Wilder's *Our Town*, Burns broke down the fourth wall between performer and audience, making observations on the action onscreen or spying on Allen or the neighbors. In playing characters based on themselves, they proved to be outstanding role models for the stand-up stars of their grandchildren's generation, like Garry Shandling and Jerry Seinfeld. George and Gracie may have said good night, but not good-bye.

12. **Andy Griffith** For a lot of folks, the '60s were a volatile, confusing time. But for eight years, there was a weekly respite from all the turmoil—that Shangri-la with grits, that cornpone Camelot called Mayberry. What made this oasis so comforting was the reassuring presence of Griffith. As Andy Taylor—the wavy-haired, guitar-toting sheriff with the endearingly broad, lippy grin and the wisdom of Solomon—Griffith played (and seemed to be, in real life) a solid, sensitive, stand-up guy we could trust and admire. As the sole reasonable person in a bubbling mash of Gomers and Goobers and Barneys and Floyds, he could have played it just for laughs, but he played it for heart . . . and smarts. Later, we trusted and admired him again as savvy defense attorney Ben Matlock. (He's what might have become of Andy Taylor if he hadn't gone fishing so often with Opie, but instead had followed the dirt path not taken.) "I would like to continue to give people some small

thing to make them laugh," he once said, "and to say some small truth." Attention to those little details is what makes Andy Griffith so big.

11. **Lassie** How could you resist that face? How could you not love a creature of such unchanging, wistful, windblown beauty who also (1) had the ability to communicate whole sentences and abstract concepts to fairly dense humans simply by barking at them; (2) could tussle with a grizzly, run through over-grown forests, and swim across flood-swollen streams and still look great in the closeup; (3) saw to it that the mine-shaft-prone Timmy somehow survived to adulthood; and (4) was mom to her spunky litter—no mean feat, considering that all eight Lassies through the years were male? Lassie went through a passel of "masters" and homes during her two decades on the air, from 1954 to 1974. That's 140 in dog years and an eternity for a TV series. In all that time, she never once let us down.

10. **Dick Van Dyke** With his current show, *Diagnosis Murder*, Van Dyke has been a series star in each of the last five decades. Of course, there's a reason for that longevity. The lanky, likable actor from Danville, Illinois, combines inspired timing, a physical agility unmatched since Donald O'Connor, and enough warmth of personality to power a

sauna. Those irresistible hallmarks were best displayed in the actor's shining achievement, *The Dick Van Dyke Show*, which ran on CBS from 1961 to 1966. Let's leave the valediction to Van Dyke's TV soulmate, Mary Tyler Moore: "Despite his lack of ego and paranoia, the usual requirements for cultivating genius, the seemingly uncomplicated all-around good guy that is Dick Van Dyke is also a genius."

9. **Bill Cosby** He has the résumé of 10 men. In 1965, he became the first African-American to costar in a prime-time dramatic series—winning three Emmys in as many seasons as the smarter half of the *I Spy* espionage team. At the same time, he was the most successful stand-up comic of his generation; during the '60s, he had as many as six comedy albums on the charts at the same time. His recollections of his rough-and-tumble childhood in Philadelphia spawned a seminal cartoon series, *Fat Albert and the Cosby Kids*. Among his many other gifts, Cosby always had an intuitive understanding of children—what they think, what they feel, what they need. That in turn made him an incredibly popular commercial pitchman for products like pudding. But he was just warming up. He reached the pinnacle of his career with *The Cosby Show*, which premiered in 1984. Wise, witty, warm, and dignified, this unassuming comedy about a well-off black family in Brooklyn was credited with restoring the fortunes of NBC and with reviv-

ing the sitcom as a TV genre. Time to rest on his laurels? Not for the Cos. He's had three series since; currently he stars as a down-sized airline worker on *Cosby*. It's an incredible body of work, even for 10 men.

8. **Michael Landon** "People aren't just surprised that I write scripts," Landon once commented during his *Bonanza years*. "They're surprised I can even write my name." That's because viewers believed he really was Little Joe: happy-go-lucky, easy to laugh, a few ounces light on the brain scale—a nice, hunky boy next door with that amazing head of hair. But Landon was something else: a driven perfectionist, the product of a lonely and painful childhood who saw television as the ideal way to exorcise his private demons while reaching the hearts of his audience with small, personal stories—*Little House on the Prairie, Highway to Heaven*—stories about loving families, guardian angels, and victorious underdogs. These were all the things he dreamed about, believed in, and hoped for—and so did those who watched his shows and loved him. And when he died young, after a public battle with cancer that almost made us believe he'd beat it—just like in one of the scripts we were no longer surprised he wrote (and produced and directed and acted in)—we felt a blow, as though we'd lost a member of the family. And in a way we had—he'd spent more good times with us in our living room than many relatives,

and he'd helped shape America's image of what a loving family can be.

7. **Carol Burnett** "That girl can do anything!" Lucille Ball once marveled about the world's most celebrated ear-tugger. And who's to quarrel with Lucy? Burnett could dance, sing, and perform melodrama, but, most of all, she could make us laugh, which she did for 11 years on her supernal variety show. With that amazingly elastic face, she could play virtually any type of character, but she preferred visual and character humor to wisecracking. Her creations—the shrill Eunice Higgins battling with her husband and mother; wacko silent-film star Nora Desmond rattling around her decaying mansion—earned our sympathy and made us chuckle at the same time. She managed to appeal to both heartland farmers and big-city sophisticates. "I'm not a striking beauty, which works in my favor," she once said. "I'm not really slick, either. I still have that tinge of being amateurish. I get embarrassed and can't take a bow that doesn't look like I'm kicking dirt." From where we sat, awkward never looked so regal.

6. **Oprah Winfrey** If imitation is indeed the sincerest form of flattery, Winfrey is the most admired woman in television (as well as the best paid). The last few years of daytime have been a seemingly never-ending parade of Jennys, Jerrys, and Rickis, all try-

ing to do what Oprah does. And all coming up more or less short. From the beginning, we connected with this effervescent survivor from Kosciusko, Mississippi. When Oprah told us about her history as a victim of abuse, our hearts went out to her. When her weight rose and fell, we all watched our diets a little closer. She has brought us a makeover with Cindy Crawford and an interview with Lee Harvey Oswald's widow, Marina, with the same enthusiasm and candor. "Spontaneous, intelligent, subjective . . . a homey personality that invites confidences." That was how *TV Guide*'s own Don Merrill saw her back in 1987. But what makes Oprah so special shines through in her irrefutable sincerity, her inexhaustible compassion, and her spiritual second sight. She simply has the biggest heart that television has ever seen.

5. **Mary Tyler Moore** By the time *The Mary Tyler Moore Show* debuted on CBS in 1970, its star had already been a big hit on TV (as Dick Van Dyke's wife, the lissome Laura Petrie). In the opening episode, Lou Grant told her, "You know what? You've got spunk. . . . I hate spunk." No one else did, though. At least not Mary's infectious brand of it. For seven years, this 30-ish career woman who came to a Minneapolis TV station looking for a new start in life did indeed "turn the world on with her smile," and in the process altered the

American lifestyle—suddenly 24 million people were building their Saturday nights around watching TV. Since *The Mary Tyler Moore Show* left the air in 1977, Moore has gone on to well-deserved success in feature films (*Ordinary People, Flirting with Disaster*). We always knew she'd make it after all.

4. **James Garner** Garner is, hands down, TV's all-time most affable star: easy to take, easy to like, easy on the eyes. Let's face it, he just makes everything he does look so darned easy. That's his genius: He doesn't seem to be acting when he's acting, which, of course, is acting at its highest level. That's why he outlasted most of his contemporaries, who merely traded on their hunkiness. Garner was able to jump comfortably between small- and big-screen projects, and he's had the range to play everything from a corporate shark in TV's *Barbarians at the Gate*, to Doris Day's dopey husband, to a guilt-ridden and responsibility-shackled brother in *Promise*, to a gender-bent suitor in *Victor/Victoria*. And that's why he gets an Emmy nomination every time he gets in front of the camera (13 in all). This tall, craggy natural, who still retains his native Oklahoma twang, can do farce and drama, romance and adventure—even his commercials become instant classics. We like him, we really like him, in just about everything, but what we can't get enough of, and want to keep seeing more of, are the two roles he made us

love him in: the wry cowboy con man with a heart of gold and a yellow streak in *Maverick;* and the Firebird-driving modern knight of *The Rockford Files*. Even after 40 years of nearly constant company, we still like having the guy around.

3. **Jackie Gleason** Orson Welles dubbed him "The Great One," and it was hard to deny the truth of that assessment. Gleason filled our TV screens like no other star before or since—in pounds and power, in sweat-soaked, top-of-the-lungs emotions and in the sheer force and raw intensity of his complex personality. He was the ultimate showman, hosting a three-ring variety hour that included a full orchestra and the leggy, synchronized June Taylor dancers—and then in that same hour acting in a skit that absolutely broke your heart. And Ralph Kramden—his crowning, undying achievement—was everything rolled into one: an explosive guy you wouldn't want sitting next to you in a bus (let alone driving it), but someone you wanted to hug for all his great hopes and dashed dreams. Gleason knew that even though they called them "situation" comedies, it was character that made audiences tune in. And his one-man repertoire—Kramden, Reggie Van Gleason III, Joe the Bartender, the Poor Soul—was filled with memorable, Chaplinesque characters. The Great One? Seems right to us.

2. **Johnny Carson** He was television's Prince Charming. For three decades—spanning eight presidential administrations—he kept America up past its bedtime with his graceful balancing act: skillfully juxtaposing his Midwestern gosh-golliness with a New York/ Hollywood clubbiness; hosting a show that veered between the spontaneous and the scripted; knowing when to be the straight man and when to be funny. Carson packaged his combination of comic influences—his idol Jack Benny's sense of timing, Oliver Hardy's mastery of the drawn-out reaction, Fred Allen's feel for sketch comedy, Groucho Marx's talent at delivering a well-placed double entendre—in the persona of the slightly naughty neighborhood kid who had the ability to chat up anyone, from Liz Taylor to a septuagenarian sardine-packer from Bangor, Maine. He presided over the Oscar ceremonies five times, with an easy poise that has been jealously emulated by every host since. It's only after he left the air that we realize how monumental Carson's achievement was: For 30 years, he threw the world's greatest party, night after night. There's no denying it: Johnny really was magic.

1. **Lucille Ball** For 24 seasons, through 179 *I Love Lucy*s, 156 *Lucy Show*s, 144 *Here's Lucy*s, numerous specials, and, what the heck, even the handful of *Life with Lucy*s, Ball was remarkably consistent. "I never changed," she

once said. "People could tune in to see what they expected to see." What we always got was a flamboyant redheaded firecracker with a fabulously expressive face and a genius for physical humor who'd do anything—anything—for a laugh. She'd stomp on grapes barefoot, set her putty nose on fire, imitate Harpo Marx—all the while projecting a child-like, never childish, innocence that endeared her to viewers. But she wasn't just influential as a performer. Lucy owned and ran (after buying out her former husband Desi Arnaz) a powerful Hollywood studio. (The original *Star Trek* and *Mission: Impossible* were both developed by Desilu on her watch.) Of course, audiences loved this high-school dropout and one-time Goldwyn Girl best as Ricky Ricardo's perpetually thwarted wife in TV's first hit sitcom, a show that debuted October 15, 1951, and continues to air somewhere in the world every day. Without a doubt, we'll be loving Lucy forever.

(from TV Guide, *December 14, 1996. By Ed Weiner, Art Durbano, Andy Edelstein, Joanne Kaufman, and Stephanie Williams)*

TV's 20 Most Romantic Moments

These are the moments when love and passion on the small screen took our breath away. They're stories both uplifting (the rapture of a first kiss, the union of two soul mates) and heartrending (the death of a lover, the breaking asunder of a perfect couple). Get out your handkerchiefs . . .

20. ***Moonlighting*—Dave and Maddie Get Down and Dirty** To make love, or war? That was the question that plunged Maddie and David into their fiercest battle and their first liaison. When a bizarre chain of events made naked bedfellows out of them in 1987, David wanted to seize the moment, while Maddie's impulse was to send him packing. Tempers flared, insults flew, crockery crashed—but by the time the Ronettes' song "Be My Baby" was

cued, the two were ready to give in to their ravenous, rapturous, wrecking-ball desire.

19. *Star Trek: The Next Generation*—**Picard's Grand Sacrifice** Fate played a cruel joke on Jean-Luc Picard in 1992 when he fell in love with Kamala, an empath who was betrothed to a man she had never met. It was Picard's mission to bring Kamala to her fiancé as a peace offering between two warring factions. Neither the captain nor his charge could bear to part, but they knew if they didn't the peace would never last. Their good-bye was both excruciating and heroic: Picard escorted his love to the wedding and gave her up to a man he knew would never love her.

18. *The Addams Family*—**"Tish, You Spoke French!"** To their suburban neighbors, Morticia and Gomez were a gruesome twosome, permanently prepped for Halloween. But au contraire, every day was Valentine's Day chez Addams. Morticia's very presence mesmerized Gomez, but when she casually dropped bon mots in "the language of love," she sent him into a spin of uncontrollable passion. She basked in serene delight as he caressed her with a trail of kisses, from her pale fingertips to the nape of her alabaster neck.

17. *Dr. Kildare*—**Dr. Kildare Breaks the Waves** During a two-part 1964 episode called "Tyger-Tyger," which featured rising movie star

Yvette Mimieux, Dr. Kildare learned the hard way that loving a wild thing is no walk along the beach. The young resident fell for Pat Holmes, "the best surfer girl on the whole coast," when she was brought in to Blair Hospital after suffering an epileptic seizure. He urged her to give up surfing, but ended up hanging ten just to be with her, and they basked in the sun—until she suffered another seizure and drowned in the ocean. Fighting tears, Kildare took his love in his arms for one last time and carried her to shore.

16. *L.A. Law*—**Grace Goes Ape** Hopeless romantics, take heart. In 1986, when lawyer Michael Kuzak found out that his new love interest, assistant district attorney Grace Van Owen, was moments away from getting married, he didn't give up. Taking inspiration from *The Graduate* and *King Kong*, he marched to the courthouse to break up the wedding—in a gorilla suit. Grace was understandably thrilled to be the object of such animal passion, and walked off with him, hand in paw.

15. **Ahmad Rashad Proposes and Phylicia Says "Yes"** He made bending down on one knee seem, well, halfhearted. It was Thanksgiving Day, 1985, and sportscaster Ahmad Rashad was on the field at Detroit's Silverdome (covering a Jets-Lions game). He asked his colleague in New York, Bob Costas, to relay a message: "Phylicia, would you marry me? Either I will be the happiest person in the

world or the biggest turkey on national television." Before game's end, Cosby Show star Phylicia Ayers-Allen joined Costas in the studio, and gave Rashad, who was wiping the sweat from his brow with a tissue, the answer he was hoping for. He beamed, and we sighed in relief.

14. *The Honeymooners*—**"Baby, You're the Greatest!"** What draws a sensible woman to a childish man? In the Kramdens' case, the answer was clear: humor. Ralph got into many a pickle, but his panicky brand of remorse was too funny for Alice to resist. Equally laughable was his "Right to the moon!" threat. Everyone (especially Ralph) knew that without Alice, he'd be like a bus without a steering wheel. Come to think of it, the only time we took Ralph seriously was when he grabbed Alice and cried, "Baby, you're the greatest!" Right from the heart.

13. *The Brady Bunch*—**Marcia Meets Davy** Every girl who's ever swooned over a rock star swooned anew when Marcia Brady— president of the local Davy Jones Fan Club— received a visit from her idol in 1971. He came to her door, handed her a copy of his latest album, and offered not only to sing at her prom, but to be her date. Crush fulfillment has rarely been so satisfying (although Tom Cruise's recent visit to Rosie O'Donnell's show did come close).

12. **"Sunshine"—In Your Eyes Can Make You Cry** Kleenex was not an optional but rather a compulsory accompaniment to this 1973 movie about a 20-year-old mother dying of cancer. Throughout Kate's ordeal, her guitar-strumming lover, Sam, stood by her side, proposing marriage the day before her first radiation treatment. The hospital-room ceremony—in all its hippie-era glory—showed that even in the face of mortality, undying love can still flourish.

11. *Miami Vice*—**Sonny Is Smitten** Sometimes there's no use fighting love, even when it's a bad idea. By the time Sonny Crockett found out Christine Von Marburg was a madam—and she found out he was a cop—they were both hooked. The smoldering sex scenes between Don Johnson and his ex-wife, Melanie Griffith, were especially titillating in this 1988 episode because the actors were in fact rekindling their real-life romance.

10. *Friends*—**Ross and Rachel's Big Kiss** He had always loved her. She never knew, or cared—until he was happily involved with another woman. The prelude to a kiss we'll never forget began a year ago, when Ross received a phone message from a drunk Rachel: "I am over you!" (His response: "When were you 'under' me?") Later, Ross showed up at Central Perk to tell Rachel she was too late, that his ship had sailed. Their argument sent

him storming out the door. Moments later, he was back inside, and the pain of his pent-up passion was finally erased as they melted together in a glorious kiss.

9. *Life Goes On*—**Becca Remembers Jesse** Becca and Jesse had everything going for them—they were young, bright, and artistic—but they chose not to consummate their relationship because Jesse was HIV positive. Their romance came to its inevitable, tragic end, but the moment we'll always remember came in the series' 1993 finale: In a flash-forward, we see Becca as a 40-something woman, tucking her young son into bed and telling him the story of her first love. As she gives him a kiss and turns out the light, she looks lovingly at the boy and murmurs, "Good night, Jesse."

8. *Hill Street Blues*—**Frank and Joyce's Pillow Talk** On the job, Frank Furillo and Joyce Davenport treated each other with cool professional respect. But after hours, they lapsed into lovey-dovey mode, complete with pet names, passion, and plenty of bubble bath. The steely police chief (she called him "Pizza Man") and prosecutor (he called her "Counselor") might have seemed like an unlikely duo, but their steamy end-of-episode trysts were a weekly reminder that the night has a logic of its own.

7. *Frasier*—**Niles and Daphne Tango** Unrequited love never looked so good. In 1996,

when Niles and Daphne took to the floor at his country club's annual winter ball, our hearts beat in time to the music. After almost three years of dancing around his feelings for Daphne, Niles finally had her in his arms, and he savored every dip and turn. She'd agreed to pose as his adoring lady, a part she played too well. After she urged Niles to let the music carry him away, he blurted, "Oh, Daphne, I adore you"—and she reciprocated the sentiment. The dance ended with a soft kiss. Afterward, Niles was quietly crushed when Daphne complimented him on his fine "acting."

6. **Royal Wedding—*Charles and Di Tie the Knot***
We didn't know then that their union wouldn't last. The pretty young bride, in a billowing silk-and-lace gown and a diamond tiara, rode to London's St. Paul's Cathedral in a Cinderella-inspired glass-covered carriage, on July 29, 1981. As all the world—an estimated 750 million people—watched in awe, she walked down the red-carpeted aisle and met her attentive prince at the altar. Even Diana's flubbing of the vows (she called him "Philip Charles") couldn't diminish the grandeur of this fairy-tale wedding come to life.

5. ***My So-Called Life*—Jordan Catalano and Angela Hold Hands** When a teenage girl is being romanced by the hunkiest boy alive, she wants the whole world to know—or at

least the whole high school. But when that hunk is the brooding Jordan Catalano, it comes as no surprise that he wants to keep the whole thing secret. Of course, Jordan didn't know what he was up against when he fell for Angela Chase in 1994. Realizing that he might lose her if he didn't let his love show, he took a deep breath, sauntered down the hall, and took Angela by the hand—as the whole school watched in wonder.

4. *Family Ties*—**Alex Declares His Love to Ellen**
Cold rationalism melts in the presence of desperate affection. Alex P. Keaton was not supposed to fall helplessly in love with anyone—let alone left-leaning art major Ellen Reed. Had she not been on the brink of marrying someone else, he would never have driven to a train station seven and a half hours away to say "I love you." In retrospect, it's no wonder Michael J. Fox and Tracy Pollan seemed like so much more than sitcom sweethearts: Three years later, in 1988, they married.

3. *Beauty and the Beast*—**Catherine Dies** The deck was stacked against them from the start. Catherine was an assistant district attorney; Vincent was a man-beast exiled to New York City's secret tunnel world. They managed to forge a one-in-a-million romance, which Catherine called "a bond stronger than friendship or love." But the love that would not be denied was doomed to come to a tragic end. In 1989, Vincent, who had protected Catherine from

danger so often, was powerless when a crime lord gave her a lethal injection—just after she gave birth to their son. Vincent arrived at her side only in time to hold her tenderly as she died in his arms.

2. **General Hospital—Luke and Laura's Wedding** No other couple in soap opera history has captured the viewing public's fascination like Lucas Lorenzo Spencer and Laura Webber Baldwin. So, when the lovebirds finally sealed their rocky courtship at the altar in November 1981, more than 16 million viewers stopped to witness the two-day extravaganza. As the bride and groom pledged their eternal love to one another on the mayor's lawn, the good people of Port Charles and fans everywhere took heart at this happiest of all endings.

1. *The Thorn Birds*—**Ralph and Meggie: On the Beach** Love doesn't get any more forbidden than this: In the 1983 miniseries, Ralph de Bricassart, a Roman Catholic archbishop, cast aside God and ambition for a few stolen days at a remote beach with Meggie, the woman he had loved since she was a child and desperately wanted since she was a teen. Their frenzied tumbles on the beach (with that poignant melody soaring in the background) were terribly moving: Each knew well that this would be their only time together.

(from TV Guide, *February 8, 1997. Reported by Stef McDonald, Stephanie Williams, and Elisa Zuritsky)*

The 100 Greatest Episodes of All Time

Gunsmoke alone has 635 of them. *Seinfeld* is at 149 and counting. We're talking about episodes, those distinctive storytelling units of series television, and there are a million of them. So when *TV Guide,* in conjunction with the television history experts at Nick at Nite's TV Land, set about assembling and ranking the 100 greatest episodes of all time, we searched for classics of both the sitcom and TV-drama formats—shows that mingled elements of great writing and acting, of serendipity and inspiration, of ambition and artistry. Our favorites may not be the same as yours, but you'll have to agree: Episodes like these reflect TV at its best—and make for wonderful and enduring memories.

100. *Friends* (February 1, 1996) How to put Ross and Rachel (David Schwimmer and Jennifer

Aniston) in each other's arms after a season and a half of false starts? Give them an audiovisual aid. Looking at footage from high school in "The One with the Prom Video," Rachel finally recognizes Ross's long-suffering devotion to her. Ever so slowly she crosses the room and kisses him. The fateful video also reveals a chunky teenage Monica (Courteney Cox). When she insists that the camera adds 10 pounds, Chandler (Matthew Perry) asks, "So how many cameras are actually on you?"

99. *The Untouchables* (October 13, 1960) In "The Rusty Heller Story," Elizabeth Mont-gomery took Prohibition-era Chicago by storm as Heller, a seductive Dixie damsel who pits a newly arrived mob faction against Al Capone's teetering empire and then plays both against the cops. "Now don't you go appealing to my decency, because I ain't got any," she drawls to a clearly smitten Ness (Robert Stack). This episode records Capone's arrest and conviction, but it's the glint of a grin Heller brings to Ness's granite mug that carves this episode in TV history.

98. *The Outer Limits* (December 30, 1963) In "The Zanti Misfits," our military forces have cordoned off a California ghost town awaiting the arrival of a spacecraft from the planet Zanti. The leaders of that world have decided that Earth is the perfect place to exile their undesirables. They threaten "total destruction" if their penal ship is molested. But a bank robber on the lam (Bruce Dern) crosses the cordon and

approaches the Zanti ship, triggering an ugly jailbreak. Earth's nervous soldiers launch an anti-Zanti attack, killing all the aliens—and fearfully awaiting the expected reprisal. Instead, they get a message of thanks from the Zanti leaders. It seems they can't execute their own kind, so they sent them to the experts on killing—us.

97. ***Little House on the Prairie*** (February 6 & 13, 1978) Under trying frontier conditions, Charles Ingalls (Michael Landon) does the best he can for his wife and four daughters. And he is usually up to the challenge, except in the two-part "I'll Be Waving as You Drive Away"— when he learns that his beloved eldest daughter, Mary (Melissa Sue Anderson), is going blind, the result of an arduous bout with scarlet fever. The devoted father almost comes undone when he has to give the girl the news. Television series, even those that pride themselves on realism, rarely make the afflictions of leading characters permanent conditions. But however gentle *Little House*'s spirit, the show doesn't take the easy way out here. Blind Mary is, and blind she will stay; both she and her family learn to cope and hold on to hope in this deeply affecting episode.

96. ***Picket Fences*** (October 27, 1995) What happens when you explore the "Heart of Saturday Night" in Rome, Wisconsin? Nothing much . . . just love and death and friendship and dreams and stars. Just life. Young Matthew Brock

(Justin Shenkarow) goes cruising with the guys, ends up at a party with the in-crowd, and acts as a go-between in a domestic dispute. Jimmy and Jill (Tom Skerritt and Kathy Baker) try to rekindle their romance until a zipper accident douses their ardor. Judge Bone and Wambaugh (Ray Walston and Fyvush Finkel) see a friend die and end the night standing in a lake, their pants rolled up like Huck Finn and Tom Sawyer, contemplating eternity. Saturday night in Rome: boring, sad, frustrating, ethereal—a miracle. And based on this marvelously subtle, sweet, and profound episode—which has the strength and integrity of TV's Golden Age dramas—it's hard to imagine a better place to spend an evening.

95. *The Mod Squad* (February 17, 1970) Pete, Linc, and Julie (Michael Cole, Clarence Williams III, and Peggy Lipton) were the grooviest TV detectives ever—long-haired hipsters in bell-bottoms who should have been throwing pots in a commune but became crime-solvers instead. In the audaciously Oedipal "Mother of Sorrow," a deranged young man (Richard Dreyfuss) stages a mock murder to gain the attention of his neglectful artist mother (Lee Grant). Film actors Dreyfuss and Grant sizzle as emotional adversaries who share a Victorian house and an intense hatred of the father and husband who walked out on them. Part therapy session, part whodunit, this episode was innovative entertainment for a generation hell-bent on self-discovery.

94. ***Mork & Mindy*** (May 6, 1980) Robin Williams's outrageous, turbo-comic brilliance has never been better showcased than in "Mork's Mixed Emotions." A kiss from Mindy (Pam Dawber) uncorks the entire gamut of the space cadet's long-pent-up feelings. What follows is a dizzying, dazzling display of Williams's unfettered inventiveness and versatility. One after another, Mork's carefully repressed emotions come ricocheting out, each of them punctuated by a different voice. He is by turns loving, fearful, joyful, guilty, envious, hopeful, disgusted, and grateful. And that's the warm-up. Thank goodness for the commercials, or you'd never have a chance to catch your breath.

93. ***Naked City*** (June 7, 1961) In the sinuous "Sweet Prince of Delancy Street," Richie Wilkins (Robert Morse) has no sooner confessed to killing a factory guard and stealing $15,000 of industrial diamonds than his father (James Dunn) walks into the police precinct. "I don't know what my boy told you," he says. "I killed the guard." The cops don't believe either guy. We soon meet the real culprit, played by a young man with a mop of dark hair and a distinctive, nasal voice. It was Dustin Hoffman's first major TV role.

92. ***Star Trek*** (April 6, 1967) Captain Kirk (William Shatner) and Mr. Spock (Leonard Nimoy) travel back to Earth during the Great Depression to correct a temporal anomaly. While there, Kirk falls in love with the altruist Edith Keeler (Joan

Collins). But a makeshift computer, rigged by Spock from his tricorder and some vacuum tubes, informs them that Keeler must die or Nazi Germany will prevail in World War II. In the provocative "City on the Edge of Forever," Kirk balances his one true love against the lives of untold millions. No adventure ever affected the captain—or us—so deeply.

91. *L.A. Law* (March 21, 1991) Leland McKenzie (Richard Dysart) has just rejected a marriage proposal from steely Rosalind Shays (Diana Muldaur). She rings for the elevator, steps in . . . and plummets down the open shaft. As the firm's partners fret over being sued while "her body's not even cold," Shays' attorney jokes, "If anything, death probably warmed her up a few degrees." Black humor and a tender love scene between Susan Dey and Jimmy Smits—that's what viewers get in "Good to the Last Drop."

90. *Miami Vice* (October 18, 1985) Boasting Hugo Boss suits, two-day beard growth, and a sleek Ferrari convertible, Sonny Crockett (Don Johnson) and Rico Tubbs (Philip Michael Thomas) were the first TV cops to have as much flash as the bad guys they chased. In "Out Where the Buses Don't Run," series creator Michael Mann updates Edgar Allan Poe's "The Tell-Tale Heart" with glitzy visuals and a throbbing rock-music soundtrack (The Who, Dire Straits). Former vice cop Hank Weldon (Bruce McGill) tags along with the squad to

catch a cocaine kingpin who disappeared long ago, Hoffa-style. Is Weldon nuts? Says Crockett: "My head tells me he's stone-cold insane, but my gut says let's go with him on this." The chilling finale proves Crockett's gut wrong: A guilt-wracked Weldon rips down a wall to expose the corpse of the drug king he actually murdered six years earlier.

89. *Speed Racer* (Fall 1967) (U.S.) Okay, maybe it isn't quite up there with "Who shot J.R.?" But for aficionados of *Speed Racer*, the irresistibly cheesy Japanese-import cartoon of the '60s, "Who is Racer X?" (the mysterious Masked Racer, who always seemed to cause disaster) was just as tantalizing a mystery. In this pivotal, two-part episode, we learn of the existence of Speed Racer's older brother, Rex—and see in flashback how he cracked up in a race he had entered (against his father's wishes) and left the family after a bitter quarrel. This is a *Speed Racer* of unusual emotional nuance and narrative complexity. But there's more: a midnight duel between Speed and Racer X and the climactic Trans-Country Race, in which every rule of international racing and physics is shattered in one unforgettable sequence.

88. *Happy Days* (October 14, 1975) A top-20 series for eight of its 11 seasons, *Happy Days* often focused on the brotherly relationship between two '50s stereotypes: Richie Cunningham (Ron Howard), the clean-cut boy next door, and his

idol, Fonzie (Henry Winkler), the coolest motorcycle-riding high school dropout in all of Milwaukee. "Richie Fights Back" finds straight-arrow Richie being tyrannized by a pair of bullies. "I'm going to teach you the secret of being tough," Fonzie assures Richie, who has already tried studying jujitsu with Arnold (Pat Morita). "Of course, with that Howdy Doody face, you can only be so tough." The secret is nothing earthshaking: Act tough, sound tough, and maybe people will think you are tough. But in the end, it works. Richie stands up to the bullies all by himself. Howdy Doody gets his self-respect back—with a little help from his leather-clad friend.

87. **China Beach** (January 25, 1989) A series set in Vietnam could hardly ignore the Tet offensive, the turning point of the war. "Tet '68" opens with Wayloo (Megan Gallagher), the ambitious TV personality, cheerily describing the upcoming holiday as "the Vietnamese Fourth of July, Christmas, and New Year's Eve, all rolled into one. We can sense the magic of the new year." Then the shooting starts. Beckett (Michael Boatman) is held hostage by his lady friend's VC brother; McMurphy (Dana Delany) is stuck at headquarters with the strung-out K.C. (Marg Helgenberger); Dr. Dick (Robert Picardo) and Dodger (Jeff Kober) are at an evac hospital; and Red Cross worker Cherry (Nan Woods) is caught in a bunker. Morning finally breaks, and all have survived.

But then Cherry, stepping outside the bunker, is killed by a bomb. It's an unflinching look at the indiscriminate ruthlessness of war, one that viewers would not soon forget.

86. *Batman* (March 16 & 17, 1966) In his first two months in prime time, the Caped Crusader battled the Joker, the Riddler, and the Penguin— and became a national obsession. But when Catwoman (Julie Newmar) steals his heart (not to mention two priceless gold cat statues) in "The Purr-fect Crime" and "Better Luck Next Time," Batman (Adam West) meets his match. Pursuing the lost treasure of pirate Captain Manx, Catwoman lures Batman and Robin (Burt Ward) to her hideout. She nearly does them in, but they break free and track her down. In the chase, she falls off a rocky ledge into a bottomless pit. But Catwoman had nine lives and appeared in eight more episodes. Although Newmar turned over her cat ears to Eartha Kitt, the first Catwoman remains the best. Meow and forever.

85. *Dragnet* (January 12, 1967) When *Dragnet* returned to prime time after an eight-year absence, Jack Webb's hard-boiled cop show had clearly left the '50s behind. The story we were about to see was not only true, it was ripped from the headlines: Sergeant Friday and his new sidekick, Officer Bill Gannon (Harry Morgan), must investigate the spread of a new hallucinogenic drug among L.A. teens. The episode plays like a more subdued version of

"Reefer Madness," highlighted by director Webb's version of a "psychedelic" party and Friday's hip lingo. "You're pretty high and far out. What kind of kick are you on, son?" he grills his prisoner, Benjie "Blue Boy" Carver (Michael Burns), an 18-year-old who paints half his face blue and the other half yellow. Do we have to tell you how "The LSD Story" ends up when the final dum-de-dum-dum is heard?

84. *Mad About You* (February 16, 1995) "The Alan Brady Show" turns reality inside out and brings to life the fictional Alan Brady (Carl Reiner), who once terrorized the characters of *The Dick Van Dyke Show*. But when Brady threatens to bail out as the narrator of Paul's documentary on the history of—what else?— TV, *Mad* really goes mad: Jamie (Helen Hunt) gets so upset she bursts into tears the way Laura Petrie used to, sobbing, "Oh, Paul." Where is Mel Cooley when you need him?

83. *Have Gun, Will Travel* (April 12, 1958) Cultured, dapper, and literate, Paladin (Richard Boone) was a professional gunslinger with a sense of honor. The series was not afraid to use controversial issues as plots, even painful chapters from America's past, such as the exploitation of Chinese immigrants. In "Hey Boy's Revenge," Paladin's Chinese friend Hey Boy (Kam Tong) gets into trouble for trying to solve the murder of his brother, a new immigrant who protested the deplorable working conditions of his railroad gang—and was killed

for it. Always using his might for right, Paladin not only frees Hey Boy, he brings the killer to justice.

82. ***The Love Boat*** (October 12, 1985) Andy Warhol is on board the *Pacific Princess*, and he wants to paint a portrait of Kansas housewife Mary Hammond (Marion Ross). But Mary will be sunk if her conservative husband, George (Tom Bosley), finds out she once had 15 minutes of fame as a green-haired bohemian named Marina Del Rey who appeared in a Warhol art movie, *White Giraffe*. Perhaps the campiest of all *Love Boats*, "The 200th Episode" not only reunites *Happy Days* stars Ross and Bosley, it features a then-unknown Teri Hatcher as one of the ship's singing-and-dancing Love Boat Mermaids.

81. ***Maverick*** (November 23, 1958) No episode better exemplified the mellow maneuvering of Bret and Bart Maverick—the Brothers Grin— than "Shady Deal at Sunny Acres." Swindled out of $15,000 by a banker, Bret (James Garner) pulls up a rocking chair and starts whittling, assuring everyone who comes by to make fun of him that he'll get his money back. Bart (Jack Kelly) lures the banker into a stock swindle, then rides into the sunset—after giving Bret the money. "You can fool all of the people some of the time, and some of the people all of the time," concludes Bret, "and those are very good odds."

80. *M*A*S*H* (February 24, 1976) The heart of this superlative series was Captain Benjamin Franklin "Hawkeye" Pierce (Alan Alda), an insubordinate surgeon whose tongue was as sharp as his scalpel. While his surgical tools were used to put young soldiers' bodies back together, his rapier wit was usually employed to skewer military pretension and hypocrisy. Hawkeye puts both his cutting instruments to optimal use in "The Interview," in which a television correspondent visits the 4077th to shoot a documentary. The episode, filmed in black and white, records staff members giving their alternately amusing, moving, and painful takes on everything from the madness of war to what they miss most about home. The "film" ends with the inevitable arrival of a new batch of casualties and the unit mobilizing to do the work it does best, but which it would rather not be doing at all, in a place it would rather not be.

79. *Law & Order* (April 13, 1994) In Harlem, a 12-year-old African-American boy is fatally struck by a hit-and-run driver. The boy's friend (Omar Sharif Scroggins) tells the police, "It was a Jew." "What, was he wearing a little hat?" asks Detective Briscoe (Jerry Orbach). "You don't think I know a Jew when I see one?" says the boy. That's the provocative opening of "Sanctuary," a powerhouse episode. The incident escalates into a race riot, and an innocent man (Italian, as it happens) is killed by an African-American youth. When the prosecution of the youth ends in a mistrial, the DA, in a controversial decision, elects not to retry the case in order to let the city heal. Fittingly, this all-too-real dramatization of society's deep racial rifts has a conclusion in which no one wins.

78. *The Partridge Family* (January 29, 1971) In "Soul Club," a plucky, ambitious road trip, the singing family finds itself mistakenly booked into a black nightclub in Detroit. Complication: The club's broke owners (Richard Pryor and Louis Gossett, Jr.) will lose their business if the night's turnout isn't huge. When only one customer shows up, Mrs. Partridge (Shirley Jones) decides to throw a block party the next day and charge admission. Keith (David Cassidy) even writes a song for the occasion, declaring, "It's sort of an Afro thing." Everyone from local merchants to a Pantheresque group in black berets attends the event, and the club is saved. This may be the most outlandish episode on our list; it's certainly one of the best intentioned.

77. *Barney Miller* (December 16, 1976) Wojo's hippie girlfriend bakes a batch of brownies, which the amiable detective (Max Gail) shares with his fellow cops in the 12th Precinct. What he doesn't know: The sweets are laced with hashish. Before long, dour Detective Yemana (Jack Soo) wobbles by, saying with a giggle, "Anybody seen my legs?" The reserved Harris (Ron Glass) greets a jailed suspect with "What's happening, baby?" Stooped, stone-faced Phil Fish (Abe Vigoda) even chases a rob-

ber across a rooftop. This humane series always treated its working-class detectives as real people, not stereotypes. That's why "Hash" remains so raucously relevant.

76. *Lost in Space* (February 28, 1966) Hey, plants have feelings, too! This is the theme of "The Great Vegetable Rebellion." The Jupiter II module is orbiting a planet that appears to consist only of flora when Dr. Smith (Jonathan Harris) jumps ship. Down on the planet's surface, the scheming stowaway is captured by an overgrown talking carrot. It may look like it stepped out of a bad commercial, but on this planet, veggies rule! The Space Family Robinson saves the mewling doctor just before he is turned vegetative himself. Lettuce be thankful.

75. *3rd Rock from the Sun* (September 29, 1996) While High Commander Dick (John Lithgow) and his beloved Mary (Jane Curtin) are at a sci-fi convention in Cleveland where *Star Trek*'s George Takei (Mr. Sulu) is plugging his new book, *Warp Speed, Dammit! The Complete Rants of William Shatner*, the rest of the crew is back at the hotel discovering the ineffable joys of room service—massages, robes, bubbly, chocolates, lobster, and more lobster. And what's this—a Cleveland phone book? No, that's the bill. Welcome to "Hotel Dick."

74. *Combat!* (March 12, 1963) The talents of director Robert Altman and actor Vic Morrow blend beautifully in "Survival," a strikingly cine-

matic episode of this 1960s World War II drama. Sergeant Saunders (Morrow) gets separated from his platoon behind enemy lines. Instead of dialogue, we get stark images: Saunders staggering in shock out of a burning farmhouse; a soldier without boots struggling in agony to keep up; Saunders staring hungrily at an apple that dangles enticingly out of reach of his scorched hands. In a medium of constant, relentless talk, Altman lets the pictures tell the story—memorably.

73. *Mister Ed* (September 29, 1963) With the Los Angeles Dodgers in a slump, manager Leo Durocher gets a helpful dugout phone call from architect "Wilbur Post," but in fact he's getting advice straight from the horse's mouth. Mister Ed's tip works: the Dodgers win. Before you know it, Wilbur (Alan Young) and Mister Ed are at Dodger Stadium, where the golden palomino takes batting practice. Stepping to the plate against Sandy Koufax, Ed hits one to the outfield wall and gallops around the bases. When Johnny Roseboro sees the hard-charging charger round third and head for home, the Dodgers' catcher immediately climbs the backstop to avoid him. This could be an inside-the-park homer. Slide, Mister Ed, slide! Okay, an ersatz Ed may have been yanked down the third-base line by visible wires, but there's certainly nothing fake about the place "Leo Durocher Meets Mister Ed" has in sitcom-sports history.

72. **The X-Files** (April 20, 1997) Fans patiently waiting for the sparks between Mulder and Scully to explode are finally rewarded in "Small Potatoes"—sort of. A loser named Eddie (Darin Morgan) uses his "striated muscle tissue" to bed women by morphing into the men they love—leading to a rash of babies born with tails. When Mulder uncovers the scam, Eddie knocks him out and assumes his shape. What follows pokes fun at every hallowed *X-Files* tradition, with Eddie, now played artfully by David Duchovny, slouching into Mulder's shoes and ridiculing everything from his first name (Fox) to his geeky friends. He even discovers a message from a phone-sex operator on Mulder's answering machine. The finest touch comes after Eddie (as Mulder) is busted while putting the moves on Scully over a bottle of wine. Eddie disappointedly confides to Mulder, "I was born a loser, but you're one by choice." A superbly twisted, yet oddly unsettling, romp.

71. **The Patty Duke Show** (May 24, 1964) This episode recreates the first meeting between those "identical cousins" Patty and Cathy Lane, in which cultured Cathy gets her Uncle Martin (William Schallert) fired from his job as managing editor of the *New York Daily Chronicle* and breaks up Patty's romance with Richard (Eddie Applegate)—all before the second commercial. This frothy family comedy boasted good writing and clever camera work, but its real distinction was Patty Duke's extraordinary dual

performance—never more noticeable than in "The Cousins," in which she plays Cathy imitating Patty and vice versa. You can lose your mind when cousins are two of a kind.

70. **Star Trek: The Next Generation** (week of June 18, 1990) *Star Trek: The Next Generation*, the whippersnapper spin-off that few took seriously at first, triumphantly came of age with "The Best of Both Worlds, Part I." This third-season finale saw the villainous Borg enter Federation space, kidnap Picard (Patrick Stewart), and transform him into one of its own. The surprise-a-minute teleplay by *Trek* producer Michael Piller—who broke Gene Roddenberry's number-one rule by allowing intense conflict among the Feds—climaxes with Commander Riker (Jonathan Frakes) weighing the lives of his crew against that of his beloved captain. He issues the command to destroy the Borg ship carrying Picard. Three of the most frightening words in *Trek* history— "Mr. Worf, fire!"—are followed by three of the most exultant—"to be continued"—for, with this episode, *TNG* boldly went into a fourth season, a feat the original series never managed.

69. **Buffalo Bill** (January 5, 1984) No sitcom was ever edgier than this one: Its pre-PC humor was so dark that some never saw it. In "Jerry Lewis Week," the browbeaten station manager, Karl Shub (Max Wright), finally stands up to his star's bullying. He steals a stuffed bear that Bill (Dabney Coleman) has been using on air to

plug his mechanic (in exchange for free repairs). This insurrection occurs during WBFL's tribute to Jerry Lewis, which has brought on a locustlike infestation of Lewis lookalikes, all braying "Hey, lady!" One is played by an unbilled 21-year-old Jim Carrey. Plenty more would be heard from Carrey, but sadly, *Buffalo Bill* would last only 12 more episodes.

68. *Family Ties* (March 12, 1987) Alex P. Keaton, whose life revolves around himself, money, family, money, school, money (and money), realizes the value of life in the one-hour "'A' My Name Is Alex," written by Alan Uger and series creator Gary David Goldberg. A friend is killed in a car accident, and Alex (Michael J. Fox) is overcome with grief. In *Our Town*–like flashbacks, he talks to an unseen psychiatrist and grapples with big questions about God and a person's place in the grand scheme of things. Great sitcoms are not always all about jokes. The best make us laugh till we cry, and sometimes, when they mix in tragedy with the comedy, we cry till we laugh.

67. *Get Smart* (January 13, 1968) Would you believe the far-out opening of "The Groovy Guru"? Agent 86 (Don Adams)—wearing a Beatles wig, shades, and a Nehru shirt, and brandishing a sign exclaiming "Drop Out!"— exchanges passwords with a courier. What he doesn't know is that the courier actually works for evil KAOS's newest recruit, a renegade disc jockey (*F Troop*'s Larry Storch) who's planning to use subliminal messages in songs to brainwash teens into overthrowing the establishment! Of course, Max and 99 (Barbara Feldon) stop this fiendish plan—but not before we get to see 99 frug madly amid a psychedelic light show. Groovy, man.

66. ***The Simpsons*** (May 13, 1993) Krusty the Clown has always beaten the competition. "I slaughtered the Special Olympics," he muses. But that was before the arrival of Gabbo, the ventriloquist's dummy. "Gabbo Is Fabbo," gush the trade papers. Krusty is soon reduced to standing by the road with a sign that says, "Will Drop Pants for Food." Bart and Lisa to the rescue! They plan a comeback special and recruit Johnny Carson, Hugh Hefner, Bette Midler, Luke Perry, and the Red Hot Chili Peppers for the show. It's a smash, and so is "Krusty Gets Kancelled."

65. ***Northern Exposure*** (August 30, 1990) Who wouldn't want to live in Cicely, Alaska, the most mystical oasis in TV history? Something unusual is always happening in this border town that brims with imagination, but never more than in "The Aurora Borealis." When Bernard (Richard Cummings, Jr.), a befuddled accountant, motorcycles into town, he and Chris, the DJ (John Corbett), discover they share more than a few genes. Meanwhile, Dr. Fleischman (Rob Morrow), stranded in the wild, comes face to face with the region's

feared and mythical "bigfoot," Adam (Adam Arkin)—who ends up grudgingly teaching the doctor how to cook Chinese dumplings.

64. ***The Many Loves of Dobie Gillis*** (October 6, 1959) Dobie Gillis (Dwayne Hickman) was nothing if not ardent, and he was most ardent about the blond, avaricious Thalia (Tuesday Weld). In "The Best Dressed Man," Dobie, a grocer's son, only has eyes for Thalia, but she only has eyes for rich, fashionable Milton Armitage (Warren Beatty). Determined to beat the clotheshorse at his own game and win Thalia's heart, Dobie persuades the local haberdasher to outfit him in snappy duds as an advertisement for the man's store. To his sorrow, though, Dobie learns that, as far as Thalia's concerned, it takes more than clothes to make the man—it takes deep pockets.

63. ***Taxi*** (September 25, 1979) "Reverend Jim" Ignatowski (Christopher Lloyd), a remnant of the '60s who's eaten one magic mushroom too many, is sitting at the bar in Mario's. Bobby (Jeff Conaway) comes up to him and says, "Hey, Jim, my friends and I were wondering if you'd like to come over and join us." Jim replies, "What did you decide?" "Reverend Jim: Space Odyssey" is a rolling snowball of laughs. First the cabbies have to persuade Louie DePalma (Danny DeVito) to take Jim on. Louie takes one look at the wild-eyed ex-hippie and says, "Get him outta here!" But Jim slips a tranquilizer into Louie's coffee, and the pint-size tyrant of Sunshine Cab Co. is soon crooning, "We were sailing along . . . on Moonlight Bay. . . ." Reverend Jim is in. All he has to do now is take a driver's test. He sits down, reads the first question, knits his brow, and whispers to the waiting cabbies, "What does a yellow light mean?" "Slow down!" Bobby whispers back. "Okay," says Jim, "What . . . does . . . a . . . yellow . . . light . . . mean?"

62. ***The Beverly Hillbillies*** (October 14, 1964) Part sitcom, part silent movie, "Hedda Hopper's Hollywood" features the legendary Hollywood columnist, who persuades Jed Clampett (Buddy Ebsen) to buy a movie studio. She tells Clampett that to make "great pictures" he'll need "great stars" and takes him to Grauman's Chinese Theater. "Somebody has sure gone and messed up this poor man's cee-ment," Jed says. Soon he and Jethro (Max Baer, Jr.) are paving over even Mary Pickford's prints. They're arrested. Hopper springs them, only to climb onto Jed's bulldozer herself: "Someday, Hollywood is going to thank me for this!"

61. ***Car 54, Where Are You?*** (February 15, 1962) Nat Hiken, one of the great comedy writers of TV's early years, had a commanding knowledge of men in uniform: Before creating New York City patrol-car cops Gunther Toody and Francis Muldoon, he gave Sergeant Bilko marching orders. Joe E. Ross plays Toody, the stocky, nonsense-spouting motormouth; Fred

Gwynne is Muldoon, his tall, thin, dour, college-educated partner. In "How Smart Can You Get?" the NYPD's personnel department decides that Toody and Muldoon are too mismatched to be partners and pairs Muldoon with a rookie named Corrigan (Richard Morse), a Harvard graduate. Muldoon eventually becomes so pre-occupied with Corrigan's highbrow conversation that he drives right past crimes in progress—and ends the episode pleading to be reunited with Toody. That's the deal with great TV odd couples: Nothing breaks them up, no matter how odd they are.

60. *Murder One* (September 19, 1995) This galvanizing courtroom thriller comes on like gangbusters. "Chapter 1," its first episode, introduces a decadent Hollywood bad boy (Jason Gedrick), an evil millionaire (Stanley Tucci), and an underage blonde found murdered in her bedroom. Called in to plumb this moral cesspool is Teddy Hoffman (Daniel Benzali), a lawyer of irreproachable integrity. Benzali is the most commanding TV presence since John Houseman. But this incisive debut is also equipped with startlingly glossy visual panache and a brisk, Byzantine script, courtesy of creator and executive producer Steven Bochco. It all adds up to a television program as slick, stylish, and satisfying as anything you're likely to see at the local cineplex.

59. *Green Acres* (April 3 & 10, 1968) It is the theatrical event of the season: the Hooterville

Barn and Repertory Company's staging of "Who." (The full title of the play was "Who Killed Jock Robin?"—but only one word will fit on the marquee, an old wooden plank.) Sophia Loren is supposed to star in the 12-act mystery, but she is unavailable. Newt Kiley's police dog, Columbo, is set to appear but bows out. Arnold the pig steps in. The big ham gets rave reviews, and in "A Star Named Arnold Is Born," he's off to Hollywood for a screen test. Arnold doesn't last long in Tinseltown, but for one shining moment a star is born. And why not? Arnold has nearly as much range as Eva Gabor.

58. *The Odd Couple* (November 12, 1971) In "Fat Farm," Felix (Tony Randall) somehow convinces junk-food junkie Oscar (Jack Klugman) to join him at a health spa run by a dictatorial diet guru and staffed by large, humorless attendants. The show's usual great one-liners—"I watched him eating six hot dogs during the game, and he only chewed two"—are supplemented with terrific physical gags. When Oscar smuggles in deli contraband, Felix blows the whistle on him, guards confiscate Oscar's pastrami, and the doctor expels him. It's a perfectly seasoned recipe for delicious, high-calorie comedy.

57. *On the Air* (June 20, 1992) In this hellzapoppin' parody of live TV in the '50s, a show starring matinee idol Lester Guy (Ian Buchanan) is nearing airtime. The director (David Lander) spews orders in an incomprehensible German

accent. The broadcast of *The Lester Guy Show* (also the episode's title) is a debacle. At one point, a jealous, gun-wielding husband rushes home to catch his wife with Lester, who has somehow managed to step into a noose and is slowly swinging across the room. "It's not what you think," he croaks. Sure it is: inspired burlesque.

56. ***The George Burns and Gracie Allen Show*** (March 29, 1954) It was a foolproof formula. George was the straight man; Gracie's scatterbrained sense of logic and inability to match pronouns with their antecedents did the rest. Case in point: "Columbia Pictures Doing Burns & Allen Story." The studio wants to make the couple's life stories and sends a team of screenwriters to the house for background. Getting nowhere with Gracie ("Were you the oldest in the family?" they ask her. "No, no. My mother and father were much older"), they inquire about George's old vaudeville partners. Announcer-pal Harry Von Zell, in all innocence, mentions Jimmy Pierce. "They worked together several months, then Pierce left George when he got married. George told me he has a wife and four sons in San Diego." That's all Gracie has to hear. TV comedy's greatest broken-field runner is off to the races—certain George is a bigamist.

55. ***The Prisoner*** (September 21, 1968) In this radical series, Patrick McGoohan played a character known only as Number 6—who, after angrily resigning from a top-secret organization, is abducted to "the village," a high-tech prison disguised as a placid English resort. Each week saw him resist the efforts of a different warder, always designated Number 2, to break his spirit. Who was Number 6? Why had he resigned? Who were his captors? In "Fall Out," the haunting finale, McGoohan finally meets Number 1 and tears a monkey mask from the man's face only to confront—himself! What did it all mean? "Pogo" cartoonist Walt Kelly may have put it best: "We have met the enemy, and he is us."

54. **The Cosby Show** (October 10, 1985) Cliff Huxtable's parents, Russell and Anna (Earle Hyman and Clarice Taylor), are celebrating their 49th wedding anniversary, and Cliff and Clair (Bill Cosby and Phylicia Rashad) want to do something nice for them. In "Happy Anniversary," they commission a portrait and surprise the couple with a cruise to Europe. They also throw a dinner party in their Brooklyn brownstone, and after the meal, Cliff and Clair's children, college student Sondra (Sabrina Le Beauf), 16-year-old Denise (Lisa Bonet), 14-year-old Theo (Malcolm-Jamal Warner), wisecracking eight-year-old Vanessa (Tempestt Bledsoe), and irrepressible five-year-old Rudy (Keshia Knight Pulliam) join their parents and entertain Grandma and Grandpa by staging an impromptu production number on the stairs, lip-synching favorite

tunes such as Ray Charles's "Night Time Is the Right Time." By showing the three generations of Huxtables together, this episode—heart-warming without being sappy—made implicit the series' underlying message: Strong, positive children are parents' most important, invaluable legacy.

53. ***The Phil Silvers Show*** (November 15, 1955) Always looking for an angle, Master Sergeant Ernie Bilko (Phil Silvers) is delighted when Corporal Ed "The Stomach" Honigan transfers into his troop in "The Eating Contest." Bilko quickly arranges a high-stakes eating contest at Fort Baxter. But Honigan—played hilariously by a boyish, rail-thin Fred Gwynne (in his TV debut)—eats only when he's miserable, and he's already over the girl from Tulsa who jilted him. This predicament sets Bilko, the unregenerate con man, into his most glorious, manipulative overdrive.

52. ***Gilligan's Island*** (October 3, 1966) In "The Producer," Hollywood deal-maker Harold Hecuba (Phil Silvers) is looking for talent in "out-of-the-way places" when his plane crashes on our favorite tropical isle. To impress the impresario, the castaways mount a musical version of *Hamlet* with Gilligan (Bob Denver) in the title role. It ain't Shakespeare, but it does get the producer's attention. He quickly rechristens it *Harold Hecuba's Hamlet* and swipes all the singing parts for himself (a quicksilver bit of shtick for Silvers). At the end of this inventive episode, Hecuba steals away—and steals the idea—leaving a sadder but wiser Gilligan to pronounce the moral: "Well, that's showbiz."

51. ***Perry Mason*** (October 17, 1963) Weren't all Perry Mason mysteries basically the same? Didn't the burly barrister (Raymond Burr) do the same thing every week: gain an acquittal? Not in "The Case of the Deadly Verdict." After almost 200 consecutive courtroom victories, Mason actually loses a murder trial to prosecutor Hamilton Burger (William Talman). No need to alert the media; Perry's loss is already headline news. Client Janice Barton (Julie Adams) is convicted of murder and sentenced to the gas chamber. Perry and his ace sleuth, Paul Drake (William Hopper), use the rest of the hour to find the real killer. A gripping, precedent-setting episode in which Perry really earns his fee.

50. ***The Bob Newhart Show*** (February 12, 1977) After a close call in the office elevator shaft, deadpan Bob takes on the panicky manner of his phobic patient Mr. Herd (Oliver Clark). "Death Be My Destiny," a deft blend of the dramatic and daffy, has a great running gag about the correct name of the Grim Reaper, from Uncle Death to Old Father Time. "I felt icy fingers up and down my spine," says Bob of his experience. That wasn't death, wife Emily (Suzanne Pleshette) reassures him. "That's old Black Magic."

49. *Hill Street Blues* (February 2, 1984) Henry Goldblume (Joe Spano) is wrapping up the morning turnout when Captain Furillo (Daniel J. Travanti) announces that Sergeant Phil Esterhaus has died of a heart attack at age 55. "This is going to be a difficult day," he says. "I know the caution Phil would urge you: Be careful out there." It would be a terrible day for the grieving officers, especially Joe Coffey (Ed Marinaro), whose girlfriend (guest star Linda Hamilton) is raped. Esterhaus's death was no ratings stunt—Michael Conrad, who played him, had died just two months before. But "Grace Under Pressure" gives Phil a droll exit: His last act was making love. It's just the kind of offbeat and human touch that made *Hill Street* one of TV's most inventive cop series.

48. *Bewitched* (May 5, 1966) Facing a tight deadline on the Stern Chemical account, overworked adman Darrin Stephens (Dick York) has to cancel a vacation with his beautiful witch of a wife Samantha (Elizabeth Montgomery). Or does he? "It's a pity you can't take the fun side of him and leave the work side at home," ponders Samantha's prankish, Pucci-clad mother, Endora (Agnes Moorehead), who promptly splits her son-in-law in two. In an athletic double performance by York, Darrin's hedonistic half becomes a Watusiing mass of irresponsibility, while his workaholic half is so all-business he nearly runs client Sanford Stern (Frank Maxwell) and boss Larry Tate (David White) into the ground. "Divided He Falls" was so delicious that when Dick Sargent replaced York on the show in 1969, the first episode he filmed was a remake of this one.

47. ***Absolutely Fabulous*** (July 24, 1994) (U.S.) "Chanel! Dior! . . . Gaultier, darling! Names, names, names!" Thus spake Edina (Jennifer Saunders) to Patsy (Joanna Lumley), summarizing the essence of their existences. Not so much victims of fashion as of their own excesses, they are the drunken, drug-soaked detritus of once-swinging London feeding off the rag trade—Edina as a PR rep, Patsy as a fashion editor. The pilot of this British import sets up Edina's topsy-turvy relationship with her prim daughter (Julia Sawalha): It's Mom who sneaks drinks and drugs behind the teenager's back. Saunders and Lumley are unafraid to look shabby; Edina and Patsy are swaddled in designer labels, but their shriveled souls are laid hilariously bare.

46. ***Brooklyn Bridge*** (September 20, 1991) Grandpa (Louis Zorich) has been telling whoppers about the old country again. There's nothing uncommon about that in this sitcom about three generations of a Russian Jewish family assimilating to life in Brooklyn in 1956. But in "When Irish Eyes Are Smiling," after Grandpa has bragged to his younger grandson (Matthew Louis Siegel) about how back in Russia he had played baseball against Brooklyn Dodgers star Gil Hodges, the youngster goes to a Hodges autograph session and asks the Dodger about the old Russian Bears. Gil gamely plays along. The grandfather tells the great first baseman, "You should know what a mensch is. Because that's you." That kind of sweetness and nostalgia suffused this resonant series, the brainchild of *Family Ties* creator Gary David Goldberg. The American melting pot has never looked as warm and inviting.

45. *Cheers* (September 24, 1987) "Home Is the Sailor" begins when Sam Malone (Ted Danson), back from his disastrous attempt to sail around the world, walks into his former bar and barely recognizes it—most of the regulars are gone. Only Carla (Rhea Perlman) and Woody (Woody Harrelson) are left, uncomfortably outfitted in the polyester uniforms required by Cheers' new owner. Sam wants work, but Carla warns him that the new manager "eats live sharks for breakfast." Enter intoxicating Rebecca Howe (Kirstie Alley), a confident and capable bar belle. Sam brags about his sexual prowess, and she rebuffs him, unable to decide if his lame come-ons are "disgusting or merely pathetic." Sam is momentarily shaken and most definitely stirred. Hey, wait a second, hadn't we already sampled a brew-haha like this? Yeah, but we couldn't wait to be served another round.

44. *St. Elsewhere* (February 19 & 20, 1986) The past is the bridge to the present—and you never stop paying the toll. So suggests "Time

Heals," a masterwork of dramatic writing that proves this most eccentric medical series was also the most mature and imaginative. The saga of St. Eligius Hospital's 50-year history is told mostly through the flashbacks of longtime employees. Every move, every utterance activates our 20/20 hindsight: When Dr. Westphall (Ed Flanders) forgets to bring home ice cream one night, we already know that the action will trigger the tragedy of his life; when the maintenance man stuffs insulation into the new emergency room's ceiling, we know it's filled with cancer-causing asbestos. This two-parter underscores the lie of its title: On *St. Elsewhere*, time merely puts a bandage on the wound and hopes you find your way home.

43. *Frasier* (October 4, 1994) Deftly using assumptions about sexuality as grist for farce, "The Matchmaker" details a mixed-up first date. Hoping to fix up Daphne (Jane Leeves), Frasier (Kelsey Grammer) invites his station manager, Tom (Eric Lutes), to dinner, unaware he's gay. During the meal, delicately used pronouns fuel Tom's misconception that he's dating Frasier, who misreads Tom's interest for an attraction to Daphne. When Frasier learns the truth, he's stunned. "What on earth could have made him think I was interested in him?" he says. "All I did was ask him if he was attached, and then we talked about the theater and men's fashions. . . . Oh, my God!"

42. *Leave It to Beaver* (October 11, 1957) The gentle tone of this definitive '50s series was already set by its second episode, "Captain Jack." Raw eggs, Mom's beauty cream, and Dad's brandy have been disappearing for weeks before June and Ward Cleaver (Hugh Beaumont and Barbara Billingsley) figure out that Wally and "the Beav" (Tony Dow and Jerry Mathers) are hiding something big—a pet alligator. The suburbs are no place for the scaly beast, however, so Ward and June make the boys return Captain Jack, as the creature is called, to his namesake, a crusty alligator-farm operator (Edgar Buchanan). And rather than grounding Wally and the Beav for getting a gator behind their backs, Ward and June buy their sons a puppy. So much for pet peeves.

41. *Alfred Hitchcock Presents* (March 13, 1960) It's 8 A.M. in Las Vegas, and a desperate gambler (Steve McQueen) is down to $1.86 and one last chip. A strange man (Peter Lorre) proposes an even stranger wager: If McQueen gets his cigarette lighter to ignite 10 times in a row, he wins Lorre's convertible. And if he can't? He forfeits the little finger on his left hand. One. Two. Three. Four. The suspense builds in "Man from the South." Five. Six. Seven. At eight, the Zippo fails. But before Lorre's cleaver falls, his irate wife (Katherine Squire) appears. All bets are off. "He has no car! It is mine. I managed to win it all . . . in the end," she gloats, brandishing a hand missing three fingers. A deliciously macabre twist, even for the master.

40. *WKRP in Cincinnati* (October 30, 1978) TV shows traditionally greet holidays with a hug, but not *WKRP*. In "Turkeys Away," which was based on a true story, station manager Arthur Carlson (Gordon Jump) announces plans to unveil a secret promotional event, and newsman Les Nessman (Richard Sanders) shows up at the local mall to cover it live. A helicopter comes into view. Mr. Carlson is aboard. So are 20 live turkeys—which, to Les's horror, are hurled to their deaths. "Oh, the humanity," Les wails, evoking the Hindenberg while fowl balls plummet to the parking lot. Mr. Carlson is shocked. "As God is my witness," he says, "I thought turkeys could fly."

39. *The Larry Sanders Show* (November 13, 1996) Larry (Garry Shandling) is convinced that upcoming guest David Duchovny has a crush on him. When D.D. sends him a jacket emblazoned "The Truth Is Out There," Larry panics—until he realizes it's *The X-Files'* motto. Duchovny, deftly toying with his leading-man status, continues to send mixed signals and progressively unnerve Larry. Finally, Larry confronts his guest, who says he's sorry, he wishes he were gay because he finds Larry so attractive. The truth is out there: "Everybody Loves Larry," which also features a subplot about Hank (Jeffrey Tambor) feuding with singer Elvis Costello over a sports car, is a standout, even by Sanders' perfect-pitch standards.

38. *My So-Called Life* (November 10, 1994) A far cry from *Happy Days*, this series took on the anguish and anticipation of high school in the '90s. "Life of Brian" begins with a dance. No one wants to go. Everyone wants to go. Geeky Brian (Devon Gummersall) wants to ask Angela (Claire Danes). She wants to go with cool Jordan (Jared Leto). Rickie (Wilson Cruz), who's gay, has a crush on Corey (Adam Biesk), who likes Rayanne (A. J. Langer). But the counselor doesn't think Rayanne, who has a drug problem, should go. It's sad and embarrassing, like high school if you're still in it, and hilarious, which is what high school becomes after you've survived it.

37. *The Brady Bunch* (December 10, 1971) Hey! Hey! She's a Brady—and the president of her local Davy Jones fan club. Marcia (Maureen McCormick) cockily promises to get the singer to play at the prom. She and her sibs try several subterfuges, and she finally gets her man. She even gets to peck his cheek. The unstated joke, of course, is the show's choice of teen idols. The Monkees had split up two years earlier, and Jones was desperately trying to jump-start a solo career. But that sense of terminal unhipness—filtered through Marcia's sunny personality—is precisely why we love *The Brady Bunch*, and especially "Getting Davy Jones."

36. *NYPD Blue* (October 12, 1993) Before David Schwimmer became a household name as Ross on *Friends*, he left his mark on this dynamic series in "True Confessions." His twitchy, nebbishy lawyer Josh Goldstein was a neighbor of Detective John Kelly's estranged wife. When Goldstein, whom Kelly calls 4B (his apartment number), is mugged, he becomes obsessed with revenge. Though Kelly (David Caruso) tries to get him to give up his gun, 4B doesn't listen and, in a shoot-out with a mugger, gets blown away. We, too, were blown away by the emotional finality of losing a character with whom we had empathized so deeply.

35. *Ellen* (April 30, 1997) Ellen (Ellen DeGeneres) is getting ready for a date. Finally, Paige (Joely Fisher) asks through the door, "Ellen, are you coming out or not?" Indeed, Ellen's coming out to her therapist (Oprah Winfrey) and Susan (Laura Dern) was actually three years in the making and cause for much media hype. But what distinguishes this hour-long show, dubbed "The Puppy Episode" to keep its plot secret, is some of the sharpest comedy TV can offer. When an offended Ellen accuses Susan of recruiting her to homosexuality, Susan says, "I'll have to call national headquarters and tell 'em I lost you. Damn—just one more, and I would have gotten that toaster oven!" And after Ellen accidentally blurts "I'm gay" over a loudspeaker, she says, "That felt so great—and it felt so loud." It sure did.

34. *Moonlighting* (October 15, 1985) Hosted by Orson Welles, who died just five days before it

aired, this stylized, mostly black-and-white episode of *Moonlighting* blended the series' trademark banter and sexual tension with an unusual homage to film noir. In "The Dream Sequence Always Rings Twice," a visit to a once-hot nightspot prompts Maddie and David (Cybill Shepherd and Bruce Willis) to dream their own versions of an old, unsolved murder. In Maddie's mind, her songbird character falls for David's horn-blowing charmer, who schemes to kill her husband; his version paints him as the innocent, framed by a conniving woman. In both dreams they make love, something that would remain merely fantasy for the characters for another two years.

33. ***Seinfeld*** (October 30, 1991) In this series that set the TV industry on its ear by boasting, proudly and subversively, that it was "about nothing," "The Parking Garage" is the ultimate nothing episode. Jerry, George, Elaine, and Kramer can't find their car in a mall parking garage and walk around looking for it. That's it. But we've come to know the idiosyncrasies and neuroses of these characters so well that we enjoy seeing them splash down in the shallow pond of a minor dilemma and sink to the bottom, while arguing about the best stroke to use to get to shore. It's theater of the absurd: Four Characters in Search of an Exit Ramp. The whole requires remarkable writing and acting, and a pact with the audience never to take anything too seriously. That's not nothing—that's everything.

32. ***Homicide: Life on the Street*** (October 18, 1996) An actor at his peak, a script that burns with intelligence and compassion, and an opportunity to have art imitate life in a way that blurs the line between fact and fiction. It's all here, as the Baltimore homicide department takes on a double killing at the state prison. Lifer Elijah Sanborn (Charles S. Dutton) witnessed the murder, but won't snitch—until the cops dangle the future of his long-estranged son, now in trouble, in front of him. It's a heartless squeeze that propels the past back at Sanborn like an exploding rocket. What gives "Prison Riot" its teeth is Dutton, who actually spent seven and a half years in prison for killing a man on those same Baltimore streets. There's hard-earned truth in his acting, and it takes this outstanding series to a new level.

31. ***The Twilight Zone*** (November 3, 1961) The premise of "It's a Good Life" is simple. A tiny town is cut off from reality by six-year-old Anthony Freemont (Billy Mumy), who combines a child's naturally amoral selfishness with limitless mental powers. Trapped in a nightmare where a mere negative thought can get them "sent to the cornfield" (i.e., winked out of existence), the terrified townspeople struggle to stay cheerful in hell. The show's impact has never lessened: On a recent episode of *The Drew Carey Show*, Drew's visiting parents go missing. "Oh, no," he says, "I hope I haven't wished them into the cornfield." It was a tribute to a classic.

30. *Playhouse 90* (October 12, 1956) It's Thursday night, nearly 9:30 in New York City, and backstage the cast is nervous: After all, it's live TV. We fade to a boxing arena as a fight ends, and Rod Serling's "Requiem for a Heavyweight" steps into the ring. Jack Palance is all angles and pain as the childlike coulda-been-a-contender "Mountain" McClintock, needing to remake his life and reeling from a low blow by a manager who'll humiliate him to square a gambling debt. The glory of the Golden Age of Television rests on the broad shoulders of this single show, which proved the medium's power and what it could do when it, like "Mount," refused to take a dive.

29. *The Wonder Years* (March 29, 1988) No series captured that tender, awkward waltz of the father-son relationship better, and especially in "My Father's Office," as it asks: What does my father do on the job, and why does he come home so grumpy? To find out, Kevin Arnold (Fred Savage) accompanies his dad (Dan Lauria) to work. There, as Kevin thrills to his dad's command and power, the boss rips his father to mortifying shreds. Later, as the Arnold men gaze at the suburban night sky, Kevin has a bittersweet realization: This wasn't at all what his dad wanted to be when he grew up. It's enough to make you cry . . . every time.

28. *Gunsmoke* (October 1, 1966) Guest stars on TV shows are usually window dressing. Only once in a very great while do they put their indelible stamp on an episode and make it theirs, and almost never does their one appearance elevate the entire series to a whole new level of excellence. But that's precisely what Bette Davis did for *Gunsmoke* in "The Jailer" as a crazed woman poisoned by revenge fantasies against Marshall Dillon (James Arness). From Davis's entrance—that widow's black dress, that hoarse and crackling voice biting off and spitting out lines like, "Don't talk flippant; y'ain't in no position" (and, yes, those Bette Davis eyes)—you can feel the power come roaring from the picture tube across the room at you. Davis takes a simple role and plays it like Medea, turning an ordinary horse opera into something akin to Greek tragedy. A peach-fuzzed Bruce Dern and an impossibly young Tom Skerritt peek out from Davis's shadow.

27. *The Mary Tyler Moore Show* (September 15, 1973) The Twin Cities become the Sin Cities when Betty White makes her *MTM* debut in "The Lars Affair" as Sue Ann Nivens, the Happy Homemaker. Actually, happy home wrecker is more like it. Invited to one of Mary's classically disastrous parties, the ever-smiling Sue Ann offers her hostess some cleaning tips, then sweeps up Phyllis's never-seen dermatologist husband, Lars, and leaves the party with him. Mary and Rhoda (Valerie Harper) are baffled—

Sue Ann, after all, is an unlikely seductress. In fact, she's exactly the sort of woman you'd leave for someone else. But Phyllis (Cloris Leachman) has the perfect explanation for her husband's unfaithfulness: her own inexhaustible feminine allure. "I've been too much of a real woman," she declares. In the '70s, adultery was not an issue frequently handled on television, certainly not on a sitcom, but this cheating heart was served up with wit and style.

26. *The Honeymooners* (October 1, 1955) Alice (Audrey Meadows) is dying to have a TV set. But cheapskate Ralph (Jackie Gleason) lamely claims he's holding off until 3-D TV is developed. He finally agrees to go in halfsies with Norton (Art Carney), rigging a coin toss so the set stays in the Kramden apartment. No sooner is the set plugged in than Ralph becomes a total zombie in thrall to the new medium, the very archetype of the couch potato: scientifically determining (in a priceless piece of physical comedy) exactly where to place his snack food so no effort is required to reach it; fighting with Norton, who wants to sit in front of the set with his space helmet on to watch *Captain Video*; and finally falling asleep with the tube on. "TV or Not TV" was the first episode in *The Honeymooners*' one and only season. All 38 shows that came after met its brilliantly simple, hilarious standard.

25. *Twin Peaks* (April 8, 1990) A bird cocks its head. Smokestacks belch exhaust. A sawmill's blades shoot sparks. A guitar plays a dreamy, sensuous adagio as white water crashes over the falls and then gently flows to Laura Palmer (Sheryl Lee), the golden girl of Twin Peaks, washed up dead onshore, wrapped in plastic. This is how the self-titled premiere episode ushered us into the shocking, surreal, sui generis world of Twin Peaks, a piney realm populated with bizarre characters—barking teens, a mystical FBI agent, a finger-snapping, dancing midget. Director David Lynch's risky, murky, over-the-top amalgam of murder mystery, soap opera, and phantasmagoria left an indelible impression on the medium.

24. *The Andy Griffith Show* (September 30, 1963) This series was at its down-home best when it focused on the sweet relationship between Sheriff Taylor (Griffith) and Opie (Ron Howard), a bond endearingly explored in "Opie the Birdman." After accidentally killing a mother bird with his slingshot, Opie dutifully raises her three nestlings until they are big enough to fly. After releasing them, Opie sadly notes how empty their cage looks. "It sure does," answers his proud and knowing pa as he watches the birds swoop skyward, "but don't the trees seem nice and full?" And aren't our lives nicer and fuller for having dallied in Mayberry?

23. *The Fugitive* (August 29, 1967) After a four-year marathon of running and chasing and hiding—always one step ahead of the tireless Lieutenant Gerard (Barry Morse) and one step behind the nefarious one-armed man (Bill Raisch)—how would it end for Dr. Richard Kimble (David Janssen)? On a warm Tuesday night, 25.7 million American households tuned in to find out. What they got was a flashback to a senseless murder; a cowardly eyewitness who could have cleared Kimble; a suspenseful fight atop a tower in an abandoned amusement park; a confession; and, ironically, Kimble's obsessed pursuer, who becomes his sharp-shooting rescuer. "The Judgment, Part II" was one of those rare TV events that the whole country seemed to share.

22. *thirtysomething* (May 15 & 22, 1990) The signal achievement of "The Towers of Zenith," a two-part episode about a hostile corporate takeover, is that it turns dry boardroom machinations into an electrifying suspense thriller: *All the President's Men* meets *Wall Street.* Michael (Ken Olin) and Elliot (Timothy Busfield) are caught up in an age-old play of ambition versus loyalty in their attempts to wrest control of their ad agency from their ingeniously calculating boss, Miles Drentell (David Clennon). It's chilling, unforgettable television with dazzling work on every level.

21. *Roseanne* (October 5, 1993) When Roseanne finds a baggieful of pot in one of the kids' rooms, she's angry—and worried about how Dan (John Goodman) is going to react. (He has

been in a foul mood since being promoted to foreman.) He does go ballistic—until he realizes the stash is a 20-year-old relic of his and Roseanne's youth. Inevitably, they roll a joint for old times' sake, and before you can say "Like, wow," Dan, Roseanne, and her sister, Jackie (Laurie Metcalf), are adrift in a Cheech-and-Chong time warp. At first, they have fun sneaking around like they did in the '70s, hoping not to get busted by their children. But then adult realities stick a sharp pin in their buzz. "A Stash from the Past" is a wise, waggish, and exceedingly daring episode from a sitcom renowned for its unflinching audacity.

20. *M*A*S*H* (March 18, 1975) If war is hell, the staff of the M*A*S*H 4077th unit was in the inferno's innermost circle. In "Abyssinia, Henry," the hospital's beloved commander, Lieutenant Colonel Henry Blake (McLean Stevenson), is going home to his family in Illinois. After a night of wine, wontons, and song, and a touching good-bye with his surrogate son, Radar (Gary Burghoff), Henry takes off on a plane that is shot down over the Sea of Japan. When Radar stumbles into the operating theater with the news, it is a shattering moment—a measure of just how precious these characters had become to us.

19. *Taxi* (May 21, 1981) Poor Latka—sick and tired of being the lovable, but lonely, grease monkey at the Sunshine Cab Company. All he wants is to become "an American fun guy taking each day in high gear"—which for him would require inventing a whole new type of transmission. And that's just what he does. Laden with copies of *Playboy* and a tape of a smooth-talking FM DJ, Latka (Andy Kaufman) goes off "to alter my lifestyle to fit the fast lane." He returns with a flashy new lounge-lizard alter ego: Vic Ferrari—slick, suave, oversexed, and beyond obnoxious. Showing off Kaufman's genius for utilizing multiple personalities (Latka started out as Foreign Man, one of Kaufman's uncanny comedy-club guises), "Latka the Playboy" was an inventive, outrageous episode that led to equally imaginative sequels—and even more splintering of Latka's breakaway ego. Sharp-eyed viewers will notice a pre-*Cheers* George Wendt in a bit part as an exterminator in this wonderful episode.

18. *I Love Lucy* (April 16, 1956) We could describe this episode as the one in which the famous redhead gets into trouble trying to break into show business. But that synopsis would cover almost every *I Love Lucy*. So let's amend things to say that in this outing Lucy (Lucille Ball) gets into a bunch of trouble. On the train to Rome, site of one of Ricky's European gigs, Lucy is spied by an Italian movie producer who thinks she'd be perfect for a role in his new film, "Bitter Grapes." Determined to research her role, Lucy hies herself to a vineyard where she's assigned the job of stomping grapes. That leads to some uproariously funny

folk-dance moves—and a near-stomping by her testy coworker. "Lucy's Italian Movie" is a vat of fun, stirred up by Ball's inimitable, extravagant flair for slapstick.

17. ***The Simpsons*** (April 15, 1990) A Simpsons episode très extraordinaire! Principal Skinner ships Bart off to France as an exchange student because of a cherry-bomb-in-the-toilet incident. ("I have a weakness for the classics," the young vandal explains.) This allows *The Simpsons'* creative team to deal with a few classics of their own, as Bart rides through a French countryside that looks suspiciously like famous paintings, one after another. "We had to figure out a way to draw those paintings in a Simpson style," recalls director Wes Archer. That eye-popping sequence helped push this episode past all the other crackerjack *Simpsons* clamoring for a spot on this roster. Even without it, "The Crepes of Wrath" is more savory than Provençal cuisine, as Bart is enslaved by his wine-making sponsors while, back home, an Albanian exchange student-spy relieves Homer of countless nuclear secrets. And while foiling a plot to lace the Beaujolais with antifreeze, Bart discovers he can speak fluent French! Incroyable! "The Crepes of Wrath" is vintage *Simpsons.*

16. ***Columbo*** (September 15, 1971) "Uh, sir? There's only one more thing I'm not clear about." "Uh, ma'am, I'm making a pest of

myself, but . . ." These words were like nails on a chalkboard or, more to the point, nails in the coffin for Lieutenant Columbo's suspects, murderers who constantly made the mistake of overestimating their smarts and underestimating his. Behind the scenes of "Murder by the Book," the first *Columbo* episode of the regular series (two earlier mysteries starring the disheveled detective were made-for-TV movies), star Peter Falk almost underestimated the talent of his young director (whose scant credits included an installment of Rod Serling's *Night Gallery*). He was some kid named, uh . . . uh . . . Steven Spielberg. But Falk gave him a chance and reaped the reward: Spielberg turned out a sleek, stylishly shot, and suspenseful thriller. The masterful script, written by another kid named Steven Bochco, centers on a smarmy coauthor of best-selling mysteries (Jack Cassidy) who kills his more-talented partner to prevent him from going solo. The cunning cat-and-mouse interplay between Falk and Cassidy set the tone for the entire series. Cassidy went on to be the culprit in two other *Columbo*s. As for Spielberg and Bochco—well, where are they now?

15. *The Dick Van Dyke Show* (February 6, 1963) Of *The Dick Van Dyke Show*'s characters, Rob Petrie (Van Dyke) was the one who usually kept his head, while Sally, Buddy, Laura, and Mel were losing theirs all around him. That's a big part of the appeal of this utterly surreal episode, in

which Rob seems to be losing not just his head but his imagination—and both his thumbs. He stays up late one night watching a thriller about an alien from the planet Twilo who wants to take over the world. The extraterrestrial has eyes in the back of his head, eats walnuts, speaks with a British accent, and looks just like Danny Thomas—in fact, the creature is played by Thomas himself, who, insiders know, co-owned the company that created *The Dick Van Dyke Show*. People who are exposed to Absorbitron, a chemical the alien possesses, lose their thumbs and their imaginations. When Rob wakes up the next morning, he finds the living-room carpet strewn with walnuts. In the kitchen, a smiling Laura (Mary Tyler Moore) opens an egg carton and offers him a walnut omelette for breakfast. At work, Buddy (Morey Amsterdam) is eating walnuts, not his usual pistachios, and there are walnuts in Rob's typewriter. Is Rob, pardon the expression, cracking up? He thinks so—until he wakes up from his nutty nightmare. Seventeen-hundred walnuts were used in "It May Look Like a Walnut"; the ones that didn't open on cue were sent back, and that is what executive producer Sheldon Leonard wanted to do with the extravagant script when he first read it. But when Leonard saw how well the inventive walnut episode played in front of an audience, he gave it the thumbs-up.

14. *Wiseguy* (February 22, 1988) On its surface, Wiseguy was just one more action show created

by Stephen J. Cannell (*Hunter, The A-Team*), this one about undercover Fed Vinnie Terranova (Ken Wahl). But the series pioneered an unusual structure: multi-episode arcs that unfolded like miniseries within the series. Over the weeks, viewers, like Vinnie, came to know and even identify with the bad guys, sharing the peculiar intimacy the undercover agent has with his quarry. *Wiseguy* was about the seductiveness of evil, and rarely has evil been more appealing than in the form of sinister siblings Mel and Susan Profitt. Played with almost gleeful intensity by Kevin Spacey, Mel runs guns, topples governments, shoots dope, believes in the power of crystals, and admires 19th-century economist Thomas Malthus—as well as his own sexy sister (Joan Severance). In "Blood Dance," Mel cracks when an agent shatters the crystal he believes harbors his soul. "Send me home," he begs his sis. She obliges, giving him a drug overdose and a Viking funeral.

13. ***All in the Family*** (February 19, 1972) Six months before Sammy Davis, Jr., hugged Richard Nixon at the Republican National Convention, he kissed America's most lovable bigot. Davis's guest appearance raised the groundbreaking sitcom's level of racial repartee to new heights. In "Sammy's Visit," Davis comes to Archie Bunker's home to retrieve a briefcase he left in Archie's cab. The script captures the mixed feelings someone like Davis might elicit from someone like Archie: respect

(Archie lets Davis sit in his chair) and awkwardness (the classic gaffe, "Do you take cream and sugar in your eye?") mingle with prejudice (Archie refuses to drink a toast from a glass that has touched Davis's lips). "If you were prejudiced, you'd go around thinking you're better than anyone else in the world, Archie," says Davis. "But I can honestly say you've proven to me that you ain't better than anybody!" This dis is followed by that kiss—planted on a startled Archie. Davis, incidentally, was a huge *AITF* fan; he considered his guest shot here as thrilling as his first big break in showbiz.

12. *Fawlty Towers* (1980) One of the rock-ribbed rules of American programming is: Nobody wants to watch a show about someone who isn't likable. (This is sometimes called the Dabney Coleman rule, after the actor who has had a few critically acclaimed but low-rated sitcoms about less-than-admirable characters.) Thus it falls to the British to give us an *Absolutely Fabulous* (see number 47) or a *Fawlty Towers*. Basil Fawlty—the English innkeeper cocreated and portrayed by Monty Python alumnus John Cleese in 1975 (the U.S. debut came in 1980)—is definitely not likable. He is, in fact, sly, sarcastic, suspicious, rude, raging, and resentful, particularly of his wife, Sybil (Prunella Scales). When Sybil starts a three-day hospital stay for an ingrown toenail—coinciding with the arrival of German guests—Fawlty's faults run riot in an achingly funny episode.

"The Germans," which includes a talking moose head and a fire that breaks out during a fire drill, climaxes when Basil gets a concussion and cannot follow his own urgent advice to the inn's staff about their new guests: "Don't mention the war!" Not only does the befogged Fawlty mention it, but he launches into a hysterical Hitler impression; and the unforgettable sight of the 6'5" Cleese goose-stepping through Fawlty Towers and shrieking in mock German puts "The Germans" high in our pantheon.

11. *The Twilight Zone* (March 2, 1962) "Respectfully submitted for your perusal: a Kanamit," intones Rod Serling in his distinctive voice. "Height: a little over nine feet. Weight: in the neighborhood of three hundred and fifty pounds. Origin: unknown. Motives? Therein hangs a tale." Serling's teasing introduction notwithstanding, the Kanamits' origin is obvious enough: They're from outer space. As for their motives—well, they're here to help. At least that's what their "spokesman"—a big, bald fellow with hugely protruding brain lobes—tells the United Nations. A day after arriving, these well-meaning aliens are demonstrating new fertilizers that will eradicate famine. Thanks to Kanamit force-field technology, the nations of Earth no longer need armies, and in the spirit of transgalactic understanding, earthlings by the thousand soon rocket off on all-expenses-paid vacations to Kanamit. Too good to be true? You bet. The one real clue we have to Kanamit

motives is a book of theirs. A government cryptographer, played by Lloyd Bochner, and his crew have translated the title as *To Serve Man* (also the name of the episode). It's only as Bochner himself is about to board the ship for Kanamit that his assistant (Susan Cummings) comes up with the episode's punch line—and with it, the essence of edginess and bitter irony that made The Twilight Zone such a memorable place to visit: *To Serve Man* is a cookbook!

10. ***The X-Files*** (October 13, 1995) Though alien abductions, freaks of nature, and sinister conspiracies among governments-within-governments are its stock-in-trade, *The X-Files* is never more profound and moving than when it explores the heart in darkness: "Clyde Bruck-man's Final Repose" is the finest achievement in a series that continues to break, then rewrite, the rules. It's a scary, sad, often marvelously goofy tale of a life-insurance salesman whose ability to predict people's deaths puts him in a serial killer's path; the premise serves as a jumping-off point for heavy-duty subjects like life after death, predestination, and the possibility of grace in a world of insane violence and despair. Peter Boyle gives an astonishing performance in this quirky death of a salesman—his transitions in and out of trances are simply breathtaking. The episode marches to an unavoidable, but nonetheless amazing, conclusion. And when Scully (Gillian Anderson), who will soon be diagnosed with an inoperable brain tumor, asks Bruckman

how and when she will die, he looks at her and mysteriously replies, "You don't." How can that be? How can she avoid the inevitable? What's in store for her . . . and us? For hard-core fans, it's *The X-Files'* supreme moment.

9. **The Bob Newhart Show** (November 22, 1975) "Over the River and Through the Woods," the craziest *Bob Newhart Show* episode of all time, begins sanely enough: Emily (Suzanne Pleshette) announces her intention to visit her family in Puget Sound over the Thanksgiving holiday; psychiatrist Bob begs off, saying he wants to be available to his neurotic patient, the endlessly depressed and depressing Mr. Carlin. But Carlin (Jack Riley) can't be happy unless he's making others miserable, so he invites himself over to watch football with Bob, Jerry (Peter Bonerz), and ever-present neighbor Howard (Bill Daily). Of course, there are certain customs that must be observed. "We take a slug of this every time the other team scores," says Jerry, offering an enormous jug of grain alcohol to Bob. Soon things get loco; it's a high-scoring game. Smashed, starving, and facing a frozen turkey, the boys consider cooking the bird at 2,000 degrees for a half hour—but the oven only heats to 500. "Then we'll use four ovens," suggests Howard. That's when they decide to call out for Chinese food—to be precise, for moo goo gai pan (to be more precise, for moo goo goo goo gai pan). And lots of it. So much that it has to be delivered with a hand truck.

Luckily for Bob, Emily arrives just in time to pick up the tab—and put on a pot of coffee.

8. ***The Dick Van Dyke Show*** (September 15, 1965) History's three best-kept secrets were the location of King Solomon's mines (never disclosed), the plans for D day (made manifest on June 6, 1944), and the fact that Alan Brady wore a toupee, which suddenly became common knowledge when Laura Petrie accidentally blabbed it to a national audience as a contestant on the *Pay As You Go* TV game show. Big oops. "What do you think Alan will do?" asks a quivery lipped, impeccably coiffed Laura (Mary Tyler Moore). "It's not what," replies her stammering husband and possibly soon-to-be-ex-Brady employee Rob (Dick Van Dyke), "but how." And indeed, in the bright, witty, Emmy-winning script for "Coast-to-Coast Big Mouth" that kicked off this magical series' fifth and final season, hell hath no fury like an egomaniacal TV star who's had the rug pulled out from over him. Series creator Carl Reiner, in one of his 12 appearances as Brady, is incensed and cutting, especially when addressing a desktop of heads, each sporting one of his wigs: "Fellas," says Reiner (who revealed his own baldness in this episode), "there she is—there's the little lady who put you out of business." More than 30 years after it aired, "Big Mouth," a caustic meditation on male vanity and office etiquette, is still one of the most precise, cohesive, and funny half hours of TV ever produced.

7. **Cheers** (November 27, 1986) In "Thanksgiving Orphans," the holiday is looming, and most of the *Cheers* gang has nowhere to go. Diane's solution is simple: Why don't they gather at Carla's house? "What could be more enjoyable than opening your heart with holiday cheer?" she asks. Carla (Rhea Perlman) responds, "Opening yours with a can opener?" Nevertheless, Woody (Woody Harrelson), Frasier (Kelsey Grammer), and Cliff (John Ratzenberger) agree to spend the holiday with Carla. As the afternoon wears on, they're joined by Sam (Ted Danson), Diane (Shelley Long), and Norm (George Wendt), who arrives with "birdzilla," a turkey so huge it takes all day to cook. Before this episode ends, nerves will fray, and the famished guests—arguably the most adept sitcom ensemble ever cobbled together—will indulge in the funniest food fight in TV history. The final arrival at the party is Norm's never-seen wife, Vera—who winds up getting smacked in the kisser with a pie just before we catch sight of her face.

6. **The Honeymooners** (January 28, 1956) Ralph Kramden's get-rich-quick schemes were a *Honeymooners* staple, but the pipe dream in "The $99,000 Answer" may be the funniest. The episode plays off the then-popular mania for quiz shows: Convinced beyond all reason that he will triumph on *The $99,000 Answer*, popular-music expert Ralph (Jackie Gleason) intensely prepares at home, aided by piano-playing pal Ed Norton (Art Carney), who warms up for each

song with a few bars of "Swanee River." Of course, the second he's on live TV, Ralph's bravado vanishes. Going into the classic Kramden meltdown—the eyes bugging, the lips quivering, the tongue stuttering "humminahummina"—he identifies the composer of "Swanee River" as Norton before being escorted offstage, reduced to an object of pure pity. Unlike most *Honeymooners* episodes, there's no redemption, no "Baby, you're the greatest" clinch with wife Alice. Of course, no actor could shift from humor to poignancy as deftly as Gleason.

5. ***The Odd Couple*** (December 1, 1972) The password is "hilarious." Felix Unger and Oscar Madison were always perfectly mismatched. The two men—one a neurotic neatnik, the other a compulsive slob—had absolutely nothing in common except a Manhattan apartment. In "Password," Felix (Tony Randall) and Oscar (Jack Klugman) make the worst team since oil and water. The popular game-show host Allen Ludden is a fan of Oscar's sports columns, and approaches him to be a celebrity panelist playing against Ludden's real-life wife, Betty White. Felix is ecstatic; he can be his roommate's partner. Oscar takes some convincing—first to be on the show and then to be on it with Felix—but he finally agrees. As bad choices go, this is right up there with Lincoln's decision to go to Ford's Theater. Speaking of the Great Emancipator, during one match, Felix hears the word mayonnaise and comes back with "Lincoln." Lincoln?

Lincoln? As Felix explains, it's a well-known fact that Lincoln loved mayonnaise. The pair's utter failure to communicate finds its fullest, most sidesplitting expression in this sparkling episode.

4. *Seinfeld* (February 12, 1992) How do we treasure "The Boyfriend"? Let us count the ways. This is the episode in which Jerry "dates" former New York Mets first baseman Keith Hernandez but eventually loses him to Elaine (Julia Louis-Dreyfus); in which George (Jason Alexander) tries to get an extension on his unemployment benefits by fabricating a bogus job selling "latex and latex-related products"; in which Kramer (Michael Richards) ruins George's scam by forgetting to answer the phone as "Vandelay Industries," forcing George to come scurrying out of the bathroom with his pants around his ankles; in which George sinks so low he even dates his caseworker's ugly daughter to ensure that his benefits continue; in which a pair of pixilated new parents keep nagging Jerry and Kramer, "You gotta see the baby"; in which Jerry sneers "Hello, Newman" for the first time; in which Kramer and Newman (Wayne Knight) unveil their own conspiracy theory in a brazen satire of the JFK/Zapruder film. Just about every other current TV comedy prays that it could come up in its entire run with as many time-capsule highlights as this single one-hour episode contains. *Seinfeld* makes this funny, smart, ingenious, and risk-taking hour look effortless.

3. _ER_ (March 9, 1995) Sure, we know it's just actors speaking lines from a script on a soundstage. . . . But tell that to your pounding heart and explain it to your rocketing blood pressure and your dry throat and your panting lungs. After the explosive, almost-too-painful-to-watch "Love's Labor Lost"—perhaps the most riveting, harrowing, and visceral hour of medical drama ever aired—we all could use a stay in the recovery room. What seems like a routine day in the ER—gunshot wounds, hemorrhoids, a guy who tries to remove one of his tattoos with a power sander—turns sour for Dr. Mark Greene (Anthony Edwards). Normally a steady hand at the throttle of the racing locomotive that is the ER, Greene derails: Distracted by personal and professional problems, he misdiagnoses a pregnant woman and begins a downward spiral of missteps and questionable procedures that continues until all present are in over their heads, panic is thick in the air, and, just as in real life, bad things happen to good people—with shocking speed. Edwards's performance in this unforgettably scorching episode is his best work in this extraordinary series.

2. _I Love Lucy_ (May 5, 1952) Fittingly, the show is pure Lucy—sidekick Ethel (Vivian Vance) doesn't even have a cameo. As the Vitameatavegamin Girl on a TV variety show, Lucy Ricardo (Lucille Ball) is supposed to "spoon her way to health," but instead gets totally snockered on the health elixir she's promoting.

In the classic "Lucy Does a TV Commercial," Ball's talent for physical comedy is at its most vibrant and resourceful. Using her usual treachery to get the job, Lucy begins to run through her spot for the director (Ross Elliot). From the first spoonful she squeamishly swallows to her early, slightly sloshed queries—"Do you pop out at parties? Are you unpoopular?"—to her final drunken swig right out of the "bittle lottle," Ball builds the mirth to a riotous climax. After mangling the product's name in every imaginable way, Lucy finally resorts to calling it "this stuff." By any name, this heady concoction continues to make "happy, peppy people" of us all.

1. **The Mary Tyler Moore Show** (October 25, 1975) One little miscalculation can just ruin your whole day. Take Chuckles the Clown, WJM-TV's kiddie-show host. Named grand marshal of the circus parade, he shows up dressed as Peter Peanut, and, as news director Lou Grant (Ed Asner) later explains to his troops, "a rogue elephant tried to shell him." And so begins "Chuckles Bites the Dust," unquestionably the best remembered, most discussed, most supremely influential episode of all time. Chuckles's nutty demise becomes the source of dark jokes for everyone in the office—except somber Mary, who can't see the absurdity of the incident, the humor in the clown's passing . . . until the funeral when, in a sublime example of poor timing, it suddenly hits her during the

eulogy. Surrounded by stony-faced mourners, striving to maintain proper decorum, squirming for control, trying to cover her giggles with coughs and throat clearings, Mary finally lets loose. Surprisingly, the preacher encourages her unseemly outburst as something the deceased would have wanted. No sooner does he say, "So go ahead, my dear, laugh for Chuckles," than Mary breaks down in tears. This unforeseen final twist, and Moore's bravura bipolar performance, make this exquisite episode a sitcom landmark and proof positive that TV can explore a social taboo with sophistication, wit, irreverence, and impeccable good taste.

(From TV Guide. *Contributors: Mark Bautz, Myles Callum, Daniel Howard Cerone, Frank DeCaro, Art Durbano, Ari Karpel, Joanne Kaufman, Mark Lasswell, Michael Logan, Bruce Newman, Rick Schindler, Ray Stackhouse, Ed Weiner, and Elisa Zuritsky. Research assistance provided by Rich Sands and by the Museum of Television & Radio.)*

The 100 Most Memorable Moments in TV History

A treasury of television events—from news to cartoons—that are truly unforgettable

When television is good, it entertains or educates us. But when it is great, it does so much more. At times, the medium touches our deepest emotions—wonder, delight, joy, sadness, shock, fear. Moments like these, when TV moves us profoundly, become like mental snapshots that never fade. We recall treasured highlights of *I Love Lucy* and *The Twilight Zone* just as clearly as we do last week's episodes of *Home Improvement* and *ER*.

So here at *TV Guide*, when we set about ranking a selection of these indelible TV moments from 100 to 1, it was a unique challenge and a special pleasure. We don't expect you to agree with all our choices; in fact, this issue sparked a number of heated debates in our offices (sample objections: "Where's Uncle Miltie?" "How about the demolition of the Berlin Wall?"). But as you pore over our choices, there's one thing on which we hope you will agree: These are all exceedingly vivid moments. In other words, great TV.

100. Mork and Mindy's Baby (October 15, 1981) When the irrepressible alien (Robin Williams) married his human ally (Pam Dawber) on *Mork & Mindy* and started a family, Mom was a little put out. Their "baby," after all, hatched from an egg and looked like an old man (in fact, it was Williams' comic idol, Jonathan Winters). But Mindy hung in there: "I'm sure with enough time, I'll grow to love every hair on his chest."

99. *Miami Vice* Premiere (September 16, 1984) Don Johnson's Sonny, a vice cop with a two-day growth and expensive accessories, is on his way to meet a coke kingpin. He pulls his Ferrari over to a phone booth, calls his estranged wife, and says, "Caroline, I need to know something. It was real, wasn't it?" The answer is yes, but Sonny sadly shuffles back to his car and zooms through the glistening tropical night as Phil Collins' "In the Air Tonight" plays at length. Stylized and atmospheric, this cop show introduced the adrenalized mood of MTV to prime time.

98. **The "1984" Macintosh Commercial** (January 22, 1984) Part of the mystique of this legendary ad is its inaccessibility: It aired for just a little over a week. But that doesn't mean its creators spared any expense. The 60-second commercial presented a grim and haunting vision of a dystopian future, one that borrowed from both George Orwell and *The Prisoner*. A group of men with shaved heads and identical gray outfits are saved from brainwashed conformity by one determined woman with vibrant clothes and a sledgehammer.

97. **The Two Faces of Latka** (May 21, 1981) Latka Gravas (Andy Kaufman), *Taxi*'s timid immigrant mechanic with the continually apologetic expression, needs to break out. Frust-rated by his notable lack of success with the ladies, the squeaky-accented Latka adopts an alter ego: the ultra-suave, self-absorbed singles-bar lizard known as Vic Ferrari. It is TV's most offbeat transformation.

96. **Police Brutality in Birmingham** (May 3, 1963) Peacefully protesting segregation in local stores and restaurants, a group of more than 1,000 blacks, led by Dr. Martin Luther King, Jr., marched through this Alabama city. They were met with unprovoked and terrifying violence by the Birmingham police, goaded on by Commissioner "Bull" Connor. First, attack dogs were set loose on the protesters, then the marchers were blasted with fire hoses shooting water at

100 psi, enough force to knock bark off trees. The evening news programs on all three networks showed extensive footage of the appalling police response. The broadcasts awakened the nation to the barbarity being committed in the name of racial segregation and added considerable impetus to the civil rights movement.

95. ***One Life* on the Stand** (March 6, 1979) On *One Life to Live*, Karen Wolek is torn. The wife of one of Llanview's leading doctors, she can provide an alibi for Viki Riley, on trial for murder, but only by divulging her shameful secret. Under intense grilling, she finally erupts: "What do you want from me, Mr. Callison? Do you want me to tell the court that I'm a common street hooker?" A riveting performance by Judith Light and a shocking social issue (housewives who hook) made this one of daytime's most potent scenes.

94. **The Theme Music from *Mission: Impossible*** (September 1966–May 1973) "Good morning, Mr. Phelps." So began the taped message that would propel our favorite espionage operative and his handpicked team on another daring sortie. After briefing Phelps (Peter Graves), the tape would self-destruct in a miasma of white smoke. Then came the really cool part: the syncopated, staccato strains of Lalo Schifrin's thrilling theme, a scintillating sonata for brass, flute, and bongo drum. Hey, who needs Tom Cruise?

93. Tonya Harding at the Olympics (February 25, 1994) Incredibly, after all the scandal and criminal matters surrounding the attack on rival skater Nancy Kerrigan, Tonya Harding was still allotted a place on the Olympic skating team in Lillehammer. The stage seemed to be set for the redemption of this talented but troubled rink rat from Oregon. But Tonya was no Cinderella. Just 45 seconds into her long program, she skated over to the judges' table, crying petulantly and pointing at the laces on her skate. She was given yet another chance. Missing her trademark triple axel, she finished eighth. Her tawdry but fascinating saga was over.

92. *The Simpsons'* Conclusion (September 17, 1995) In part two of the mock-mystery "Who Shot Mr. Burns?"—a clear parody of *Dallas* (see #13)—the Simpsons are watching a TV news broadcast when the prime suspect in the shooting is cleared (his alibi involves watching Comedy Central). "Hmmm," says Marge, "I guess it's never the most likely suspect." "Actually, Mom," notes Lisa, "in 95 percent of cases it is. The rest of the time, it's usually some deranged lunatic who did it for no reason." With that, every head in the room turns to Homer.

91. Rhoda's Wedding (October 28, 1974) For the nuptials of Rhoda Morgenstern (Valerie Harper), all her friends from Minneapolis come to town—Mary, Lou, Murray, and the rest. And 51 million viewers turn up, too, by far the largest audience this *Mary Tyler Moore Show* spin-off ever attracted. But Phyllis forgets to pick up the bride to take her to the ceremony in the Bronx. So plucky Rhoda, already dressed in her gown and veil, does what any determined New Yorker would do. She runs out in the street and tries to hail a cab. And when that fails, Rhoda hops the subway to her mom's house. Here comes the bride . . . on the D train!

90. Jack Paar Walks Off (February 11, 1960) The previous night, *The Tonight Show* host told a labored but innocent joke about a British term for bathroom—WC. The NBC censors bleeped it, and the prickly Paar took umbrage. During his next monologue, he explained what had happened and declared he wouldn't stand for it. He began to choke up as he announced he was quitting and then left the stage. A shocked audience watched second banana Hugh Downs take over a show that included Orson Bean and Shelley Berman. After predicting to the press that the show would crumble without him, a contrite Paar was back one month later.

89. The Fonz's Entrance (September 1974–July 1984) He was the showstopper on *Happy Days*. Sauntering into Arnold's Drive-In with his sculpted hair, black leather jacket, white T-shirt, and blue jeans, he would growl, "Aaayh!" and the studio audience would go nuts. He was the Fonz, the coolest man on the planet, or at least Milwaukee. When the sitcom debuted in January 1974, Henry Winkler's character had been in the background, dressed in a gray windbreaker. But as his image became flashier, he came to dominate the show. Today, the Fonz's biker jacket resides in the Smithsonian.

88. **Pee-wee's Big Comeback** (September 5, 1991) It happened at the MTV Music Video Awards. An announcer asked us to welcome an old friend, and out walked Paul Reubens, better known as inventive Saturday-morning star Pee-wee Herman. Reubens had been in virtual seclusion since his arrest at an X-rated theater, but he gleefully accepted the audience's raucous ovation and insouciantly asked, "Heard any good jokes lately?" Indeed they had.

87. **Tom Jordache Is Slain** (March 15, 1976) Back in the days when miniseries really were mini series, ABC spun out the Irwin Shaw epic *Rich Man, Poor Man* in grand style, taking 12 hours to tell the story of the embattled Jordache brothers. But the emotional payoff came right at the conclusion, when former boxer, seaman, and general knockabout Tom Jordache (Nick Nolte, who became an overnight sensation) was set upon and stabbed by two thugs—just when happiness was within his grasp. That left just enough time for a touching, 10-hankie deathbed reconciliation between

Tom and his high-society sibling, Rudy (Peter Strauss). This Cain and Abel saga did everything in a big way—it even earned 23 Emmy nominations.

86. **Kookie Combs His Hair** (October 10, 1958) Actor Edd Byrnes played a homicidal thug named Smiley in the movie pilot of the detective show *77 Sunset Strip*. But his James Dean flair and wavy hair caught on with audiences immediately, so the producers rechristened him Kookie and brought him back as a regular. Kookie's hepcat phrases, like "the ginchiest" (the greatest) or "piling up the Zs" (sleeping), were adopted by teenagers everywhere, and his trademark gesture—sliding his comb sensuously through his pomaded pompadour—spawned the hit song "Kookie, Kookie, Lend Me Your Comb."

85. **Plop-Plop Goes Letterman** (September 6, 1984) Clothes make the man. At least they did for David Letterman. Back in his NBC days, the sardonic late-night host gained a reputation for skits involving surreal suits made of sponge, Velcro, even potato chips. His most celebrated garment, however, was festooned with 3,400 Alka-Seltzer tablets. Sporting plastic goggles and an oxygen tank (so the gas soon to be released by the effervescent tablets wouldn't make him pass out), Dave was dangled over a 900-gallon water tank. "Boy, if I die," he mused, "this is the worst possible way to go, isn't it?" Down went Dave,

and up came a satisfying cloud of vapors. The stunt was the masterstroke in Letterman's plan to put the fizz back in late night.

84. **The Alexis and Krystle Catfight on _Dynasty_** (April 13, 1983) Alexis (Joan Collins) always likes to go for the soft underbelly. So when she sees Krystle (Linda Evans) sitting placidly and prettily by the lily pond, she starts needling the current Mrs. Carrington mercilessly about her inability to conceive. Now the gloves are off. "You miserable bitch," cries Krystle, diving at her tormentor. They plunge into the pond and start _whaling_ on each other, wet hair, soggy silk and all. When Alexis tries to escape, Krystle says, "Oh, no, you don't," and cracks her one right on the kisser.

83. **The Debut of _NYPD Blue_** (September 21, 1993) Almost a quarter of ABC's 225 affiliates refused to air the first episode of Steven Bochco's daring drama. Their viewers missed an extraordinary hour of TV, during which the relationship between detectives John Kelly (David Caruso) and Andy Sipowicz (Dennis Franz) was delineated with unusual rawness—and poignance.

82. **POWs Return from Vietnam** (March 19, 1973) Shortly after the Paris cease-fire agreement was signed, North Vietnam began releasing American prisoners of war. The most touching reunion seen on TV took place at California's Travis Air Force Base, as

Lieutenant Colonel Robert Stirm stepped onto the tarmac. His eldest daughter, Lorrie, 15, beamed as she rushed at her father with arms outstretched, followed closely by her brothers, her sister, and her mother, Loretta. The scene personified Operation Homecoming, during which 591 serviceman were released.

81. The U.S. Hockey Victory Over the U.S.S.R. at the 1980 Olympic Games (February 22, 1980) They said it would never happen, but with only five seconds to go, and the U.S. holding on to a tenuous lead of 4–3, ABC Sports announcer Al Michaels asked, "Do you believe in miracles?" then answered his own question with a resounding "Yes!" Michaels' words were immortalized—and, he said, unplanned, because "the thought of the American team winning that game was ludicrous."

80. Jeff Baker's Car Wreck on *As the World Turns* (August 23, 1962) *TV Guide* called it the "automobile accident that shook the nation." Actor Mark Rydell, who had played Jeff Baker for six years on the top-rated CBS soap, refused to sign a long-term contract. And so, the producers ripped asunder America's favorite daytime sweethearts in a blur of twisting metal: Jeff died instantly; his wife, Penny (Rosemary Prinz), fell into a lengthy coma.

79. The Fire in Waco (April 19, 1993) After a 51-day standoff between federal agents and Branch Davidian leader David Koresh, the FBI decided it could wait no longer for Koresh to surrender on a weapons charge (a previous raid had left four agents dead). On April 19, six hours after tanks pounded holes in the Branch Davidian compound and pumped in tear gas, bright orange fireballs erupted and black smoke cast a dark shadow over the grounds. Agents waited for cult members to pour out of the burning buildings and were horrified when they didn't. More than 80 members of the religious sect were killed, including Koresh and many young children. It was the apocalyptic ending Koresh had predicted for his followers.

78. **The Final Episode of** *M*A*S*H* (February 28, 1983) Betraying mixed emotions, Hawkeye (Alan Alda) gazes for the last time at the 4077th Mobile Army Surgical Hospital as his chopper rises in the air. Then, in the distance, he spies a giant "good-bye" etched in the dust by his departing buddy B. J. Hunnicut (Mike Farrell) on his trademark yellow motorcycle. So ended the Korean War adventures of our favorite medical unit after 11 critically lauded and audience-grabbing years (eight years more than the actual war lasted). *M*A*S*H* mania ruled the country on the night the two-and-a-half-hour series finale aired, and the episode set a Nielsen ratings record that has yet to be beaten.

77. **Maddie and David Make Love on** *Moonlighting* (March 31, 1987) In an episode entitled

"The Big Bang," battling detectives Maddie Hayes and David Addison finally put two seasons of bickering behind them and "got horizontal." Pottery, glassware, and various objets d'art flew about the room as the two tangled to the tune of the Ronettes' "Be My Baby." Though fans had begged for this moment, "The Big Bang" soon turned into "The Big Bust," and a valuable lesson was learned: no sexual tension equals no sizzle.

76. **Paul Newman in** *Bang the Drum Slowly* (September 26, 1956) Newman was at the peak of his blue-eyed beauty when he played a star pitcher who befriends an unpopular but cancer-stricken catcher (Albert Salmi). In the live broadcast, Newman noticeably flubbed a line from his final soliloquy, but his stumbling speech somehow added even more pathos to the moment. Describing the sparsely attended funeral, the remorseful Newman movingly declares, "From here on in, I rag nobody."

75. **Clarabell Speaks** (September 24, 1960) "Say kids, what time is it?" asked Buffalo Bob Smith. The response was a high-pitched chorus of delight: "It's Howdy Doody time!" Since 1947, children had been devoted to Howdy, the freckled cowboy marionette. When it came time to pack up Doody-ville, who got the last word? Clarabell, the mute clown who had communicated only with horns and seltzer bottles. On the last show, he found his voice, saying sadly, "Good-bye, kids."

74. The Bookworm Episode of *The Twilight Zone* (November 20, 1959) All meek Henry Bemis ever wanted was to be left alone to read. And as the sole survivor of a nuclear holocaust, he gets his wish, sitting contentedly on the steps of a library, surrounded by books and rubble. Then the compulsive reader (played by Burgess Meredith) trips and shatters his only pair of glasses, and all those beautiful pages are just an indistinct blur. TV's most mordant twist ending.

73. Ruby Shoots Oswald (November 24, 1963) Still numb from the assassination of President Kennedy two days before, the nation tuned in to see JFK's presumed assassin, Lee Harvey Oswald, being transferred from one Dallas jail to another. Bodies jostled in the crowded jailhouse basement and then a shout—"Here he is"—rose above the hubbub as the slight Oswald was led in. Then a burly man, Dallas strip-joint owner Jack Ruby, stepped in front of the cameras, and a shot rang out. CBS's Harry Reasoner, desperately trying to sort out the commotion, finally announced, "What you saw very clearly is a man in a dark hat step out from the line and shoot Lee Harvey Oswald." The next day we would gather in front of the TV again for JFK's funeral (see #3).

72. Barbara Walters Interviews Sadat and Begin (November 20, 1977) Who else but Walters could have convinced Egypt's Anwar Sadat and Israel's Menachem Begin to sit down for a televised tête-à-tête? The heads of state seemed content to bask in the symbolism. But Walters wanted this memorable moment to be a historic one, repeatedly pressing them for possible peace concessions. Finally, Sadat objected. "Politics," he said, "can't be conducted like this."

71. **Dan Jansen Skates to Victory** (February 18, 1994) Sometimes good guys do finish first. Speed skater Jansen had known nothing but Olympic disappointment. Favored in the previous two Winter Games, he failed to earn a medal. (In 1988, he had been distraught over the death of his sister.) Then, in Lillehammer, having slipped again in his favored event, the 500 meters, he faced his last chance but came through, winning the 1,000-meter gold. His setbacks only made the triumph sweeter, and he skated a victory lap with his baby, Jane, named after his late sister.

70. **Halting the Tanks** (June 5, 1989) After six weeks of prodemocracy demonstrations by students and workers, the Chinese government ordered the Army to retake Tiananmen Square. As a convoy of tanks rolled into the city, a lone man carrying groceries stepped in front of the lead tank, stopping the column. This intrepid act, seen worldwide, was a potent symbol of individual will.

69. **Terrorists at the Olympics** (September 5, 1972) In the middle of the night, Arab guerillas stole into the athletes' compound at the

Munich Olympics, killing two Israelis and taking nine hostage. After negotiations failed, West German police made a rescue attempt that resulted in a tragic firefight in which all the hostages died. Pressed into service to cover the 23-hour crisis, ABC Sports announcer Jim McKay somberly reported, "They're all gone."

68. ***Star Trek*'s "City on the Edge of Forever"** (April 6, 1967) In the original series' most provocative episode, Captain Kirk and Mr. Spock pursue Dr. McCoy through a time portal to Depression-era New York, where Kirk falls for a social worker (played by a radiant Joan Collins). But Kirk faces a torturous dilemma: If she does not die young, her subsequent activities will result in the Nazis' winning World War II. So, as a truck barrels toward the woman, Kirk restrains McCoy from saving her. "Do you know what you've just done, Jim?" asks the horrified doctor. "He knows, Doctor," says Spock, his Vulcan reserve cracking. "He knows."

67. **A Visit to Neverland** (March 7, 1955) Fueled by a sprinkle of fairy dust, NBC's *Producers' Showcase* reached the pinnacle of live television with a lavish mounting of the musical *Peter Pan*. Custom-built machinery was shipped in from England to make the flying as convincing as possible. In the case of Mary Martin, they probably could have saved on the special effects. She was so effervescent

and evocative as Peter, it seemed she could soar at will. The production was such a huge critical and popular success that NBC reprised it twice more live—in 1956 and 1960.

66. **Oprah's Little Red Wagon** (November 15, 1988) It was the most notorious engagement in the daytime queen's battle of the bulge. On a show about dieting, talk-show titan Oprah Winfrey threw off an overcoat and dramatically revealed her newly trim, size-10 body. Then, using a toy wagon, she wheeled out a remarkable visual aid: a huge slab of animal fat wrapped in plastic. "This is what 67 pounds of fat looks like," she said triumphantly. "Is this gross or what? It's amazing to me that I can't lift it, but I used to carry it around with me every day."

65. *Hill Street* **Blue** (January 15, 1981) Captain Furillo locks up the bad guys and feisty public defender Joyce Davenport springs them. By the second commercial in *Hill Street Blues'* dazzling debut, she has called him a fascist and promised to bring him up on charges. So when she's at home at episode's end, kissing her lover's chest, and we see it is Furillo, we realize this is a couple that will create some sparks.

64. **Edith Is Raped** (October 16, 1977) *All in the Family* had a unique ability to raise serious topics within a sitcom format. Never more so than in the episode in which Edith Bunker

was sexually assaulted by a stranger in her living room. There are jokes early on (her attacker compliments her scent, and Edith says, "That's Lemon Pledge"). But her vulnerability and shame become almost tangible. The episode was used at rape crisis centers for years.

63. **Al Campanis on** *Nightline* (April 6, 1987) It was supposed to be a celebration of progress—marking the 40th anniversary of Jackie Robinson's entry into the major leagues. But Ted Koppel's guest, Al Campanis, a front-office executive with the Los Angeles Dodgers and a former teammate of Robinson's, was busy proving how deeply entrenched prejudice remains. He amiably asserted that blacks "may not have some of the necessities to be a . . . field manager or perhaps a general manager." Campanis was fired almost immediately, but his comments revealed how racism can fester, blithely unchecked, beneath a smiling facade of tolerance.

62. **The Oscar Streaker** (April 2, 1974) David Niven was terribly nervous about cohosting the Academy Awards. That's ironic, since he would go down as the show's most unflappable master of ceremonies. As he was in the process of introducing Elizabeth Taylor, a mustachioed man with no clothes ran across the stage. (Streaking was a popular college fad in those days.) Niven licked his lips, did a double take, tugged at his ear, and tossed off

such a witty ad-lib, many people assumed it was scripted. "Well, ladies and gentlemen," he said, "that was almost bound to happen. But isn't it fascinating to think that probably the only laugh that man will ever get in his life is by stripping and showing off his shortcomings."

61. Namath in Panty Hose (1974) With sensuous languor, the camera panned up the shapely, clean-shaven legs of a reclining model. The effect was somewhat marred by a pair of green shorts. As the camera continued up, we saw a hairy arm emerging from a football jersey emblazoned with the number 12 and, finally, the grinning face and twinkling blue eyes of New York Jets quarterback Joe Namath. As promised, the ad proved "to the women of America that Beautymist Panty Hose can make any legs look like a million dollars." Using Namath, a symbol of cocky machismo, made the spot the ultimate gender bender.

60. Darrin's Dastardly Doppelgänger (September 18, 1969) It certainly looked like the Stevenses' cozy home as the sixth season of *Bewitched* opened. But who was that guy talking with such familiar irritation to Samantha? And why was she calling him Darrin? Well, ongoing back problems and an addiction to painkillers had led to the departure of Dick York and the arrival of Dick Sargent. Or maybe it was just one of Endora's evil spells.

59. Watergate Breakthrough (July 16, 1973) After two frustrating months of uncooperative witnesses, the Senate Watergate Committee called in self-effacing bureaucrat Alexander Butterfield on short notice. Unexpectedly he provided a major revelation. Butterfield disclosed the existence of a taping system in the Oval Office, with reels kept and catalogued. The senators were incredulous. Surely the president wouldn't discuss sensitive matters on tape? "As a matter of fact," said Butterfield, "the president seemed to be totally, really oblivious or certainly uninhibited by this fact." For the first time, unraveling the whole knotty coverup seemed like a real possibility.

58. The Kiss on *Cheers* (September 29, 1983) Sam and Diane are fighting again in his office. But this time they're really riled up. "You know, you know," he says, barely able to spit out the words, "I've always wanted to pop you one. Maybe this is my lucky day, huh?" "You disgust me," she yells. "I hate you!" Then the mood shifts radically. "Are you as turned on as I am?" he asks. "More," she pants. And suddenly these two antagonists are kissing with hungry passion. Out in the bar, Cliff notes how quiet it's gotten. Norm muses that maybe Sam's killed Diane. And Carla observes, "Nah, even in death she wouldn't be that quiet."

57. Death Comes to *Sesame Street* (November 24, 1983) When Will Lee, the actor who played kindly storekeeper Mr. Hooper, died at 74,

Sesame Street waited until the following Thanksgiving Day, when they were sure parents would be home with their kids, to explain the concept. Big Bird had to be reminded by Susan, "When people die, they don't come back." "Ever?" he whispered. The finality of it sank in, but all the adults were there to comfort Big Bird as the camera craned away.

56. **Golfing on *The Honeymooners*** (October 15, 1955) As usual, Ralph has bitten off a good deal more than he can chew. He's got a golf date with a big shot at the bus company in two days and he doesn't know a putt from a potato. Well, first things first: the clothes. Let's see, plaid pants, argyle socks, and a floppy Scottish tam with a little ball on top. "How do I look, Norton?" he asks. "Deee-vine!" enthuses his pal. Now it's time for the lesson. Norton reads from a manual. Address the ball, it suggests. Norton grabs a club, works his body like a double-jointed hula dancer, salutes, and shouts, "Helloooo, ball." Hole-in-one humor.

55. **The Louds' Divorce** (March 8, 1973) The PBS documentary *An American Family* turned out to be a surprisingly involving portrait of the Loud family of Santa Monica, California. First came the issue of son Lance's homosexuality. Then Pat dropped a real bombshell on her husband. When he returned from a business trip, she handed him a card from her lawyer and said, "I'd like to have you move out." The camera maintained a tight, blurry closeup of

Bill's face. The father of five accepted the dissolution of his marriage with odd equanimity. "Well, that's a fair deal," he said.

54. Ali Defeats Foreman (October 29, 1974) Awesome. Invincible. That's how writers described domineering heavyweight boxing champ George Foreman. Muhammad Ali, then 32, was given no chance when he faced Foreman in a steamy soccer stadium in Kinshasa, Zaire, at 4 A.M. (The starting time was designed to accommodate millions of Americans watching on closed-circuit TV.) For eight rounds Ali employed his passive "rope-a-dope" technique, leaning back and letting Foreman pound away at Ali's arms and elbows. Then Ali turned the tables, unleashing a quick and devastating flurry. Foreman buckled and ever so slowly toppled to the canvas.

53. The Contest on *Seinfeld* (November 18, 1992) All the show's endearing hallmarks are on display in this episode: deft ensemble work, catchy buzz phrases ("master of your domain"), and a witty, self-referential script that folds back on itself like a Möbius strip. The premise is that Jerry, George, Kramer, and Elaine make a wager to see who can go the longest without pleasuring himself or herself. Finally Kramer, tempted by a naked lady in the building across the way, bolts into Jerry's apartment, slams down a pile of cash, and declares, "I'm out!"

52. Bobby's in the Shower on *Dallas* (May 16, 1986) Pam Ewing—still pining for her do-good hubbie, Bobby, who had died the previous year—woke up one morning to the sound of the shower. She swung open the door of the steam-filled shower stall to find a cheery, lathery Bobby. "Good morning," he said—season-ending freeze-frame. In the fall, we found out Bobby's death—in fact, conveniently, the whole misbegotten preceding season—had just been a dream of Pam's.

51. The Bombing of Baghdad (January 16, 1991) Operation Desert Storm was a made-for-TV military operation with satellite correspondents like Arthur Kent, the "Scud Stud," filing reports from the war zone and incredible footage of smart bombs finding their targets with unerring precision. It all started with CNN's gripping footage of Baghdad under siege. As sirens blared, antiaircraft tracer rounds drifted up into the night sky in a scene right out of "War of the Worlds."

50. The Borg on *Star Trek: The Next Generation* (June 18, 1990) Federation starships have massed to fight the Borg, the indomitable antlike race that is rapidly conquering the universe. Captain Picard has been captured, and Officer Riker is sitting at the helm of the *Enterprise* when the ship is hailed. On the viewscreen, we see Picard—or a half man, half machine that looks like Picard—on the enemy vessel. "I am Locutus of Borg," he says in a dead voice. "Resistance is futile. Your life as it has been is over." Riker knows what he must do: "Mr. Worf," he orders. "Fire!"

49. Cal Ripken, Jr., Breaks the Record (September 6, 1995) Boy, did we need a hero! Baseball fans were still disillusioned by the previous year's major league strike that had robbed them of a World Series for the first time since 1904. So the soft-spoken Baltimore Orioles shortstop had the ideal summer in which to play his 2,131st consecutive game, thus shattering a seemingly unbreakable mark set by legendary Iron Horse Lou Gehrig. As Ripken came out of the dugout in the fifth inning, after the game had become official, it wasn't just his athletic prowess that prompted the 22-minute standing ovation. (ESPN motormouth Chris Berman honored the occasion with silence.) No, we were saluting Cal's more heroic, but all too easily overlooked, accomplishment: doing his job with consistent devotion.

48. Hertz Puts Us in the Driver's Seat (1961) A riderless convertible rolls along the road. Then, as if from the clouds, a smiling man in a suit and tidy snap-brim hat floats down and lands snugly behind the wheel. Cue the jingle: "Let Hertz put you in the driver's seat/ Let Hertz take you anywhere at all. . . ." The levitating motorist ad campaign—a technical tour de force—changed car rental, previously considered the province of the rich, into a mass-market commodity.

47. **The Hug on *The CBS Morning News*** (May 15, 1985) The latest body in the revolving anchor chair of CBS's morning show belonged to Phyllis George, a former Miss America. Her guests were Gary Dotson and Cathleen Webb (who had already made appearances that morning on *Today* and *Good Morning America*). After six years in prison for raping Webb, Dotson had just been released after Webb recanted the charge. George complimented Dotson on his autograph-signing technique and inquired brightly about TV-movie offers. As the awkward interview ground on, George suggested Dotson and Webb shake hands "after a long day's work." When they stiffly complied, she followed up with four career-ending words: "How about a hug?" It was the dismal nadir of bubbly, happy-talk news.

46. **Mary Lou Retton Scores a 10** (August 3, 1984) Talk about pressure. Retton was attempting to accomplish what no American woman ever had: win an Olympic gold medal in all-around gymnastics. But her principal rival, Ecaterina Szabó of Romania, had just scored an astounding 9.9 on the uneven bars. That all but mathematically eliminated Retton, the spunky 16-year-old from West Virginia. She would need a perfect score in her final event—the vault—to overtake Szabó. Inhaling deeply, Retton rose on her toes, bounded down the runway, and launched herself at the

vault. After catapulting through the air, she stuck her landing as the crowd at UCLA's Pauley Pavilion rose to their feet to cheer. Retton flung up her fists in exultation and flashed that infectious, megawatt smile. When the score was posted, it confirmed what everyone already knew: 10.00!

45. **"Where's the Beef?"** (January 1984) Three white-haired ladies stand just able to peer over the counter of a brand-X fast-food eatery. Confronted by a minuscule hamburger patty sitting on an enormous bun, the lady in the middle squawks, "Where's the beef?" The expression became a national catchphrase, a favorite Johnny Carson punch line, and even a sound bite in that year's presidential race. The ad for Wendy's restaurants made a star out of grandmotherly Clara Peller, a retired beautician from Chicago who was so hard of hearing that a hidden stagehand had to tap her ankle to cue her famous line.

44. **"Your Money or Your Life"** (January 15, 1956) The star of *The Jack Benny Program* is given that simple, seemingly obvious option by a holdup man. But Benny, whose comic persona was built around his notorious stinginess, has no response. Catching on to the gag, the audience begins laughing (just as they did when Benny first performed this skit on radio). Finally, the robber prods the comedian with the gun and barks, "I said, 'Your money or your life.'" Whereupon Benny delivers in a

piteous wail his most famous punch line: "I'm thinking it over!"

43. Jacqueline Kennedy at the White House (February 14, 1962) Speaking in her refined murmur, Jackie Kennedy took CBS newsman Charles Collingwood on a guided tour of the presidential residence. (The special aired simultaneously on NBC and ABC as well.) The show was part art-history lesson (as Mrs. Kennedy knowledgeably lectured on paintings and furnishings) and part house tour (for the first time, a camera was allowed inside the Lincoln and Monroe rooms). But it was most remarkable for the unusual access it afforded to our charmingly enigmatic First Lady.

42. *Monday Night Football* (October 9, 1972) Down on the field, the Raiders are blowing out the Oilers. The camera flashes up to the stands, where a disgruntled Oilers fan slumps, surrounded by a sea of empty seats. As Howard Cosell begins to pontificate ("Right there is a very vivid picturization . . ."), the fan makes an obscene gesture on live TV. Dandy Don Meredith quickly quips, "He's saying they're No. 1 in the nation," and everyone in the booth cracks up. The incident reflected the chemistry that made the show such a captivating TV institution.

41. "Went With the Wind" (November 13, 1976) *The Carol Burnett Show* got its longest sustained laugh during this loopy spoof of "Gone

With the Wind." Starlett (played by Burnett) is in a tizzy because Ratt Butler (Harvey Korman) is returning to Terra and she doesn't have a thing to wear. As he strides into the front hall and calls to her, Starlett imperiously descends the staircase wearing an emerald green gown that is obviously made from the curtains we just saw hanging in the window. In fact, the curtain rod is still intact, lying across Starlett's shoulders. When Ratt compliments her on the dress, Starlett says, "I saw it in the window and I just couldn't resist it."

40. The Premiere Episode of *Roseanne* (October 18, 1988) The kitchen was a mess, cereal littered the table, the furnishings looked shabby, and the kids were sniping at each other. Right from the opening scene, this groundbreaking sitcom plunged us into a very different sort of American family than we were used to seeing. Then came Rosey: bumptious, brazen, crabby, and brutally honest. Wearily watching her kids squabble, she drawled, "Now I know why some animals eat their young." The show's raw, blue-collar tone clashed emphatically with everything on prime time.

39. Columbo's First Case (February 20, 1968) He wasn't your typical police investigator, with his crablike gait and wrinkled raincoat. He seemed so goofy and distracted—the kind of guy who couldn't find his car keys, much less ferret out a killer. Especially one as clever and self-possessed as Gene Barry's character. Barry made the mistake countless villains would with Peter Falk's dumpy detective: He underestimated him. About the third time Columbo popped back in the room to croak, "One more thing," Barry was truly exasperated. At home, however, we were beginning to understand that Lieutenant Columbo was one deceptive detective.

38. The Black Power Salute (October 16, 1968) At the 1968 Olympics in Mexico City, U.S. sprinters Tommie Smith and John Carlos finished first and third in the 200-meter dash. On the victory stand, as "The Star-Spangled Banner" began to play in the Olympic Stadium, each athlete lowered his head and raised a gloved fist, a gesture associated with black militants. It was a shocking incident, jarringly incongruent with the usual patriotic flavor of that moment—a sign that racial politics had splashed over into the world of sports.

37. Shatner at the *Star Trek* Convention (December 20, 1986) In an inspired *Saturday Night Live* skit, William Shatner fulfills his official duty as the former Captain Kirk of the Starship *Enterprise:* attending one of those Trekker conventions. Looking balefully out at the all-male audience, he sees attendees in Federation uniforms, sporting pointy Vulcan ears or proudly wearing T-shirts with slogans like "I Grok Spock." Finally he addresses this motley multitude who gaze up at him so raptly: "Having received many of your letters over the years—and I've spoken to you, and some of you have traveled hundreds of miles to be here—I'd just like to say, 'Get a life, will you, people!'" It was satire with a wicked bite of reality.

36. Michael Jackson Performs "Billie Jean" (May 16, 1983) It made musical history. After performing a medley of Jackson 5 hits with his brothers on the *Motown 25th Anniversary Special,* Michael remained alone on the darkened stage. The insistent pulse of Michael's new hit began to throb and the singer seemed to be consumed by the music, erupting into a dance that was part mechanical, part balletic, and totally funky. The crowd went into a frenzy when Michael unveiled his Moonwalk, a backward-gliding move that suggested magic, not choreography. In the span of three minutes, he had established himself as the most electrifying performer of his generation.

35. The Tomahawk Incident (April 29, 1965) Ed Ames of *Daniel Boone* came on *The Tonight Show* to demonstrate tomahawk tossing. Winding up, he buried the weapon right in the crotch of the silhouetted target. Johnny Carson's wincing reaction had the audience howling interminably. Ames asked Johnny if he wanted to try throwing it. "Well," said the host, "I can't hurt him any more than you did."

34. Rather Tangles with Bush (January 25, 1988) Bombs away! In a live interview on *The CBS*

Evening News, Dan Rather grilled then–Vice President George Bush about his role in the Iran-Contra affair. Bush fired back, chiding the anchor for having walked out of the studio the previous year in a snit, leaving six minutes of dead air. Rather shouted, "You've made us hypocrites in the face of the world!" It was a moment of unrivaled rancor.

33. Chuckles the Clown Dies (October 25, 1975) When Chuckles, a recurring character on *The Mary Tyler Moore Show*, is killed at a circus parade, it occasions a flood of silly jokes. Ted's on-air tribute to the fallen entertainer? "A little song, a little dance, a little seltzer down your pants." Mary is infuriated by all the levity, but, later, at the funeral, when everyone else is somber, Mary cannot stop giggling. Noticing this, the minister asks her to stand up and laugh out loud. Of course, she is immediately wracked with loud, convulsive sobs. Only our Mary could make mood swings this extreme seem so lovable.

32. Nixon Waves Farewell (August 9, 1974) They were scary and, at times, surreal days for the country. The previous night President Richard Milhous Nixon, facing certain impeachment, had announced in a nationwide broadcast that he would be resigning his office "effective at noon tomorrow." In the morning, he addressed White House staffers, emotionally unspooling as he invoked his long-dead mother. Afterward, marching out stiffly to the waiting helicopter, he turned, smiling broadly, and flung out both hands in victory signs. It was an ambiguous final flourish, yet somehow fitting for this complex and confounding character.

31. The Premiere Episode of _The Cosby Show_ (September 20, 1984) Theo explains to his father that he isn't interested in having a career. "Dad," he implores, "can't you just accept me and love me 'cause I'm your son?" Giving this serious thought, Cliff Huxtable says, "That's the dumbest thing I've ever heard." The early exchange was emblematic of this landmark sitcom: smart but amusing family dynamics presided over by parents (Bill Cosby and Phylicia Rashad) who were affectionately authoritative.

30. Clarence Thomas's Rebuttal (October 11, 1991) The confirmation hearings of this Supreme Court justice took a startling turn when law professor Anita Hill came forward with graphic allegations of sexual harassment by Thomas. The embattled nominee responded by indignantly denying all charges and assailing the hearings. "I would have preferred an assassin's bullet," he fumed, "to this kind of living hell." Thomas's ringing defense may have saved his confirmation. It certainly made for gripping TV.

29. _Bonanza_ Debuts (September 12, 1959) "Look at it, Adam," said Ben Cartwright to his saturnine eldest son as they sat on horseback. "Feast thine eyes on a sight that approaches heaven itself." And the Ponderosa certainly had some impressive vistas, particularly if you were one of the few Americans lucky enough to own an RCA color set in 1959. *Bonanza* was the first hour-long series to employ the new technology (preceded by a handful of game and variety shows). Of course, the open-hearted adventures of the Cartwrights made for a pretty engaging series, even in plain old black-and-white.

28. **The Dismemberment of Kunta Kinte** (January 25, 1977) Few television events merit the designation "epic." *Roots* unquestionably does. Airing over eight consecutive nights, this profoundly affecting miniseries presented the multigenerational saga of a black family brought to this country by slave traders.

   The atrocious cruelty of human bondage was distilled on the third night. Kinte, shipped to this country at age 17 from his native Gambia, refused to live as a slave and kept trying to escape. His disgruntled owner (*Bonanza*'s Lorne Green) finally said, "I don't care how you bring him back. Frankly, I prefer him dead." The slave catcher had a more sadistic solution: hacking off Kinte's foot at the ankle. The ruthlessness of that act resonated deeply with viewers, as did everything else about this watershed miniseries. *Roots* remains the most-watched drama in the medium's history.

27. **Buckner Muffs the Ball** (October 25, 1986) The Curse of the Bambino was finally about to be put to rest. The Boston Red Sox had not won a World Series since 1917, a losing streak superstitious fans attribute to the team's trading of Babe Ruth to the Yankees. But at long last the Bo Sox had one in the bag. The Red Sox needed only one out to win the Series against the Mets, and Mookie Wilson had just tapped a weak grounder to Boston's first baseman Bill Buckner. Incredibly, the ball rolled right between Buckner's legs. The Mets went on to win that game and then the Series. Curses! Foiled again.

26. **The Birth of Air Jordan** (April 20, 1986) The Boston Celtics' Larry Bird scored 36 points. Pretty impressive. Until you realize that his opponent on the Chicago Bulls, a 23-year-old sapling out of North Carolina named Michael Jordan, almost doubled Bird's output. In an incredible offensive display, the second-year pro knocked in 63 points, erasing Elgin Baylor's playoff scoring record. Boston won the game 135–131 in double overtime and subsequently swept the series. But everyone who witnessed that incendiary performance recognized that the NBA landscape had just shifted.

25. **Kennedy Debates Nixon** (September 26, 1960) Television can be a cruel mistress. Republican presidential candidate Richard Nixon found that out in the very first of his four broadcast debates with his Democratic

opponent, John F. Kennedy. Of course, Nixon's most glaring problem was flop sweat. He repeatedly had to wipe beads of perspiration off his lip. Even his chin grew noticeably moist. Kennedy, looking cool and poised, assiduously maintained eye contact with the camera and spoke in melodious phrases: "In the election of 1960, the question is whether the world will exist half-slave or half-free." Nixon's eyes seemed to avoid the lens, and he based his arguments on dry facts and statistics. If you read the transcript of the debate, Nixon is the more substantive candidate; watch the tape and it's a different story. The camera doesn't lie, but it can flatter.

24. **Rather Gets Roughed Up** (August 28, 1968) Outside, chaos reigned as police clashed repeatedly with student demonstrators who had been drawn to Chicago for the Democratic convention. Mayor Richard J. Daley knew only one way to maintain order: squeeze tighter. Inside the International Amphitheatre, Daley's repressive tactics found an unlikely victim in a young CBS correspondent, Dan Rather. Near the Georgia delegation, Rather was set upon. "Excuse me being out of breath," he reported to Walter Cronkite, "but a security man just slugged me in the stomach." He was knocked to the floor and shoved toward the exit. "Get your hands off me," he shouted. The incident, which incensed Cronkite ("It looks like you have some thugs down there, Dan"), indicated how deep

and dire the divisions in our society were growing.

23. ***The Andy Griffith Show* Opening Credits**
(1960–1968) First you hear the folksy whistle of the theme song. And down this backcountry dirt path come Sheriff Andy Taylor and his son, Opie, toting their fishing rods. Opie stops to skim a rock and Andy calls to him. The boy runs to his father not out of fear, but because he likes being with his dad—and who wouldn't? Note that Andy's wearing his uniform. Either it's before work or after . . . or maybe Andy has just decided to leave the town in the jittery hands of Barney Fife. Through the turbulent '60s—the years of assassinations, social upheaval, and foreign wars—that serene opening offered a gracious invitation to America's favorite rusticom. Was this nirvana or Mayberry?

22. ***Requiem for a Heavyweight*** (October 11, 1956) The '50s, a time of ambitious live dramas on television, are often referred to as the medium's Golden Age. And no event possessed the luster of this supernal *Playhouse 90* production, written by Rod Serling. Jack Palance played Mountain McClintock, a boxer forced into retirement. Desperate for money to help his unscrupulous manager, Maish (Keenan Wynn), Mountain is reduced to professional wrestling. Dressed up in a hillbilly costume and stripped of his dignity, he confronts himself in the mirror. Soon after, he

finds out that his own manager bet against him in his last fight. "You know," he says, "in all the dirty, crummy fourteen years I fought for you, I never felt ashamed. . . . Now I feel ashamed." It is perhaps TV drama's most heartbreaking moment, rendered with exquisite pathos by Palance.

21. Murrow Skewers McCarthy (March 9, 1954) Conducting a witch hunt against Communists in the government, Senator Joseph McCarthy of Wisconsin had become one of the country's most powerful and dangerous men. Then, TV's most august newsman, Edward R. Murrow, devoted an installment of his CBS investigative show, *See It Now*, to McCarthy, using the senator's own comments and speeches to reveal him as a blustering demagogue. McCarthy never recovered from the devastating exposé. It was an early and powerful testament to television's ability to influence public opinion.

20. The White Bronco Chase (June 17, 1994) The networks broke into regularly scheduled programming with a news bulletin that looked like a bizarre episode of *Cops*. A white Ford Bronco drifted slowly down a Los Angeles freeway with a phalanx of LAPD cruisers trailing behind. Maybe it was the parade-route pace, but the police cars seemed to be escorting the Bronco rather than pursuing it. Crouched inside, we were told, was a desperate O.J. Simpson, wanted for a heinous double murder. The strange but curiously mesmerizing spectacle marked the beginning of our national obsession with the Simpson case.

19. Laura Petrie Gets Stuck in the Tub (March 31, 1965) Like many episodes of *The Dick Van Dyke Show*, this sharp farce unfolds in flashback, as Rob (Van Dyke) and Laura (Mary Tyler Moore) recall their second honeymoon. Rob dresses up for champagne and caviar in their hotel suite, while Laura soaks in the tub. But she gets her big toe stuck in the faucet and the bathroom door is locked. Eventually, Rob grabs the gun of the hotel detective, shoots the lock off the door, and collapses in giggles at the sight that greets him off-camera: a wet, naked Laura. After a commercial, the camera goes inside the bathroom, but—big tease—Moore is now wrapped in a raincoat.

18. Hank Aaron Hits #715 (April 8, 1974) He was so steady, so workmanlike. Although Aaron ended 1973 one home run shy of Babe Ruth's record of 714, there was little drum-beating or merchandising in the off-season. The slugger from Mobile, Alabama, simply refused to participate in the hype. We didn't have to wait long to celebrate. Aaron tied Ruth on the first day of the new season and, the same week, swatted an Al Downing fastball into the left-field bleachers. The fans went crazy—in fact, Aaron had to shrug off two of them who tried to join him as he circled the bases. At home plate his teammates waited, whooping and jumping up and down. Then this remarkable, stoic man, never varying his deliberate, dignified trot, disappeared into the welcoming maelstrom.

17. **The Challenger Explodes** (January 28, 1986) After being rescheduled numerous times, the space shuttle *Challenger* is cleared for takeoff. Earlier, viewers had seen the smiling crew— Scobee, Smith, Resnik, Onizuka, McNair, Jarvis, and "teacher in space" Christa McAuliffe—make the traditional walk to the craft. Three, two, one ... on the launchpad, sparks fly, engines bellow, and the *Challenger* rises majestically, clearing the gantry. Then, 73 seconds into the flight, a whoosh, a ball of fire, and smoke. For an instant, we think it's planned—a booster rocket igniting. But debris careers from the fireball and the two solid-fuel rockets zigzag out of control. The cameras switch to the astronauts' families in a bleacher by the launch site, their expressions shifting from awe to concern, shock, and, finally, terrible certainty. Ten miles up, shards of a dream continue to fall and melt in a cloudless sky.

16. **The Wedding of Luke and Laura** (November 16–17, 1981) On the lawn of the Port Charles mayoral mansion, on a perfect autumn afternoon, Laura Webber Baldwin—a vision in white—and Lucas Lorenzo Spencer—in a gray cutaway, his permed hair rustling in the breeze—spoke their vows with quivering lips.

It had been a stormy romance, starting with the night a drunken Luke raped Laura in a deserted disco. Ah well, the course of love never runs smooth on daytime. But their relationship on *General Hospital* resulted in the most celebrated wedding in the annals of soaps. As they walked down the aisle, Luke pumped his two fists in a show of giddy victory. Then we heard a shadowy, uninvited guest (okay, it was Elizabeth Taylor) swear, "Curse you, Laura and Luke!" So much for happy endings.

15. **LBJ Announces He Will Not Seek Reelection** (March 31, 1968) President Lyndon Johnson looked notably glum as he began his televised address to the nation. True, he was having a bad year, between the Tet offensive and Bobby Kennedy's decision to run against him. Johnson announced he was ordering a virtual halt to all bombing of North Vietnam in a unilateral gesture of peace. After discussing Vietnam for nearly 40 minutes, he added an astonishing codicil to his address: "I shall not seek, and I will not accept the nomination of my party for another term as your president." On live TV, without warning and without a fight, the century's consummate politician had just surrendered the highest office in the land.

14. **Samurai Delicatessen on *Saturday Night Live*** (January 17, 1976) Guest host Buck Henry walks into a deli, finds a kimono-clad, sword-wielding samurai (John Belushi)

behind the counter, and orders a sandwich. There follows a flurry of strenuous physical comedy and pseudo-Japanese double-talk worthy of Sid Caesar. Belushi uses the sword to chop salami, spread dressing, and slice a tomato in midair. Presented with his order, Henry asks, "Do you think you can cut it in half?" Belushi cocks his eyebrows slyly at the camera, emits a samurai shriek, draws the sword way up over his head and . . . brings it down ever so gently to delicately divide the sandwich in two.

13. **Who Shot J.R.?** (March 21, 1980) It is night, and coldhearted J. R. Ewing sits in his office alone. And no wonder: In the course of the previous 50 minutes, he has managed to alienate, infuriate, and betray most of Texas and all of his relatives. It's Miller time! Then a door in the outer office opens and someone enters. "Who's there?" J.R. asks. BLAM! He clutches his chest. BLAM! He hits the floor, exhales and . . . dies? The following November, more than 80 million viewers—nearly as many as voted in the presidential election that month—tuned in to *Dallas* for the resolution of this tantalizing cliffhanger. In case you forgot: It was Kristin who wounded J.R.

12. **The Final Episode of *The Mary Tyler Moore Show*** (March 19, 1977) Minneapolis's WJM has just been bought by a new owner who has made it clear he will be clearing out some of

the deadwood on the news staff. Most assumed it would be Ted Baxter's empty head that would roll. The staff was summoned and the verdict was swift: "Ted, you're staying. And the rest of you guys, I'm gonna have to let you go." After their last broadcast together was over, they stood in the newsroom until gruff news director Lou Grant blurted out, "I treasure you guys." In a flash, they were locked together in a weepy group hug. Said Lou, "I think we all need some Kleenex." Georgette replied, "There's some on Mary's desk." No one wanted to let go, so the whole gang, like some gigantic, ungainly crab, scuttled over to the desk in one of TV's most hilarious, touching, and inspired bits of physical comedy.

11. **Reginald Denny Beating** (April 29, 1992) The events were linked by grotesque irony. The videotaped bludgeoning of black motorist Rodney King by white policemen led to the riots in South Central Los Angeles. Now another camera, in a news chopper covering the riot, was capturing a racially motivated attack sickeningly reminiscent of King's battering: Denny, a white truck driver, was pulled from the cab of his vehicle by a black man, then beaten and smashed in the head with a brick, kicked, and trampled on. The two related attacks indicated to a horrified nation that race relations—and basic human conduct—were in worse shape than anyone had imagined.

10. **Elvis' 1968 Comeback Special** (December 3, 1968) The psychedelic era had dawned, the time of the Magical Mystery Tour, and most trend-followers had written off the King. With this electrifying televised special, Elvis reclaimed his throne. The opening salvo showed Presley in an ultratight closeup, his face filling the screen. There were the low, dark eyebrows, the simmering eyes, a red bandanna tied around his throat above a black silk shirt, his famously full lips an inch from the microphone, as he sang, "If you're lookin' for trouble/You came to the right place." This was Elvis in his electrifying adult prime, taking care of business as only he could.

9. **Bette Serenades Johnny** (May 21, 1992) How do you say good-bye to a legend? Yes, there'd be another show the next night, but that was to be one of *The Tonight Show*'s patented reeling-through-the-years retrospectives. So this was really Johnny's swan song. And what a chanteuse he got to sing it! Suitably dressed in black, Bette Midler crooned "You Made Me Love You" with lyrics adapted to the occasion. When she began "Here's That Rainy Day"—a Carson favorite—Johnny joined in and the two, faces inches apart, warbled a sweet impromptu duet. Then, perched on a stool, Midler said, "I can't believe it, the last guest, the last fool Mr. Carson will have to suffer gladly." She swung into the Johnny

Mercer–Harold Arlen standard "One for My Baby (and One More for the Road)," again tailoring the lyrics ("Well, that's how it goes/ And, John, I know you're getting anxious to close"). Carson, a closeup on him now, sniffed and wiped away a tear. Song done, Midler ran over and placed a red lei around his neck. And at the end, after nearly 30 years of always having something smart and funny to say, Johnny Carson was left speechless.

8. **The Wedding of Charles and Diana** (July 29, 1981) Only a few thousand people received invitations to St. Paul's Cathedral for the royal nuptials. But 750 million showed up—via worldwide TV, including throngs in this country who got up in the middle of the night to witness all the glorious pomp. First, the processional, as carriages conveyed Queen Elizabeth and Prince Philip, princes Charles and Andrew, and finally, Lady Diana Spencer past the cheering crowds from Buckingham Palace. Then the breathtaking ceremony. A camera affixed to the cathedral ceiling provided a magnificent tableau: the bride making her way down the aisle, the long white train of her gown flowing behind her as the organ played, a chorus sang, and the man who would be king awaited her at the altar. After conducting the vows, the Archbishop of Canterbury expressed a universal sentiment, noting, "This is the stuff of which fairy tales are made."

7. The O.J. Simpson Verdict (October 3, 1995) The "trial of the century" had dragged on for more than a year, yet it took the jury only four hours to reach a verdict. The entire country, it seemed, paused to witness the outcome. At Judge Lance Ito's instruction, the nattily dressed defendant warily turned to the 12 unseen determiners of his fate as the court clerk read the verdict: "We, the jury, in the above entitled action, find the defendant, Orenthal James Simpson"—America held its breath—"not guilty of the crime of murder." Across the nation, people either gasped or cheered. In the courtroom, Simpson blinked twice and bit his lip. Then the second count was read—again not guilty—and attorney Johnnie Cochran hugged Simpson from behind. The Simpson family rejoiced; the victims' families appeared shocked, particularly Fred Goldman, who sat openmouthed while his daughter, Kim, sobbed. Relieved and exhausted, Simpson himself finally smiled, then nodded toward the jury and mouthed, "Thank you, thank you."

6. The Final Episode of *The Fugitive* (August 29, 1967) Convicted of killing his wife, Dr. Richard Kimble (David Jansen)—"an innocent victim of blind justice"—was finally able to vindicate himself in the second half of a two-parter that was the most-seen regular series episode at that time. (The show attracted 72 percent of the viewing audience.) Kimble convinced Philip Gerard, the police lieutenant obsessed with his capture, to grant him 24 hours to track down the real killer, the notorious one-armed man. The confrontation took place at an abandoned amusement park at the top of the towering Mahi-Mahi ride. The killer's confession was heard by Kimble alone before the one-armed man plunged to his death. Fortunately, a witness finally came forward and Kimble was acquitted. As he walked from the courtroom, a free man at last, a squad car screamed up to the curb and two policemen hurried out. In that moment, we saw in Kimble's haunted eyes and tensed body that he was getting ready to flee. But the cops walked right past him and then, only then, did Kimble realize that this was the day the running stopped.

5. *Newhart* **Final Episode** (May 21, 1990) Japanese speculators had bought up a rustic Vermont village, lock, stock, and cracker barrel—all except for stubborn holdout Dick Loudon (Bob Newhart), whose Stratford Inn was left sitting forlornly on the 14th fairway of a golf resort. When Dick's flaky old staff and former neighbors, now all millionaires, show up for a reunion, Dick can take it no more. "I've got to get out of this madhouse," he splutters. Throwing open the front door, he is hit by a golf ball and slides to the ground. Cut to a pajama-clad Dick in bed, saying, "Honey, wake up. You won't believe the dream I just had."

Whoa, we're not in Vermont anymore. That's the Chicago apartment of mild-mannered psychologist Bob Hartley, and the woman in bed next to him is Emily (Suzanne Pleshette). We're not only in an alternate reality—we're in a whole different series (the comic's previous sitcom, *The Bob Newhart Show*). As Bob explains his eight-year dream, Emily, in that deep, smoky voice, says, "That settles it—no more Japanese food before you go to bed." Unquestionably, the cleverest sitcom finale in TV history.

4. **The Beatles' First Appearance on *The Ed Sullivan Show*** (February 9, 1964) "Ladies and gentlemen," intoned Sullivan, "the Beatles!" With that, the variety-show host turned stiffly to the studio audience, gesturing for a reaction. His prompting was utterly superfluous. The ecstatic screams of the predominantly female audience all but drowned out Sullivan's next words: "Let's bring them on!" As the Fab Four launched into "All My Loving," the camera moved to the crowd, where a plump, dark-haired girl stood poleaxed, in an advanced state of shock. Nearby, another girl couldn't stop bouncing, clutching her hair, and screaming. As the band downshifted into the ballad "Till There Was You," graphics appeared on the screen, identifying each of the Beatles by name. Under John's tag, it read: "Sorry girls, he's married." The frenzy reached a peak as the

boys jolted into "She Loves You," singing, "Yeah, yeah, yeah," and shaking their hair. They would return for two more songs later in the show and again a week later for another appearance from Miami, but pop-culture history had already been rewritten. This was one of those seismic events about which people ask, "Where were you when . . . ?"

3. **John-John's Salute** (November 25, 1963) As a mourning nation watched on TV, a subdued parade of dignitaries and heads of state marched behind the flag-draped caisson and the riderless black horse from the Capitol to St. Matthew's Cathedral in Washington, D.C. After the service, conducted by Cardinal Cushing (who had presided at President Kennedy's wedding and inauguration), an honor guard carried the casket down the steps of the church and loaded it onto the caisson for the ride to Arlington National Cemetery. John-John, standing between his veiled mother and his heartbroken uncle Robert, raised his hand in salute at his mother's gentle urging. It was the boy's third birthday.

2. **Lucy in the Candy Factory** (September 15, 1952) To prove a point to their spouses, Lucy (Lucille Ball, right) and Ethel (Vivian Vance) get jobs at Kramer's Kandy Kitchen. After failing at a number of tasks around the plant, the gals get one last chance in the wrapping department. Their mission: Make sure every

bonbon that comes down the conveyor belt gets a paper cup. Miss even one and they're fired. "This is easy," says Lucy. Famous last words. And classic slapstick—the chaotic, crowning moment of *I Love Lucy*. Suddenly the conveyor belt speeds up and the chocolates are bunched closer together. Unable to keep up, Lucy and Ethel begin frantically gobbling candies, shoveling them into their chef hats, and scooping them into their blouses. The supervisor returns. Seeing everything perfectly wrapped, and oblivious to Lucy and Ethel's panic, she says, "Well, you're doing splendidly." And then, to the conveyor operator, "Speed it up a little!"

1. **Armstrong Walks on the Moon** (July 20, 1969) It was the culmination of a national goal, set by President Kennedy, to land an American on the moon before the decade's end. After flying 240,000 miles through airless and soundless space, the buglike lunar module separated from the ship and began its jerky descent to the surface. On living-room sets, on giant outdoor screens, and in appliance-store windows, the drama unfolded. The module's thrusters kicked up lunar dust and, transfixed, we saw—actually saw—the craft cast a shadow on that dust. Then, at 4:17 P.M., EDT: "Houston, Tranquility Base here. The Eagle has landed." The first words from the moon. (Oddly, the picture was far clearer than the audio.) More than six hours later, a hatch

opened and the bulky, silhouetted figure of astronaut Neil Armstrong cautiously descended the ladder, leaping the final three feet to the powdery surface. "That's one small step for man," he intoned over his headset, "one giant leap for mankind." Nothing on television before or since has approached that unforgettable and triumphant moment.

(From TV Guide. *Contributors: Ed Weiner, Alan Carter, Mike Hammer, Lisa Miller, Ileane Rudolph, Rick Schindler, Annabel Vered, and Stephanie Williams.* TV Guide *would like to acknowledge the invaluable assistance of the Museum of Television & Radio in compiling this list.)*